IBSEN : PLAYS

AN ENEMY OF THE PEOPLE
THE WILD DUCK
ROSMERSHOLM

IBSEN : PLAYS

AN ENEMY OF THE PEOPLE

THE WILD DUCK

ROSMERSHOLM

Translated with an Introduction by
JAMES WALTER McFARLANE

OXFORD UNIVERSITY PRESS

LONDON OXFORD NEW YORK

1971

Oxford University Press

LONDON OXFORD NEW YORK
GLASGOW TORONTO MELBOURNE WELLINGTON
CAPE TOWN SALISBURY IBADAN NAIROBI DAR ES SALAAM LUSAKA ADDIS ABABA
BOMBAY CALCUTTA MADRAS KARACHI LAHORE DACCA
KUALA LUMPUR SINGAPORE HONG KONG TOKYO

ISBN 0 19 281109 6

First published by Oxford University Press, London, 1960

First issued as an Oxford University Press paperback 1971

The text of this edition of *An Enemy of the People*, *The Wild Duck*, and *Rosmersholm* is taken from Volume VI (1960) of The Oxford Ibsen, an edition of the plays newly translated and edited by J. W. McFarlane. That volume also contains earlier drafts of *The Wild Duck* and *Rosmersholm*, a commentary on each of the three plays giving dates of composition and other background material, and a list of productions of Ibsen in English on stage, radio, and television, together with a full bibliography.

Printed lithographically in Great Britain by The Camelot Press Ltd., London and Southampton

CONTENTS

PREFACE

The translations in this volume are based on the Norwegian text as printed in the Centenary Edition (*Hundreårsutgave*, 1928–57), edited by Francis Bull, Halvdan Koht, and Didrik Arup Seip.

All three plays represented here have been translated a number of times before, and I have not left these earlier versions unregarded—in addition to the Archer versions, I might mention in particular those of R. Farquharson Sharp, Una Ellis-Fermor, and Eva Le Gallienne—but neither have I paid them any importunate attention, preferring to approach them more as a possible contributor to their fascinating conversation than as a potential borrower; and it is as such that I feel I owe them a general debt of gratitude for their company rather than specific debts in respect of particular items. Nevertheless, there are of course frequent coincidences, not a few of which are there as a result of a decision I early made not to alter a phrase merely because (as naturally quite often happened) it turned out to have been used in one or another of the earlier versions.

The best translation, says the man with no knowledge of the original, is one that does not read like a translation; for anybody familiar with the original, on the other hand, it is imperative that he should be reminded of it at every stage, and in every possible particular. If I have had any definable policy at all in shaping the present versions, it was to reconcile as far as I was able these two factors—making something that to the knowledgeable was recognizably a 'translation' and not a 'free-rendering' or 'adaptation' or something equally undisciplined, and yet at the same time making the lines 'sayable'. One other point may be referred to here: in deciding whether characters should address each other by first name or surname, I have chosen what seemed appropriate to the equivalent English context of situation, rather than follow the Norwegian conventions mechanically; titles, such as 'Rektor', 'Frøken', and so on, have been similarly treated; and I have also tried to exploit this device to the point where it would, I hoped, deal relatively unobtrusively with the perennial problem of 'De' and 'du', the formal and familiar modes of address.

In connection with the staging of Ibsen's plays, there is one point of some interest: 'left' and 'right' in the stage directions mean 'as seen from the point of view of the audience'. In a letter of 22 November 1884 to the Swedish actor-manager, August Lindberg, Ibsen wrote: 'In answer to your question, I hasten to inform you that *The Wild Duck* is disposed from the auditorium and not from the stage, as indeed all my plays are. I position everything as I see it in my mind's eye as I am writing it down.'

SCHOOL OF EUROPEAN STUDIES   J. W. McF.
UNIVERSITY OF EAST ANGLIA
NORWICH.
November 1970

INTRODUCTION

It was Georg Brandes who suggested that much of *An Enemy of the People* (1882), *The Wild Duck* (1884), and *Rosmersholm* (1886) might be traced to a point of common origin: the hurt, the distress and disgust Ibsen felt at the hostile reception given in 1881 by the Norwegian public and critics to *Ghosts*. Within a year of this bitterly resented publication, Ibsen had given his answer to those who had abused him: a play (actually begun before *Ghosts* but now splendidly appropriate to the new situation) which traces the bewilderment and incredulity and ultimate exasperation of one who, for publishing unpalatable truths about the polluted sources of the community's economy, is subjected to insult and slander and even physical violence from his fellows. After thus venting his immediate anger, Ibsen in his next play allowed himself a second and more searching look at this phenomenon of a man who makes it his mission to proclaim truth; and *The Wild Duck*, in asking whether it really does add to the sum total of human happiness to put the average person in possession of the truth, redresses a balance. The tertiary stage of exasperation was reached with *Rosmersholm*, a further exploration of the theme of one whose dementia was truth, who like his earlier counterparts had improving designs on his fellows, but whose ultimate achievement is equally unavailing, though not in the same way and not for the same reasons.

Comparable though the three plays may be in this particular respect, they nevertheless vary greatly in quality. *An Enemy of the People* generally ranks as one of the thinnest of Ibsen's maturer works, one which, to use William Archer's phrase, is 'not so richly woven, not as it were, so deep in pile'. Archer goes on: 'Written in half the time Ibsen usually devoted to a play, it is an outburst of humorous indignation, a *jeu d'esprit*, one might almost say, though the *jeu* of a giant *esprit*. . . . *An Enemy of the People* is a straightforward spirited melody; *The Wild Duck* and *Rosmersholm* are subtly and intricately harmonized.'[1] The two latter plays are often to be observed in the critics' estimates vying with each other as rivals for the top place among Ibsen's works: Nils Kjær's characterization of *The Wild Duck* as 'the master's masterpiece' has been echoed many times in the critical studies of recent decades; and

[1] *Play-Making* (London 1912), p. 79.

it is repeatedly claimed on behalf of *Rosmersholm* that never was Ibsen's constructional skill more confidently or more successfully exploited.

To plot these three dramas against the co-ordinates of technique and ultimate meaning provides evidence, however, of something more than the mere amplification, or even enrichment, of things already there in essence at the beginning; it is to testify also, and more importantly, to a distinct turning-point in Ibsen's authorship, a change of direction arguably no less profound and no less significant than his earlier abandonment of verse as the medium of his dramas in favour of prose. As a rule it was only with the greatest reluctance that Ibsen was ever drawn to comment on his own work; his letters to his publisher and to his friends tended to harden into a drily formal, almost communiqué-like phraseology whenever it was a question of reporting progress on his own work: a bare admission that he *was* busy, a hint of whether or not the thing had a contemporary theme, a forecast of the number of acts it would be in, and (for his publisher) perhaps an estimated time for completion, or some indication of the number of printed pages it would fill. Rarely was there anything else of much significance. It is precisely this habitual uncommunicativeness that makes his unsolicited comment on *The Wild Duck* the rather startling thing it is: writing to his publisher on 2 September 1884, he was moved to admit that he thought of this new work of his as something rather special, adding that his methods were new, and that some of the country's younger dramatists might possibly be encouraged by them to launch out along new tracks. It is therefore not without a certain measure of approval from Ibsen himself that one is tempted to consider *An Enemy of the People* as the culmination of a distinct 'period' in the dramatist's career, as something that set a terminus to the line of the development that had begun with *Pillars of Society* in 1877, and had continued by way of *A Doll's House* (1879) and *Ghosts* (1881). There is encouragement also to see *Rosmersholm* as the inauguration of the later mode of composition serving the group of plays that marked the end of his career: *The Lady from the Sea* (1888), *Hedda Gabler* (1890), *The Master Builder* (1892), *Little Eyolf* (1894), *John Gabriel Borkman* (1896), and *When We Dead Awaken* (1899). And—intractable, transitional, between two 'periods'—*The Wild Duck*, composed at a time when its author's dramatic *credo* was profoundly changing.

The pace of *An Enemy of the People* is unusual for Ibsen; elsewhere, at least in the later dramas, the progression is purposefully deliberate, like an exploratory advance over uncertain country which has had careful preliminary study but no close reconnaissance. In this play, by contrast, the advance is conducted with eager exuberance, moving over ground familiar as it might be from regular patrol activity, and not seeming to care greatly if on occasion it happens to put a foot wrong. Part of the terrain had in fact been one of Ibsen's favourite stamping-grounds for over ten years, if not longer: a hatred, carefully nurtured in correspondence and in conversation, of anything in the way of party or association or society or indeed any identifiable grouping that went in for 'majority' practices, that invited majority decisions or accepted majority rule. As early as 1872, he had even talked enthusiastically about undermining the whole concept of state-hood, asserting that 'the state is the curse of the individual'. Such political sympathies as he had at the time were reserved for nihilists and anarchists and the extreme left-wing, from a feeling that they at least cared about the big things in life and honestly strove to realize their ideals, whilst the larger parties with their mass appeal struck him as trafficking in nothing but sham and humbug. Organized Liberalism he considered freedom's worst enemy.

To these convictions, the events of the year 1881—the hostile reception given to *Ghosts*—brought peculiar reinforcement. To his scorn of organized politics was now added a consuming contempt for the press, especially the so-called Liberal press. Ibsen was confirmed in his view that the press as then constituted was no better than a parasite on a grotesque and deformed body politic, for ever talking about freedom, but terrified of the realities of it, for ever proclaiming independence although itself merely the slave of public opinion and organized pressure-groups and its own circulation figures.

Three items, chiefly, 'seeded' his mind, super-saturated as it was by bitterness and contempt for these things; and they provided the nuclei around which the drama eventually crystallized. One was an anecdote, reported to him by a German acquaintance, Alfred Meissner, about a spa doctor who had been persecuted by his fellow-townsmen for reporting, to the great detriment of the tourist trade, a local case of cholera. Another was the incident in February 1881 involving a chemist called Harald Thaulow and the Christiania Steam Kitchens, in which Thaulow was prevented at a public meeting from reading his indictment of the management of the Kitchens and instead delivered an impromptu speech of denunciation. And the third was the person-ality of his great contemporary Bjørnstjerne Bjørnson.

The life-long relationship between these two men was marked by almost every emotion and attitude except indifference. Never was Ibsen, the self-sufficient, introverted exile, able for long to put out of his mind the image of the popular, rhetorical, extroverted Bjørnson. His feelings were always mixed—admiration, contempt, envy, exasperation, gratitude, affection, resentment, with sometimes one thing preponderating, and sometimes another. At the time Ibsen was working on *An Enemy of the People*, he had cause to think of Bjørnson with gratitude, particularly for the latter's spirited defence of *Ghosts*; and the courage, the bluff honesty, and the fundamental decency that he acknowledged in Bjørnson reappear also in his created hero, Dr. Stockmann.

But the piquancy of the situation can surely not have been lost on the author. Ibsen *à la* Bjørnson! The opportunities were too good to be missed. And there, accompanying his quite genuine regard and affection for his hero, one finds a good deal of dry mockery, directed in particular against Dr. Stockmann's simple-minded, self-opinionated interpretation of things. (One must beware, of course, of ascribing *all* Stockmann's traits to Bjørnson or even to what Ibsen might have wanted to pin on Bjørnson—the relevance is to be found rather in the author's implicit attitude to his created character, and not in the details.) Dr. Stockmann does not find it easy to relate the immediate problem to any wider context of things; his strength and his weakness lie in his simple directness, his inability to see more than one side of the question; and his brother's remonstrance that the alleged pollution cannot be regarded in isolation as a merely scientific matter but is also political and economic, is not without justification. He lacks any deeper understanding of the motives of human conduct and is even perhaps too easily misled about his own. It is no coincidence that both Stockmann and Gregers have spent much of their adult lives in remote parts, the former stuck away in Arctic Norway as a doctor, and the latter brooding 'up at the works' in Höidal for fifteen years; their conduct lacks the corrective of the 'reality principle', that which could tell them what may be presumed socially possible, and what may not.

It is precisely these temperamental and very human weaknesses in the main character, however, that prevent the drama from degenerating into a theatrical tract; and Ibsen was able to make his Kierkegaardian points about the need for individual decision, the necessity for individual responsibility, and the value of individual courage—especially the courage of one's convictions—and to enlist the sympathies of the

audience unambiguously on the side of the lone champion without at
the same time making him too offensively virtuous. Against his hero,
Ibsen marshals an alliance of vested interest, political hypocrisy, and
editorial opportunism: the Mayor, the influential representative of
entrenched authority, not without courage of a kind and horribly
experienced in the manipulation of others by veiled threat and the
promise of favour, who masks self-interest and self-preservation as 'the
common good'; Aslaksen, embodying the inherent timidity of public
opinion, and making a virtuous 'moderation' out of his essential
servility; and Hovstad, hawking his influence to the highest bidder.
These are the elements that determine the ultimate shape of the drama,
in which principles are balanced against expediency, integrity weighed
against quick profits, and the 'individual' involved in a fight against
what Hebbel was inclined to call the Idea—the reaction of those who
wish to maintain the *status quo* and the inertia and the intolerance of the
undifferentiated masses who are their dupes.

Among the earliest jottings preliminary to *The Wild Duck* are two
which make special reference to the business of growing up, the
transition from childhood to adulthood: one of them compares the
advance of civilization to a child's growing up, whereby instinct is
weakened, the power of logical thought is developed, and 'the ability
to play with dolls' is lost; the other draws a parallel between the
revisionary changes in man's attitude to his past achievements and the
way in which a child mind is absorbed into the adult spirit. This mani-
fest interest in the phenomenon of childhood and its advance to
maturity was not without its personal side. In 1881 Ibsen had begun a
short autobiographical account which, however, never got beyond a
description of the days of his earliest childhood in Skien. One can nevertheless well imagine how his memories of those days were jogged by
this exercise: of his sister Hedvig; of his father who suffered the shame
of bankruptcy and who reduced a once prosperous family to something near penury; of the attic at Venstøp (a few miles out of Skien)
where the Ibsen family subsequently lived; of the furniture there and
the books and the other old lumber left by a previous occupant; and of
the puppet theatre, with which as a boy he had been in the habit of
devising little entertainments for family and friends. Particular details
like these can easily be picked out as having contributed to *The Wild Duck*
in fairly obvious ways; but the more reflective items in the preliminary
notes about childhood and its problems count perhaps for even more.

One way of looking at *The Wild Duck* is to see it as a dramatic commentary on the shock of growing up. The Ekdal household, seen as an entity, enjoys an innocent and child-like happiness until this is upset by its introduction, through the agency of Gregers, to a new and disturbing awareness; it gives an account of the thoughtless, brutal imposition of a new and demanding consciousness upon a ménage totally unprepared to face it, and of the sad consequences; it presents a history of shattered illusions and the destruction of make-believe, an account of what happens when a family's 'ability to play with dolls'—or as Relling puts it, its 'life-lie'—is destroyed.

Its most literal representative of childhood is, of course, Hedvig. Standing fearfully yet expectantly on the threshold of adulthood, taking a secret delight in playing with fire, she has all the genuine imaginativeness of the child, and a naïve and still active sense of mystery; responding intuitively to language's more magical powers, she is greatly impressionable and pathetically sensitive to the moods of those about her. Her death is the consequence of her being caught up in the emotional entanglements of an adult world, the result of confused loyalties; and the senselessness of her self-sacrifice and the pity of her fate are things that the drama is particularly concerned to communicate. Balancing her in the composition of the piece is Old Ekdal, who also enjoys 'the ability to play with dolls', but in his case it is the ability of one who has reached a second childhood; he enjoys dressing-up, wearing his old uniform for private and family celebrations; his enthusiasm for the surrogate reality of the attic is genuine and unassumed; helped on occasion by the brandy bottle, he can live himself without difficulty into a world of his own imagining; and his sad and —by its rather touching ridiculousness—moving presence is also an important ingredient in the whole. Between them is Hjalmar. Between the representatives of nonage and dotage, between the embodiments of the puerile and the senile is this defining figure of childishness: a child without the innocence or the sensitivity of a child, a big baby, sometimes petulant and querulous, sometimes appealing and charming, happy to let himself be spoilt by the attentions of others, skilled in tantrum but quite ready (as Hedvig knows) to be distracted by some little treat or favourite toy, by a bottle of beer or his flute. He takes refuge from the disappointments and frustrations of life in daydreams of worldly success, of clearing the family name, which provide him with a kind of substitute purposefulness. He too retains something of 'the ability to play with dolls', but it is a self-conscious, a less wholeheartedly spontaneous thing than that of Hedvig or his father; so that when he uneasily shows the loft and its contents to Gregers, he is quick to shelter behind the excuse that it is for the old man's sake.

What the drama emphasizes is that, before the coming of Gregers, this household was a generally happy one, the members of which had succeeded in amalgamating reality and dream, in bringing them both under one roof as they had conjoined their prosaic studio with their fantastic attic. Access from the one to the other was just too easy. What they do not at this stage realize is that the relative stability of their world depends on Werle's unobtrusive manipulations and the cynical adjustments of Relling. These two are the people in ultimate control, secretly supplying both the worldly goods and the stuff of fantasy without which life *chez* Ekdal would be impossible. Hidden subventions provide the material means to bear reality, inspired suggestions sustain their dream-life. That the Ekdals in return help to satisfy some craving or need in the lives of those who thus manipulate them—serving, one imagines, self-interest or conscience or cynicism or a sense of secret power—is a further integral though subsidiary element in the drama. What is important is that a balanced existence is contrived for the whole family unit, permitting all its members to fulfil themselves as completely as ever they are likely to. This existence is brought into a state of violent unbalance by the arrival of Gregers, who, seeing or suspecting something of the conspiracy that thus controls the Ekdals, feels that he has a duty to expose it; applying a moral imperative, he sets out to reveal what he regards as the dishonesty inherent in the whole situation.

Like Hjalmar, Gregers gains extra definition in the play from two flanking characters: his father Haakon Werle and Relling. To the former he stands in contrast by virtue of his lack of practical sense, his alienation from life as it is really lived; fifteen years in the backwoods is set against the father's successful business career at the centre of things; his inability even to light his own stove gives heightened emphasis to the quietly purposeful way his father, with his sure grasp of opportunity and his *savoir faire*, has organized his own life and the lives of so many of those around him. With Relling—the soul of cynicism, a maker of dreams for all but himself, whose only solution for his own problems is a good binge—the contrast is on the plane of idealism. He takes his fellows firmly by the arm, and beguiling them with pleasant fictions, leads them quietly away from their own frustrations and the jagged edges of reality; Gregers, by contrast, rubs their noses in the truth. Gregers represents what Ibsen had by now rejected—the principle of making universal demands regardless of person or situation or circumstance. He is the self-elected agent of his fellows' betterment, trafficking in truth and liberty without any sense of what is appropriate, or of what allowances to make: liberty, wrote Ibsen in one of the preliminary notes, 'consists in giving the individual the right to liberate himself, each according to his personal needs'. Gregers's approach is based on an inflexibly abstract view of life, a theorist's; wanting the best for his fellows, and convinced of their power to achieve it by heroic methods, he blunders in with his missionary fervour and upsets what he does not understand. Human kind, he fails to realize, cannot bear very much reality.

The compositional pattern of *The Wild Duck* thus poses two figures *en face*, Hjalmar and Gregers, each with his two supporting figures: Hedvig and Old Ekdal for the one, and Werle and Relling for the other. But to resolve what would otherwise be merely a dramatic encounter into a dramatic situation, there are cross-references and cross-tensions. Werle is linked to the Ekdal household by former business association and (through Gina) by illicit relations and a suspected paternity; Relling is attached to the Ekdals by his tenancy and daily association, to Gregers by earlier acquaintance up at the works; both are tenuously related to each other through Mrs. Sörby, and so on. The result is a plexus of intimacies, affinities, bonds, transactions, intrusions, importunities. It was perhaps to dispose these elements more eloquently and to control them more effectively that Ibsen seems to have been particularly concerned during the preliminary stages with what one might reasonably call 'depth', a certain quality of perspective. The drafts show how some characters were brought much nearer the foreground, others were stood back, and some even (like Old Ekdal's wife, for instance) taken out of the composition altogether. Then there were others whose actual location seems to have remained very largely unchanged yet whose focus was altered—like the three guests at Werle's party who were originally named characters and then later became anonymously typed; or like Mrs. Sörby who in the first mention was an unnamed middle-aged woman. Hand in hand with this went a certain reduction in the definition of what was supplied to the composition by past event; facts in the final version are not things to prove or determine or demonstrate, there is no concern to annex certainty, but instead the design is built up by hint, allusion, suggestion or obliquity generally: Hedvig's paternity, Ekdal's alleged crime,

Werle's treatment of his former wife, all these things are deliberately blurred in the interests of the design as a whole. Nor must one forget the extra quality of 'depth' that the language is made to sustain, the loading of it with extra and secretly shared significance, as when Gregers talks to Hedvig.

Finally, is it perhaps in some such terms that the Wild Duck itself is best explained; as something arbitrarily interposed, which additionally to its function in the drama as one of the 'Requisiten' serves also to make more explicit the relationship of the other elements in 'depth'. Because it is not difficult in the circumstances to imagine a *human* reaction without it, it gives the impression of being inserted; what really integrates it into the play is the realization that no genuinely *dramatic* reaction is possible without it. Part of its effect on the play is comparable with that produced by the traditional dramatic unities: it concentrates, it holds together a number of otherwise separate things, it permits that density by which art distinguishes itself from the more diffuse nature of life, it helps to compose the drama. To call it a 'symbol', however, is possibly to emphasize unduly the similarity of the many disparate things it is successively made to stand for: Hedvig, in its role as gift from Werle to the Ekdals; Old Ekdal, whom life has winged and who has forgotten what real life is like; Hjalmar, who has dived down deep into the mud; Gregers, who suggests that he too will soon accustom himself to his new surroundings; or the object of Gregers's mission, the thing he will, like some extraordinarily clever dog, save from the depths. It is not so much that there is some kind of identity which all these things share, there is no 'falling together' such as the etymology of 'symbol' might suggest; rather it is that the Wild Duck is at the point of convergence of a series of comparisons, the purpose of which is to enable the onlooker to discriminate among the things it serves, to sort them out rather than heap them together, and ultimately to place them in perspective. What happens is that a number of characters are moved to say, or think, or unconsciously propose: 'This or that or he or she equals the Wild Duck', so that the Wild Duck functions almost like a recurrent element in a series of simultaneous metaphorical equations about life and the living of it, a kind of 'x' quality for which a whole range of variables might be substituted in an effort to find some kind of answer to things. Express your answer (the drama seems to enjoin from those who are tempted to try to solve such problems) in terms of truth and human happiness, and comment on the degree of incompatability indicated.

One of the contributory sources of *Rosmersholm* was undoubtedly Ibsen's disappointment following his first visit to Norway for eleven years. When in the late spring of 1885 he left Italy for Norway, it was not without the hope that he might find life there congenial enough to make him want to settle; but after only four months he was away again to Munich, sickened by too many of the things he had seen and heard to want to stay in the North. 'Never have I felt more alienated by the *Tun und Treiben* of my Norwegian compatriots than after the lessons they read me last year', he wrote to Georg Brandes in November 1886. 'Never more repelled. Never more discomfited.' Many of the less admirable qualities pilloried in *Rosmersholm* have their origin in this sense of repulsion: the cruel fanaticism of Kroll, whom Ibsen created to represent extreme right-wing thought in Norway; the sacrifice of principles to expediency and party advantage that the left-wing Mortensgaard represents—both of these characters reflecting the disgust Ibsen felt for politicians, a disgust that led him in one of his notes to *The Wild Duck* to suggest that politicians and journalists might serve nicely for vivisection experiments. And there was the ineffectualness of Brendel, who with his visionary dreams and his lack of practical sense mirrored Ibsen's scorn of those who claimed to be poets in spirit, enjoying visions of great brilliance and yet nauseated, they said, by the thought of having to write it all down. Equally there is good reason to suppose that some of the more positive elements also grew out of this visit and out of the contacts he made or renewed: Carl Snoilsky, whose company he enjoyed for several days at Molde, seems to have served in some measure as the model for Rosmer; and Snoilsky's second wife provided something of Rebecca.

Above all, however, it was the pettiness and the self-seeking that he could not stomach, the air of narrow provinciality which to him seemed to characterize such a great deal of Norwegian public and private life. The speech that he delivered to a workers' meeting in Trondheim, only about a week after his arrival in the country, expressed both his impatience with democracy as it was then operating and his conviction that what was lacking was nobility of mind: 'Our democracy, as it now is [he said], is hardly in a position to deal with these problems. An element of nobility must find its way into our public life, into our government, among our representatives and into our press. Of course I am not thinking of nobility of birth nor of money, nor a nobility of learning, nor even of ability or talent. What I am thinking of is a nobility of character, of mind and of will.' These are sentiments one finds, in almost identical phrases, not only among his preliminary notes to *The Wild Duck*, but also allotted to Rosmer at that moment when he seeks to define his mission in life. Democracy is no better than the individuals who constitute it; and some form of *individual* regeneration is necessary if the ruthlessness of the party politician and the brutishness of the masses are to be vanquished.

This is one of the things Ibsen stressed when, on one of those rare occasions when he was persuaded to give an opinion about his own work, he offered an explanation of the meaning of *Rosmersholm*; in response to an inquiry from some grammar-school boys in Christiania, he agreed that the play dealt among other things with 'the need to work', but went on to draw attention to the conflict within the individual between principle and expediency, between conscience and acquisitiveness, between the 'progressive' and the 'conservative' in his nature, pointing out at the same time the difference in tempo in the way these things change. *Rosmersholm* considers the dialectics of change, and the consequences for the individuals concerned, that follow an encounter between a predominantly conservative nature and a predominantly progressive one: Rosmer, contemplative by nature, conservative by family, generous by inclination, of the highest personal integrity, and with his roots deep in a landed tradition; and Rebecca, swept along by her passions, of questionable antecedents, 'advanced' in her thinking, and with a ruthless will-power. He is stimulated by her example to act, to take personal decisions, to commit himself; and she is moved by his example to adopt some of the Rosmer scruples. Both of them have a vision of glory as the consummation of their endeavours, a glad cause, stimulating not strife but the friendly rivalry of noble minds, all splendid. But the reality of it is profound disappointment. Rebecca is 'ennobled', but in winning generosity of mind loses her power to act; Rosmer in daring to commit himself to action discovers that he has unwittingly but inevitably involved himself in guilt; and any joy they may separately have had from life is killed.

Between the policies of Rosmer and the earlier Gregers, the difference is fundamental: Gregers seeks to impose a general regulation, Rosmer wants rather to interpose *himself*, to make a personal contribution by mixing with his fellows and helping them to self-help—there is, he says, no other way. One of the reasons for his failure is that he is too fine-grained, too passively receptive, too retiring for the evangelical life. Rosmersholm is a refinery in which all the roughage is extracted from existence—is it not said that Rosmer children have never cried, nor the men ever laughed?—and in which all sense of initiative is filtered away. Rebecca testifies how it kills joy, and some of her remarks show how she suspects it kills sorrow, too; indeed, that it annihilates all the stronger, cruder, and more elemental aspects of life. The innocence of saintliness and the innocence of pathetic gullibility are equally Rosmer's, and he is greatly vulnerable; he has no idea how pitilessly he is manipulated by others, he sees very little of what really goes on. He stands there as one whose authority is largely inherited, taken from the family name; and also whose opinions are 'received', taken from the stronger personalities he yields to: first Brendel who was in the early days his tutor, then Kroll to whom he had turned for advice ever since his student days, and finally Rebecca. When ultimately his faith in Rebecca is destroyed, the ideals she has represented for him also crumble, their validity for him derives only from a faith in their guarantor, and it is characteristic of him that he turns at once to Kroll for a replacement of faith. When Brendel reappears to show himself a broken man, this betokens yet a further assault on what pass for Rosmer's convictions. His ideals, dependent as they are on the borrowed life they take from their sponsors, are not sturdy enough for independent existence, so that when at the end a final claim is made on Rosmer's faith—that Rebecca loves him—he is drawn as by an obsession to demand a living sacrifice, to request that the total personality should underwrite this new proposal.

But whereas Rosmer comes to rely utterly on this 'advanced' woman who has invaded his house, she herself, whose past has been a Nietzschean amoral life 'beyond good and evil' and who has all the instinctive ruthlessness of an animal of prey, falls victim to the insidious power of the Rosmer tradition. She encounters something, a sense of scruple, that turns out to be even stronger than her own pagan will, and she submits to it, numbed, 'ennobled'. The two things—integrity and initiative, innocence and committal, nobility of mind and tenacity of purpose, or however they are termed—seem on this evidence totally incompatible, mutually exclusive; and in this respect the play is profoundly pessimistic. The point where such destinies finally meet and merge is death; when, as Rosmer insists, the two of them become one, one course alone is adequate for *her* to prove her love, for *him* to prove his will, and for both to invite a just retribution for their guilty past.

It is this more than anything that invalidates the traditional question as to whether this play is a Rebecca tragedy or a Rosmer tragedy, for it is both and it is neither. The world that Ibsen constructs in *Rosmersholm* is a world of relationships, a lattice of conjoined characters linked each to each, in which dramatically speaking it is less important to evaluate the constituent elements as discrete phenomena than it is to see how they stand to each other; less important to see how they separately change than it is to see how, in the flux of changing circumstance, the relations between them change; less important to 'place' them by political belief, or psychological type, than it is to note the sightings they separately take on each other, and continue to take (often with unexpected results) in the light of new events; not forgetting that any change in these latticed relationships will be reflected in changes all round, in the sense that Rosmer's relations with Kroll, or Rebecca's, are also functions of their own private relationship, and that any change *there* will have its consequences *here*.

Consider, to take an extreme example, the strangely influential role of Beata, Rosmer's deceased wife, who 'exists' in the play not by reason of her physical presence but solely through the memories and through the assessments of those who remembered her. We know her only through them and what they say: Rosmer, though during her lifetime repelled by her over-passionate nature which he obviously associated with the growing insanity that drove her to suicide in the mill stream, can now think of her with tenderness; Rebecca, who at first speaks sympathetically of her until circumstances make her change her words; Kroll, whose sister she was and who puts first one and then a very different interpretation on some of her last actions; Mortensgaard, to whom she wrote a secret and compromising letter shortly before her death; and Mrs. Helseth, the housekeeper and intermediary between them. Such items constitute bearings, taken from vantage points that can be approximately determined because those who occupy them *appear* and so declare themselves. But of course there is no neat answer. Instead of all converging upon some single point of corroboration, their testimonies are so widely divergent that together they do no more than demarcate an area in which a number of different interpretations of Beata are possible. Allowances have to be made, corrections calculated—for individual bias, for distorted or defective vision, for deceit. How ignorant is Rosmer of the real state of affairs? How unscrupulous is Rebecca? How reliable Mortensgaard? Statements about Beata have not only a demonstrative but also a betrayal value; they are also *admissions*, sometimes involuntary, which provide a two-way link with every other character in the drama, except possibly Brendel. Any change in the relationships among those who make these admissions tends to be reflected there, as well as in their attitude to each other.

Further variables can add to the complexity of the dramatic structure. When, for example, Ulrik Brendel is announced, and before he shows himself, the three people assembled in the living-room line up their minds on this new phenomenon: for Kroll, it is that 'waster' whom he last heard of as being in the workhouse; for Rebecca, it is that 'strange man' of whom she wonders that he is still alive; and for Rosmer—to the astonishment of both Kroll and the housekeeper who cannot think that Brendel is a fit person for the living-room at Rosmersholm—he is, as a former tutor in the house, welcome. Three snap bearings help to locate this as yet unknown quantity. *After* he has made his appearance, and after it has been noted not only what valuation he places on himself but also what by his conduct he involuntarily reveals, the initial bearings can be given some adjustment and thus one's ideas about those who took them refined. The importance of looking to the relations, expressed and implied, *between* the characters and not merely to the characters as independent creations is underlined by the letter Ibsen wrote on 25 March 1887 to Sofie Reimers. Invited to play Rebecca in the first Kristiania production, she had begged Ibsen's advice; his answer was that she would do well to note carefully what the other characters said about Rebecca, and not make the mistake of studying the part in isolation. Expanding this, one might say that the truth about the individual characters lies within an area bounded by: what they assert is the case; what they wantonly or unwittingly conceal; what they betray of themselves; and what they draw by way of comment from others. And when it is remembered that it is quite possible for these characters to mislead, to be misled or misinformed, or to be in the grip of instincts or impulses they cannot wholly comprehend, then the unreliability of the raw, untreated evidence is at once apparent. To fit in the separate parts as coherent items in a shifting pattern of event and belief is very largely a question of allotting appropriate values to the various hints, suggestions, and allusions the play is strewn with. What hidden meanings in the opening conversation between Rebecca and Kroll, for example, are subsequently brought to light by the momentary revelation that he had once been infatuated by her? What modifications must be made to Rosmer's implicit allegation that Beata was over-sexed, when his attitude to Rebecca, and the evidence of the past year of their living alone together in the house, carries the suggestion that he himself was under-sexed? And with such suspicions, should one then begin to wonder where in fact the sterility in his marriage to Beata lay—with her, as she was given to understand, or with him? How much had Kroll suspected about Rebecca before, that his thrust about her one-time relations with Dr. West struck home? And by implanting the idea that she had been guilty of incest, was he merely taking revenge on her with the same weapon she had already employed on his sister Beata: fostering suspicion on a minimum of evidence, knowing just how vulnerable her mind was to such suggestions? All these are things that cause one to look again at remarks that are otherwise deceptively obvious or perversely obscure.

Truth, its establishment and its promotion, is a thing all three plays have something to say about. In *An Enemy of the People* truth is provable and demonstrable; it inhabits a few scribbled lines of an analyst's report, it is expressible as a chemical formula. Stockmann, in becoming its spokesman, provokes a bold pattern of communal response to the revelations which, by the authority of science, he is able to make; and the local community is goaded into disposing itself in attitudes of hostility round the main character. Truth lights up the whole as from a central pendant fitting, a naked lamp lowered into the dark places of society, making a composition in strong light and shade. Each individual is the incarnation of the principles he professes, or lack of them; attitudes are adopted and persisted in, word and deed are concerted, and there is plain speaking. In *Rosmersholm* on the other hand, truth is an equivocal thing, being no more than what anybody at any particular time believes to be the case; it is a matter of partly knowing, or not knowing any better; there is no real laying bare of fact but rather a submission of possibilities, no establishment of what in reality was so, but an appeal to plausibility; any authenticity can be substantiated only by stealthy and oblique methods. Things are as they seem, or as they can be made to seem, and genuine motives are buried beneath layer upon layer of self-deception and duplicity; secret shifts and subsidences are for ever taking place in the minds of those concerned, and lighting is dim and indirect and full of flickering cross-shadows, and the wool is pulled over more than one pair of eyes.

The path leading from the earlier drama to the later runs from the outspoken to the unspoken, from bluff honesty to shifty evasiveness, from the self-evident to the merely ostensible, from proclamation to dissimulation, from the ingenuous to the disingenuous, from open debate and public uproar to secret eavesdropping and private intimation, from events urged on by a live issue to events brought up short by a dead woman. By the polluted baths there is enacted a tableau, a positioning of one to many in a generally radial pattern of static relationships, with Stockmann as the hub and cynosure. Beside the millstream, on the other hand, none of the characters is central in the same way, and instead of the build-up of a linear pattern one finds a sequence of positional changes, a ballet of death in which the manœuvres of the principals trace out a complex pattern of movement. In *An Enemy of the People* the author fashioned a vessel, a parabolic mould, into which he poured his wrath. *Rosmersholm*, however, has no such containing walls; its parts hold together rather on the analogy of particles in a complex magnetic field, they cohere not in obedience to some central solar force but rather because the resultant of all the various and varying attractions and repulsions they exert (or have exerted upon them) moves them the way it does. There is nothing at the centre except Nothing, the great void to which Brendel is finally attracted, and which draws the two anguished principals as though into the eye of a vortex. By comparison with *An Enemy of the People*, *Rosmersholm* seems to dispose over an extra dimension, and to enjoy a dynamic rather than a static existence; it differs from the earlier drama as a mobile differs from a blue-print, the one making a seemingly arbitrary but actually carefully balanced and *necessary* pattern of movement, and the other displaying all the clarity and self-assurance of something that recognizes its own dimensional limitations. By these tokens *The Wild Duck* is photographic, rather, and so ordered as to give an astonishingly successful illusion of perspective depth.

Hand in hand with these changes went an extra care in what Ibsen termed the 'individualization' of chararacter and other 'finesses' attaching to the creation of dramatic dialogue. So, for instance, in conversation with John Paulsen some time in the early 1880s about 'the thousand and one finesses of dramatic art', he is reported to have asked whether his companion had ever considered 'how the dialogue in a play ought to have a different timbre if it was meant to be spoken in the morning from what it would be at night'. In letters written whilst engaged on revising *The Wild Duck*, he stressed that his attention was being given to the 'energetic individualization of character' and the finer formulation of the dialogue; and many years later, when replying to a young Frenchman who wanted permission to translate this play, he returned to this matter and pointed out the great demands the play makes on any translator, since 'one must be extremely familiar with the Norwegian language to be able to understand how thoroughly each separate character in the play has his own individual and idiosyncratic mode of expression'. Ibsen had always been an extremely conscientious artist, painstaking in the care that he gave the successive drafts of his work; now, and especially from *The Wild Duck* onward, he applied his massive revisionary capacity to the problem of the finer delineation of character; the separate figures are now no longer in the first instance the embodiment of general principles or attitudes, but instead personalities whose individuality and uniqueness are emphasized at every point in the drama. They cease to be object lessons, and become instead subjects of study. It is one of the chief fascinations of the draft manuscripts of these plays that they document at a number of points this process of 'individualization'.

Of the *fact* of some fundamental change in Ibsen's writing about the time of these three plays, there is general recognition, although there is not the same unanimity about where precisely to locate the turning point, nor how best to style it. Some critics have seen it as a transition from the 'social' to the 'visionary', from the 'naturalistic' to the 'symbolic', from the 'problematical' to the 'psychological'; there have been arguments in favour of calling the earlier group 'moralist' and for distinguishing *two* later phases, the 'humanist' and the 'visionary'; whilst yet another critic has argued persuasively for regarding the shift as being from a 'demonstrative' to an 'evocative' mood. It may indeed be necessary to relate the change to terms even more fundamental than these, and to see the crux as being a substantial shift in Ibsen's whole scheme of values. Writing to Theodor Caspari on 27 June 1884, Ibsen confessed that he had long since given up making general or universal demands, believing that one could not with any real justification make such blanket claims on people, and added: 'I do not believe any of us can do anything other or anything better than realize ourselves in truth and in spirit.' What seemed to matter to him now were particulars rather than generalities; his attention was addressed to private dilemma rather than public abuse, to what was individual and personal rather than typical or representative. He abandoned collective indictment for singular, distinctive investigation; he became less comprehensive in his scrutiny of things, more selective, more penetrative; and with it all went an increasing impatience with the mass mind and all its works.

AN ENEMY OF THE PEOPLE

[En Folkefiende]

PLAY IN FIVE ACTS

(1882)

CHARACTERS

DR. THOMAS STOCKMANN, doctor at the Baths

MRS. KATHERINE STOCKMANN, his wife

PETRA, their daughter, a teacher

EJLIF
MORTEN } their sons, 13 and 10 years old

PETER STOCKMANN, the doctor's elder brother, Mayor, Chief of Police, Chairman of the Board of the Baths, &c.

MORTEN KIIL, owner of a tannery, Mrs. Stockmann's foster-father

HOVSTAD, editor of the *People's Herald*

BILLING, a journalist

CAPTAIN HORSTER

ASLAKSEN, a printer

Attending a public meeting are: men of all classes, some women and a group of schoolboys

The action takes place in a coastal town in Southern Norway

ACT ONE

Evening. DR. STOCKMANN'S *living-room, simply but tastefully furnished. In the side-wall, right, are two doors, one of which up-stage leads to the hall, and the other to the doctor's study. On the opposite wall and directly facing the hall door, another door leads to the rest of the house. In the middle of this wall stands a stove; down-stage of it is a sofa; above it hangs a mirror and in front of it is an oval table covered with a cloth. On the table, a shaded lamp is burning. In the back wall, the door to the dining-room stands open. Within, the table is laid for supper; a lighted lamp stands on the table.*

BILLING, a napkin tucked under his chin, is seated within at the supper table. MRS. STOCKMANN *stands by the table and hands him a serving dish on which is a large joint of beef. The other places at table are empty, and the table is in disarray as though after a meal.*

MRS. STOCKMANN. Well, if you will arrive an hour late, Mr. Billing, you'll have to put up with everything being cold.

BILLING [*eating*]. It's absolutely delicious, really excellent.

MRS. STOCKMANN. You know how strict my husband is about keeping punctually to his mealtimes. . . .

BILLING. It doesn't matter to me in the least. In fact I almost believe it tastes better, sitting down like this to it, alone and undisturbed.

MRS. STOCKMANN. Ah well, as long as you enjoy it. . . . [*Turns to the hall door and listens.*] That's probably Hovstad.

BILLING. Quite likely.

[PETER STOCKMANN, *the Mayor, enters; he is wearing an overcoat and his mayor's hat, and he carries a stick.*]

MAYOR. A very good evening to you, Katherine.

MRS. STOCKMANN [*coming into the living-room*]. Oh. It's you! Good evening. How nice of you to drop in like this.

MAYOR. I happened to be passing, so . . . [*With a glance towards the dining-room.*] Oh, but it seems you have company.

MRS. STOCKMANN [*rather embarrassed*]. No, not really. He just happened to drop in. [*Quickly.*] Wouldn't you like to join him and let me get you something to eat?

MAYOR. Who, me? No thank you. Heavens above! A cooked meal in the evening! Not with my digestion.

MRS. STOCKMANN. Oh, couldn't you just for once. . . ?

MAYOR. Bless you, no. I stick to my tea and bread and butter. It's better for one's health in the long run . . . as well as being more economical.

MRS. STOCKMANN [*smiles*]. Now you mustn't get the idea that Thomas and I are terribly extravagant, either.

MAYOR. Not *you*, Katherine. I'd never think that of you. [*Points to the doctor's study.*] Isn't he at home?

MRS. STOCKMANN. No, he's gone for a little walk after his supper . . . with the boys.

MAYOR. I wonder if that really does one any good? [*Listens.*] That's him now.

MRS. STOCKMANN. No, I don't think it's him. [*There is a knock on the door.*] Come in!

[HOVSTAD *comes in from the hall.*]

MRS. STOCKMANN. Oh, it's Mr. Hovstad.

HOVSTAD. Yes, you must excuse me, but I got held up at the printer's. Good evening, Mr. Mayor.

MAYOR [*bowing rather stiffly*]. Good evening! A business call, no doubt?

HOVSTAD. Partly. It's in connection with something for the paper.

MAYOR. That I can imagine. From all accounts, my brother is a prolific contributor to the *People's Herald*.

HOVSTAD. Yes, whenever he wants to get any particular home-truths off his chest, he writes a piece for the *Herald*.

MRS. STOCKMANN [*to* HOVSTAD]. But won't you . . . ? [*She points to the dining-room.*]

MAYOR. Indeed, and why not? Who am I to blame him if he decides to write for the class of reader he can expect the greatest response from! And in any case, there's no reason for me to feel any personal animosity towards your paper, Mr. Hovstad.

HOVSTAD. No, I don't think there is.

MAYOR. All in all, there is an admirable spirit of tolerance in our little town . . . a sense of civic pride. That's what comes of having a great communal undertaking to unite us . . . an undertaking which concerns all right-thinking citizens in equal measure. . . .

HOVSTAD. The Baths, you mean.

MAYOR. Exactly. We have our splendid new Baths. Mark my words! The prosperity of the town will come to depend more and more on the Baths, Mr. Hovstad. No doubt about it!

MRS. STOCKMANN. Thomas says the same.

MAYOR. Just look at the quite extraordinary way things have improved, even in the last year or two. People have more money! There's more life, more things going on. Land and property are going up in value every day.

HOVSTAD. And unemployment falling.

MAYOR. Yes, that too. The burden of the poor-rate on the propertied classes has, I am happy to say, been considerably reduced—and it will be even less if only we have a really good summer this year . . . with plenty of visitors, and lots of convalescents to help to give the place a reputation.

HOVSTAD. And things are looking pretty promising in that way, they tell me.

MAYOR. The prospects are very encouraging. Every day we receive more inquiries about accommodation and things like that.

HOVSTAD. Well then, I suppose the doctor's article will just come in nicely.

MAYOR. Has he been writing something else?

HOVSTAD. This is something he wrote during the winter, giving an account of the Baths and recommending the place generally as a very healthy spot. But I didn't use the article at the time.

MAYOR. Aha! I expect there was a snag in it somewhere.

HOVSTAD. No, it wasn't that. But I thought it might be better to hold it over till the spring; now's the time when people start thinking about their summer holidays. . . .

MAYOR. Very sensible, very sensible indeed, Mr. Hovstad.

MRS. STOCKMANN. Yes, Thomas is quite indefatigable if it's anything to do with the Baths.

MAYOR. Well, as he's one of its officials it's only natural.

HOVSTAD. Besides, he was the one who started the whole thing.

MAYOR. *He* was! Indeed! Yes, this isn't the first time I've heard of people getting that idea. But I rather imagined *I* too had had a modest part in this enterprise.

MRS. STOCKMANN. Yes, that's what Thomas is always saying.

HOVSTAD. Of course, who would want to deny that, Mr. Mayor. It was you who got things moving, got it going as a practical concern, we all know that, of course. All I meant was that the idea came first from Dr. Stockmann.

MAYOR. Yes, my brother's always had plenty of ideas—more's the pity. But when it's a matter of getting things done, you have to look round for a different type of man, Mr. Hovstad. I should at least have thought that the members of *this* household would . . .

MRS. STOCKMANN. My dear Peter . . .

HOVSTAD. But Mr. Mayor, how can you . . . ?

MRS. STOCKMANN. You go and get yourself something to eat, Mr. Hovstad. My husband is sure to be back by the time you're finished.

HOVSTAD. Thanks. Perhaps just a bite.

[*He goes into the dining-room.*]

MAYOR [*lowering his voice*]. Funny, these people from peasant stock! They never have any tact.

MRS. STOCKMANN. But there's no point in upsetting yourself about it! Can't you and Thomas share the credit like brothers!

MAYOR. Yes, one would have thought so. But apparently it isn't everybody who is content to share.

MRS. STOCKMANN. Oh, nonsense. You and Thomas get on perfectly well together on this point. [*Listens.*] That's him now, I think.

[*She goes over and opens the door into the hall.*]

DR. STOCKMANN [*laughing and talking outside*]. Here we are, another visitor for you, Katherine. Isn't this fun, eh! Come in, Captain Horster. Hang your coat on that peg there. You don't bother with an overcoat, eh? You know, Katherine, I ran into him on the street. . . . Had a terrible job persuading him to come along.

[CAPTAIN HORSTER *enters and bows to* MRS. STOCKMANN.]

DR. STOCKMANN [*in the doorway*]. In you go, lads. They are absolutely ravenous again, my dear. Come along, Captain Horster, what do you say to a bit of roast beef. . . ?

[*He urges* HORSTER *into the dining-room;* EJLIF *and* MORTEN *go in also.*]

MRS. STOCKMANN. But Thomas, don't you see . . . ?

DR. STOCKMANN [*turns in the doorway*]. Oh, it's you, Peter. [*Walks across and shakes hands.*] Well, this is very pleasant.

MAYOR. Unfortunately I can only stay a minute or two. . . .

DR. STOCKMANN. Rubbish! There'll be some hot toddy coming up soon. You haven't forgotten the toddy, Katherine, have you?

MRS. STOCKMANN. Of course not! I've got the kettle on.

[*She goes into the dining-room.*]

MAYOR. Toddy as well!

DR. STOCKMANN. Yes, sit yourself down and we'll make an evening of it.

MAYOR. Thanks, but I don't care for drinking parties.

DR. STOCKMANN. This isn't a drinking party.

MAYOR. It seems to me . . . [*He looks into the dining-room.*] It's incredible the amount of food they manage to put away.

DR. STOCKMANN [*rubbing his hands*]. Yes, isn't it grand to see young people eating well? Such an appetite they've got! That's as it ought to be. They need food . . . need to build up their strength. They'll be the ones to stir things up a bit in the coming years, Peter.

MAYOR. And what, if I may ask, is it that requires 'stirring up', as you put it?

DR. STOCKMANN. Ah, you'll have to ask the younger generation about that—when the time comes. We just can't see it, of course. Stands to reason! A couple of old fogies like you and me . . . !

MAYOR. Well, really! That's a most extraordinary description. . . .

DR. STOCKMANN. Oh, you mustn't take me too seriously, Peter. Thing is, I feel so full of the joy of everything, you see. I can't tell you how happy I feel, surrounded by all this growing, vigorous life. What a glorious age this is to live in! It's as if a whole new world were springing up all around.

MAYOR. Do you really think so?

DR. STOCKMANN. Well, you can't see it as clearly as I can, of course. All your life you've lived amongst this kind of thing, and it doesn't make the same sharp impression on you. But think of me, living all those years in the North, cut off from everything, hardly ever seeing a new face, never the chance of any decent conversation . . . for me it's like coming to some great throbbing metropolis.

MAYOR. Huh! Metropolis. . . !

DR. STOCKMANN. Well, I know everything's on a small scale compared with a lot of other places. But there's life here . . . and promise . . . and innumerable things to work and strive for. *That's* what counts. [*Shouts.*] Katherine, has the postman been?

MRS. STOCKMANN [*in the dining-room*]. No, nobody's been.

DR. STOCKMANN. And then what it is to have a decent income, Peter! That's something one learns to appreciate after living on a starvation wage as we did. . . .

MAYOR. Surely now . . .

DR. STOCKMANN. Oh yes we did. Let me tell you, things were often pretty tight up there. But now I can live like a gentleman. Today, for instance, we had a joint of beef for dinner; it did us for supper, too. Wouldn't you like a taste? Or let me show it to you, anyway. Come here. . . .

MAYOR. No, no, it's not necessary. . . .

DR. STOCKMANN. Well, come here then. Look, we've got a new table-cloth.

MAYOR. So I noticed.

DR. STOCKMANN. And we've got a lampshade. See? Katherine managed to save all that. Don't you think it makes the room look cosy? Just stand over here—no, no, not there—here, that's right! See? How it directs the light down like that. . . ? I think it looks really elegant, don't you?

MAYOR. Yes, for those who can afford such luxuries. . . .

DR. STOCKMANN. Oh, yes! Of course I can afford it. Katherine says I earn very nearly as much as we spend.

MAYOR. Nearly . . . yes!

DR. STOCKMANN. But a man of science ought to have a decent standard of living. I bet you there's many a civil servant spends more in a year than I do.

MAYOR. Well, I dare say there is. A civil servant, a senior executive. . . .

DR. STOCKMANN. Well, an ordinary businessman then. I'm sure that sort of person spends very much more. . . .

MAYOR. That depends on circumstances.

DR. STOCKMANN. Anyway, I don't go throwing my money away on any old thing, Peter. But I feel I can't deny myself the pleasure of having people in. I need something like that, you see, after being out of things for so long. For me it's like one of the necessities of life—to enjoy the company of eager young people, with initiative and minds of their own. That's the kind of person you'll find sitting at my table, enjoying their food. I wish you knew Hovstad a bit better. . . .

MAYOR. Ah, Hovstad, that's right. He was telling me he's going to print another one of your articles.

DR. STOCKMANN. One of my articles?

MAYOR. Yes, about the Baths. An article you'd apparently written during the winter.

DR. STOCKMANN. Oh, that one! Well, I don't want that one in just now.

MAYOR. Don't you? This seems to me to be exactly the right time for it.

DR. STOCKMANN. Yes, that's right . . . in ordinary circumstances. . . .

[*He walks about the room.*]

MAYOR [*watching him*]. And what's so extraordinary about the present circumstances?

DR. STOCKMANN [*halts*]. In point of fact, Peter, that's something I can't tell you for the moment. Not this evening, anyway. There might be quite a lot that's unusual about the present state of affairs; on the other hand, it might be nothing at all. It might very well be just my imagination.

MAYOR. I must admit it all sounds very mysterious. What's going on? Why am I being kept out of it? I would remind you that, as Chairman of the Board of the Baths, I . . .

DR. STOCKMANN. And I would remind you that I . . . Oh, let's not jump down each other's throats, Peter.

MAYOR. Heaven forbid! I'm not in the habit of jumping down people's throats, as you put it. But I must insist most emphatically that all matters be considered and dealt with through the proper channels and by the appropriate authorities. I cannot permit any dubious or underhand methods.

DR. STOCKMANN. Since when have *I* used dubious or underhand methods?

MAYOR. You have a chronic disposition to take things into your own hands, at least. And in a well-ordered community, that can be equally reprehensible. The individual must be ready to subordinate himself to the community as a whole; or, more precisely, to the authorities charged with the welfare of that community.

DR. STOCKMANN. That may well be. But what the devil has that got to do with me?

MAYOR. Everything. Because, my dear Thomas, that's just the thing you don't seem to want to learn. But mark my words; one of these days you'll pay for it . . . sooner or later. I'm telling you. Goodbye.

DR. STOCKMANN. Have you gone stark, staring mad? You are barking up the wrong tree altogether. . . .

MAYOR. I'm not in the habit of doing that. And now if I may be excused. . . . [*He calls into the dining-room.*] Goodbye, Katherine. Goodbye, gentlemen.

[*He leaves.*]

MRS. STOCKMANN [*comes into the living-room*]. Has he gone?

DR. STOCKMANN. Yes, he has; and in high dudgeon.

MRS. STOCKMANN. Thomas, my dear, what have you been doing to him this time?

DR. STOCKMANN. Absolutely nothing. He can't expect an account from me before the proper time.

MRS. STOCKMANN. What are you expected to give him an account of?

DR. STOCKMANN. Hm! Don't bother me about that now, Katherine.— Funny the postman doesn't come.

[HOVSTAD, BILLING *and* HORSTER *have risen from the table and come into the living-room.* EJLIF *and* MORTEN *follow them after a while.*]

BILLING [*stretches himself*]. Ah! A supper like that and, damn me, if it doesn't make you feel like a new man!

HOVSTAD. Our Mayor wasn't in the best of moods this evening.

DR. STOCKMANN. It's his stomach. Digestion's none too good.

HOVSTAD. It was mainly us two from the *Herald* he couldn't stomach, I reckon.

MRS. STOCKMANN. I thought you seemed to be getting on quite nicely with him.

HOVSTAD. Oh yes, but it's only a kind of armistice.

BILLING. That's it. That describes it exactly.

DR. STOCKMANN. We mustn't forget that Peter's a lonely person, poor chap. He hasn't any proper home where he can relax. Business, nothing but business! And all that damned weak tea he keeps pouring into himself. Now then, lads, pull your chairs up to the table. Katherine, don't we get any toddy?

MRS. STOCKMANN [*makes for the dining-room*]. I'm just going to get it.

DR. STOCKMANN. Come and sit beside me on the sofa, Captain Horster. It's so rarely we see you. Do sit down, my friends.

[*The men seat themselves round the table.* MRS. STOCKMANN *enters with a tray on which there is a kettle, glasses, decanters and so on.*]

MRS. STOCKMANN. There we are. This is Arrack, and this is rum, and this is cognac. Everybody just help themselves.

DR. STOCKMANN [*takes a glass*]. Ah, we will that! [*Whilst the toddy is being mixed.*] Let's have the cigars out, too. Ejlif, you know where the box is kept. And you, Morten, can bring my pipe. [*The boys go into the room on the right.*] I have a suspicion Ejlif helps himself to a cigar now and then, but I don't let on I know. [*Calls.*] My smoking-cap as well, Morten! Katherine, could you tell him where I've put it. Ah! he's got it. [*The boys bring the various articles.*] Help yourselves, my friends. I'll stick to my pipe. Many's the time this one's done the rounds with me, fair weather and foul, up there in the North. [*They clink glasses.*] Your health! Ah, it's much better to be sitting nice and snug in here.

MRS. STOCKMANN [*sits knitting*]. Will you be sailing soon, Captain Horster?

HORSTER. I reckon we'll be ready by next week.

MRS. STOCKMANN. And then you're off to America?

HORSTER. That's the intention.

BILLING. Then you won't be able to vote in the municipal election.

HORSTER. Is there going to be an election?

BILLING. Didn't you know?

HORSTER. No, I don't bother about things like that.

BILLING. But you take an interest in public affairs, I suppose?

HORSTER. No, I don't know the first thing about them.

BILLING. I think people ought to vote, all the same.

HORSTER. Even those who have no idea what it's all about?

BILLING. No idea? What do you mean? Society's like a ship; everybody must help to steer it.

HORSTER. That might be all very well on dry land; but it wouldn't work very well at sea.

HOVSTAD. It's strange how little most seafaring people care about what goes on ashore.

BILLING. Quite remarkable.

DR. STOCKMANN. Sailors are like birds of passage, equally at home in the north or in the south. All the more reason for the rest of us to be even more active, Mr. Hovstad. Is there anything of public interest in the *Herald* tomorrow?

HOVSTAD. Nothing about municipal affairs. But I thought of putting in your article the day after. . . .

DR. STOCKMANN. Oh damn it, yes! That article. Listen, you must hold it over for a while.

HOVSTAD. Really! It just happens we have room for it now, and it seemed to be the right time for it. . . .

DR. STOCKMANN. Yes, yes, maybe you are right; but you'll have to wait all the same. I'll explain later. . . .

[PETRA, *wearing a hat and a cloak, comes in from the hall, a pile of exercise books under her arm.*]

PETRA. Good evening.

DR. STOCKMANN. Is that you, Petra? Good evening!

[*Greetings all round.* PETRA *takes off her things and puts them, along with the exercise books, on a chair beside the door.*]

PETRA. So you've all been sitting here enjoying yourselves while I've been out slaving.

DR. STOCKMANN. Now *you* come and enjoy yourself too, then.

BILLING. Can I get you something to drink?

PETRA [*comes over to the table*]. Thanks. But I'd rather do it myself. You always make it too strong. But I'm forgetting, Father, I have a letter for you.

[*Goes over to the chair where her things are.*]

DR. STOCKMANN. A letter? Who from?

PETRA [*feels in her coat pocket*]. The postman gave me it just as I was going out. . . .

DR. STOCKMANN [*gets up and goes across to her*]. And you haven't brought it out before now!

PETRA. I hadn't time to run back again with it. Here it is.

DR. STOCKMANN [*seizing the letter*]. Let me see it. Let me see it, child. [*Looks at the address.*] Yes, that's it. . . .

MRS. STOCKMANN. Is *that* the one you have been waiting for, Thomas?

DR. STOCKMANN. Yes, that's the one. Excuse me if I take it straight into . . . Where can I find a light, Katherine? Is there still no lamp in my study!

MRS. STOCKMANN. Yes, of course. There's a lamp already lit on your desk.

DR. STOCKMANN. Good, good. Excuse me a minute. . . .

[*He goes into his room, right.*]

PETRA. What can that be, Mother?

MRS. STOCKMANN. I don't know. He's done nothing else these last few days but ask whether the postman's been.

BILLING. Presumably some country patient.

PETRA. Poor Father! All this work, it's getting too much for him. [*She mixes her drink.*] Ah, I'm going to enjoy this!

HOVSTAD. Have you been taking Evening Classes again today?

PETRA [*sipping her glass*]. Two hours.

BILLING. And four hours this morning at the Institute.

PETRA [*sits at the table*]. Five hours.

MRS. STOCKMANN. And tonight I see you have essays to correct.

PETRA. A whole bundle of them.

HORSTER. You've got plenty of work to do yourself, it seems.

PETRA. Yes, but that's all right. It makes you feel so gloriously tired afterwards.

BILLING. Do you like that?

PETRA. Yes, it makes you sleep so well.

MORTEN. You must be a dreadful sinner, Petra!

PETRA. Sinner?

MORTEN. Working as hard as you do. Mr. Rörlund says that work is a punishment for our sins.

EJLIF. Puh! You must be stupid, believing a thing like that!

MRS. STOCKMANN. Now, now, Ejlif!

BILLING [*laughs*]. Oh, that's good, that is!

HOVSTAD. Don't you want to work as hard as that, Morten?

MORTEN. No, I don't.

HOVSTAD. Well, what *do* you want to be when you grow up?

MORTEN. I want to be a Viking.

EJLIF. Well, you'd have to be a heathen.

MORTEN. All right, I'll be a heathen.

BILLING. I'm with you there, Morten. I say exactly the same.

MRS. STOCKMANN [*making signs*]. I'm sure you wouldn't really do anything of the kind.

BILLING. Yes I would, so help me! I *am* a heathen, and proud of it. You watch, we'll all be heathens before long.

MORTEN. And *then* can we do exactly what we like?

BILLING. Well, you see, Morten . . .

MRS. STOCKMANN. Now, boys, off you go now; I'm sure you've got some homework for tomorrow.

EJLIF. Couldn't *I* just stay on a little bit longer. . . ?

MRS. STOCKMANN. No. Off you go now, both of you.

[*The boys say good night and go into the room, left.*]

HOVSTAD. Do you really think it's bad for the boys to listen to things like that?

MRS. STOCKMANN. Oh, I don't know. But I don't much like it.

PETRA. Oh, Mother! I think you're quite mistaken there.

MRS. STOCKMANN. Yes, that's quite possible. But I *don't* like it, not in my own home.

PETRA. All this hypocrisy, both at home and at school. At home one mustn't say anything; and at school we have to stand there and lie to the children.

HORSTER. Lie to them?

PETRA. Yes. Can't you see we have to teach all sorts of things we don't even believe in ourselves?

BILLING. That's only too true.

PETRA. If only I had the money, I'd start a school myself, where things would be run very differently.

BILLING. Huh! The money!

HORSTER. Well, if you've got anything like that in mind, Miss Stockmann, I'd be glad to offer you the necessary accommodation. My father's big old house is standing there practically empty; there's an enormous dining-room on the ground floor. . . .

PETRA [*laughs*]. Thanks, thanks very much. But nothing's likely to come of it.

HOVSTAD. No, I think Miss Petra's much more likely to join the ranks of the journalists. By the way, have you had any time to look at that English story you promised to translate for us?

PETRA. No, not yet. But you'll have it in good time.

[DOCTOR STOCKMANN *comes out of his room, with the open letter in his hand.*]

DR. STOCKMANN [*waving the letter*]. Well! Here's a bit of news that will set a few tongues wagging about the town!

BILLING. News?

MRS. STOCKMANN. What news?

DR. STOCKMANN. A great discovery, Katherine!

HOVSTAD. Really?

MRS. STOCKMANN. Which you've made?

DR. STOCKMANN. Which I've made, yes. [*Walks up and down.*] Now let them come as they always do, and say it's some madman's crazy idea! Ah, but they'll watch their step this time! They'll watch out this time, I'll bet.

PETRA. But, Father, tell us what this is all about.

DR. STOCKMANN. Yes, yes, just give me time and you'll hear all about it. Ah, if only I had Peter here! Yes, it lets you see how we men go about our affairs as blind as bats. . . .

HOVSTAD. What do you mean, Doctor?

DR. STOCKMANN [*stands by the table*]. Is it not generally believed that our town is a healthy place?

HOVSTAD. Yes, of course.

DR. STOCKMANN. A quite exceptionally healthy place, in fact . . . a place highly commended on this score both for the sick and for the healthy. . . .

MRS. STOCKMANN. Yes, but my dear Thomas . . .

DR. STOCKMANN. And have we not recommended it and acclaimed it? I myself have written repeatedly, both in the *Herald* and in a number of pamphlets. . . .

HOVSTAD. Well, what of it?

DR. STOCKMANN. And then these Baths—the so-called 'artery' of the town, or the 'nerve centre', and the devil only knows what else they've been called. . . .

BILLING. 'The throbbing heart of the town', as I was once, in a festive moment, moved to call it.

DR. STOCKMANN. Quite so. But do you know what they are in reality, these great and splendid and glorious Baths that have cost such a lot of money—do you know what they are?

HOVSTAD. No, what are they?

MRS. STOCKMANN. Yes, what are they?

DR. STOCKMANN. The Baths are nothing but a cesspool.

PETRA. The Baths, Father!

MRS. STOCKMANN [*at the same time*]. Our Baths!

HOVSTAD [*likewise*]. But, Doctor . . . !

BILLING. Absolutely incredible!

DR. STOCKMANN. The whole establishment is a whited poisoned sepulchre, I tell you! A most serious danger to health! All that filth up at Mölledal, where there's such an awful stench—it's all seeping into the pipes that lead to the pump-room! And that same damned, poisonous muck is seeping out on the beach as well!

HORSTER. Where the bathing place is, you mean?

DR. STOCKMANN. Exactly.

HOVSTAD. How are you so certain about all this, Doctor?

DR. STOCKMANN. I have investigated the position with scrupulous thoroughness. Oh, I've had my suspicions long enough. Last year there were a number of curious cases of sickness among the visitors . . . typhoid and gastric fever. . . .

MRS. STOCKMANN. Yes, so there were.

DR. STOCKMANN. It was thought at the time that the visitors had brought their infections with them. But afterwards . . . during the winter . . . I began to have other ideas. So I carried out a few tests on the water, as far as I could.

MRS. STOCKMANN. So *that's* what's been keeping you so busy!

DR. STOCKMANN. Yes, you may well say I've been busy, Katherine. But of course I didn't have all the necessary scientific equipment. So I sent some samples—drinking water as well as sea-water—up to the university to get an exact chemical analysis.

HOVSTAD. Which you have now received?

DR. STOCKMANN [*shows the letter*]. Here it is! It testifies to the presence in the water of putrefied organic matter . . . it's full of bacteria. It is extremely dangerous to health, internally and externally.

MRS. STOCKMANN. What a mercy you found out in time!

DR. STOCKMANN. You may well say so.

HOVSTAD. And what do you intend to do now, Doctor?

DR. STOCKMANN. To see the matter put right, of course.

HOVSTAD. Can that be done?

DR. STOCKMANN. It must be done. Otherwise the whole establishment is useless, ruined. But there's no need for that. It's quite clear to me what must now be done.

MRS. STOCKMANN. But, my dear Thomas, what made you keep all this so secret?

DR. STOCKMANN. Did you expect me to run all round town gossiping about it before I was absolutely certain? No thank you! I'm not such a fool as all that.

PETRA. Still, your own family . . .

DR. STOCKMANN. No, not a living soul. Still, you can run round in the morning to the old 'Badger'. . . .

MRS. STOCKMANN. Please, Thomas!

DR. STOCKMANN. All right, to your grandfather, then. Yes, now we'll give that old boy something that will really open his eyes. He's another one who thinks I'm a bit cracked—oh yes, there are plenty more with the same idea, I can see. But now these good people are going to see something—they're certainly going to see something, this time. [*He walks round rubbing his hands.*] What a commotion this is going to cause in the town, Katherine! You've no idea! All the pipes will have to be re-laid.

HOVSTAD [*rising*] . All the pipes . . . ?

DR. STOCKMANN. Naturally. The intake is sited too low down; it will have to be moved much higher up.

PETRA. So you were right after all.

DR. STOCKMANN. Ah, you remember, Petra? I wrote in opposing it, when they were drawing up the plans. But at that time nobody would listen to me. Well, now I'm going to let them have it. Naturally I've written a report for the Board—it's been lying there all ready for the past week. I was only waiting for this to come. [*He points to the letter.*] But now we'll get this off at once. [*He goes into his room and comes back with a sheaf of papers.*] Look! Four closely written sheets! And the letter attached. A newspaper, Katherine! Something to wrap it in. Good! There we are! Give it to . . . to . . . [*Stamps his foot.*] . . . what the devil's her name again? Anyway, give it to that girl, and tell her to take it straight down to the Mayor.

[MRS. STOCKMANN *takes the packet and goes out through the dining-room.*]

PETRA. What do you think Uncle Peter's going to say, Father?

DR. STOCKMANN. What do you expect him to say? He can't help but be pleased that an important matter like this has been brought to light, surely.

HOVSTAD. Do you mind if we put a little paragraph in the *Herald* about your discovery?

DR. STOCKMANN. I should be extremely grateful if you would.

HOVSTAD. The sooner the public hears about this, the better.

DR. STOCKMANN. Certainly.

MRS. STOCKMANN [*returning*]. She's just gone with it now.

BILLING. You'll be the leading light of the town, Dr. Stockmann, damn me if you won't!

DR. STOCKMANN [*walks happily up and down*]. Oh, don't be silly! I've only done my duty. It just happened to be a lucky strike, that's all. All the same . . .

BILLING. Hovstad, don't you think the town ought to organize something to show its appreciation to Dr. Stockmann?

HOVSTAD. I'll certainly put it forward.

BILLING. And I'll talk it over with Aslaksen.

DR. STOCKMANN. Please, please, my dear friends! Let's have no more of this nonsense. I won't hear of it. And if the Board starts getting any ideas about increasing my salary, I shall refuse. Do you hear me, Katherine?—I won't take it.

MRS. STOCKMANN. Quite right, Thomas.

PETRA [*raising her glass*]. Your health, Father!

HOVSTAD.
BILLING. } Your health, Dr. Stockmann!

HORSTER [*clinking glasses with him*]. Here's wishing you joy of it!

DR. STOCKMANN. Thank you, my dear friends, thank you! I am extremely happy. . . . What a wonderful thing it is to feel that one's been of some service to one's home town and fellow citizens. Hurrah, Katherine!

[*He puts his arms round her and whirls her round and round; she screams and tries to resist. Laughter, applause and cheering for the Doctor. The boys poke their heads in at the door.*]

ACT TWO

The DOCTOR'S *living-room; the door to the dining-room is shut.
It is morning.* MRS. STOCKMANN *comes out of the dining-room,
carrying in her hand a sealed letter; she crosses to the door of the*
DOCTOR'S *study, right, and peeps in.*

MRS. STOCKMANN. Are you there, Thomas?

DR. STOCKMANN [*within*]. Yes, I've just got back. [*Comes in.*] What
is it?

MRS. STOCKMANN. A letter from your brother.

[*She hands him the letter.*]

DR. STOCKMANN. Aha, let us see. [*He opens the envelope and reads.*] 'Your
manuscript is herewith returned. . . .' [*He reads on to himself in a low
murmur.*] Hm!

MRS. STOCKMANN. What does he say?

DR. STOCKMANN. Oh, just that he'll look in about midday.

MRS. STOCKMANN. You mustn't forget to be at home this time.

DR. STOCKMANN. I'll manage that all right; I've finished all my
morning calls.

MRS. STOCKMANN. I'm awfully curious to know how he's taking it.

DR. STOCKMANN. He'll not be very pleased that I was the one to make
the discovery and not he, you'll see.

MRS. STOCKMANN. Doesn't that worry you a little?

DR. STOCKMANN. Oh, he'll be glad enough really, you know. It's just
that Peter can't bear to see anybody other than himself doing things
for the town.

MRS. STOCKMANN. Well, you know what I think, Thomas? I think you
should be a dear and share the credit with him. Couldn't you drop
a hint that it was he who first put you on the track. . . ?

DR. STOCKMANN. Certainly, for all it matters to me. I only want to
see that something gets done about it. . . .

[*Old* MORTEN KIIL *puts his head round the hall door, looks round inquiringly, and chuckles to himself.*]

MORTEN KIIL [*slyly*]. This thing . . . is it true?

MRS. STOCKMANN [*crosses towards him*]. Father! What are you doing here!

DR. STOCKMANN. Well, well! Good morning, Father-in-law!

MRS. STOCKMANN. Do come in.

KIIL. I will if it's true; if it isn't, I'm off again.

DR. STOCKMANN. If what's true?

KIIL. This queer business about the water-works. Well, is it true?

DR. STOCKMANN. Certainly it's true. But how did you get to know about it?

KIIL [*comes in*]. Petra dashed in on her way to school. . . .

DR. STOCKMANN. Oh, did she?

KIIL. Yes, and from what she says . . . I thought she was just pulling my leg; but it isn't like Petra to do that.

DR. STOCKMANN. No, what made you think a thing like that!

KIIL. Oh, you should never trust anybody. You can be taken in almost before you know where you are. But it really is true, then?

DR. STOCKMANN. Definitely. Just you sit down now. [*Urges him to sit on the sofa.*] Isn't this a real stroke of luck for the town. . . ?

KIIL [*fighting his laughter*]. A stroke of luck for the town?

DR. STOCKMANN. Yes, the fact that I found out in time. . . .

KIIL [*as before*]. Oh, yes, of course! But I never thought you would try any monkey tricks on your own brother.

DR. STOCKMANN. Monkey tricks?

MRS. STOCKMANN. Really, Father!

KIIL [*resting his hands and his chin on the handle of his stick and winking slyly at the* DOCTOR]. Let me see, how was it now? Wasn't it something about some little creatures that had got into the water pipes?

DR. STOCKMANN. That's right. Bacteria.

KIIL. And from what Petra said, a whole lot of these animals had got in. An enormous number.

DR. STOCKMANN. That's right. Hundreds of thousands of them!

KIIL. And yet nobody can see them—isn't that what they say?

DR. STOCKMANN. Of course. Nobody can *see* them.

KIIL [*quietly chuckling*]. Damn me if this isn't the best you've managed yet.

DR. STOCKMANN. I don't know what you mean!

KIIL. But you'll never get the Mayor to believe a thing like this.

DR. STOCKMANN. We'll see about that.

KIIL. You don't think he's such a fool as all that!

DR. STOCKMANN. I hope the whole town's going to be such fools as all that.

KIIL. The whole town. Well, that's not such a bad idea, after all. It'll serve them right . . . do them good. They all think they're so much smarter than us older men. They hounded me off the Council, they did, I tell you. Treated me like a dog, they did. But now they'll get what's coming to them. You just carry on with your little tricks, Stockmann.

DR. STOCKMANN. But really . . .

KIIL. You just keep it up, I say. [*Gets up.*] If you can manage to put a thing like this across on the Mayor and his lot, I'll give a hundred crowns to charity on the spot.

DR. STOCKMANN. That's very good of you.

KIIL. Yes, I haven't all that much money to throw about, I'll have you know, but if you pull this off, I'll give fifty crowns to charity next Christmas.

[HOVSTAD *comes in from the hall.*]

HOVSTAD. Good morning! [*Stops.*] Oh, I beg your pardon. . . .

DR. STOCKMANN. No, come in, come in.

KIIL [*chuckles again*]. Him! Is he in on this as well?

HOVSTAD. What do you mean?

DR. STOCKMANN. Of course he's in on it.

KIIL. I might have known! It has to get into the papers. Ah! You're a right one, Stockmann. I'll leave you to talk it over; and now I'll be off.

DR. STOCKMANN. Oh, can't you stay a bit longer?

KIIL. No, I must be off now. Keep it up and bring out all the tricks you can think of. I'm damned sure you won't lose by it.

[*He goes, accompanied by* MRS. STOCKMANN.]

DR. STOCKMANN [*laughs*]. Fancy—the old man doesn't believe a word about this business of the water-works!

HOVSTAD. Ah, so that was what you . . . !

DR. STOCKMANN. Yes, that was what we were talking about. And you've probably come about the same thing, eh?

HOVSTAD. Yes, I have. Can you spare me a moment or two, Doctor?

DR. STOCKMANN. As long as you like, my dear fellow.

HOVSTAD. Have you heard anything from the Mayor?

DR. STOCKMANN. Not yet. He's coming round here later.

HOVSTAD. I've been thinking a lot about this thing since last night.

DR. STOCKMANN. Well?

HOVSTAD. As a doctor and a man of science, you regard this matter of the water-supply as something quite on its own, no doubt. What I mean is—it probably hasn't struck you that it's tied up with a lot of other things?

DR. STOCKMANN. In what way. . . ? Come and sit down, my dear fellow. No, on the sofa there.

[HOVSTAD *sits down on the sofa, the* DOCTOR *in an armchair on the other side of the table.*]

DR. STOCKMANN. Now, what was it you were saying. . . ?

HOVSTAD. You said yesterday that the water was contaminated by impurities in the soil.

DR. STOCKMANN. Yes, there's no doubt it all comes from that poisonous swamp up at Mölledal.

HOVSTAD. You'll forgive me, Doctor, but I think it comes from a very different swamp.

DR. STOCKMANN. What swamp?

HOVSTAD. The swamp that our whole community is standing rotting in.

DR. STOCKMANN. What kind of damned nonsense is this you're talking, Mr. Hovstad?

HOVSTAD. Everything in this town has gradually found its way into the hands of a certain group of officials. . . .

DR. STOCKMANN. Come now, not every one of them is an official.

HOVSTAD. No, but those that aren't officials are friends and hangers-on of those that are—the wealthy ones of the town, and the well-connected. These are the people in control.

DR. STOCKMANN. Yes, but you mustn't forget these are people of ability and insight.

HOVSTAD. How much ability and insight did they show when they laid the water pipes where they are now?

DR. STOCKMANN. *That*, of course, was a tremendous piece of stupidity. But that's going to be put right now.

HOVSTAD. Do you think it will be as easy as all that?

DR. STOCKMANN. Easy or not, it's going to be done.

HOVSTAD. Yes, as long as the press takes a hand.

DR. STOCKMANN. That won't be necessary, my dear fellow. I am sure my brother . . .

HOVSTAD. Excuse me, Doctor, but what I'm trying to tell you is that I intend taking the matter up.

DR. STOCKMANN. In the paper?

HOVSTAD. Yes. When I took over the *Herald* it was with the express intention of breaking up this ring of obstinate old buffers who'd got hold of all the power.

DR. STOCKMANN. But you told me yourself what the outcome of that was; it nearly ruined the paper.

HOVSTAD. Yes, it's true we had to pipe down on that occasion. Only because there was a danger that the whole business about the Baths might have fallen through if those men had been turned out then. But now we've got the Baths, and now these fine gentlemen can be dispensed with.

DR. STOCKMANN. Dispensed with, perhaps. But we have much to thank them for.

HOVSTAD. Full acknowledgement will be given, with all punctiliousness. But no popular journalist, such as I am, can afford to let an opportunity like this go by. This myth of official infallibility must be destroyed. A thing like this has to be rooted out just like any other superstition.

DR. STOCKMANN. I agree with you whole-heartedly, Mr. Hovstad! If there is any superstition, then away with it!

HOVSTAD. I should be most reluctant to implicate the Mayor, seeing that he's your brother. But I'm sure you agree with me that truth must come first.

DR. STOCKMANN. That goes without saying. [*Vehemently.*] Yes, but ... but ...

HOVSTAD. You mustn't think so badly of me. I am no more egotistical or ambitious than most.

DR. STOCKMANN. But, my dear fellow, who's suggesting you are?

HOVSTAD. I came from a fairly poor home, as you know. And I've had plenty of opportunity of seeing what's needed most among the working classes. And it's this: to have some say in the control of public affairs, Dr. Stockmann. *That's* the thing for developing people's ability and knowledge and confidence. ...

DR. STOCKMANN. I can understand that very well. ...

HOVSTAD. Yes . . . and that's why I think it's a terrible responsibility for a journalist if he neglects any opportunity that might bring some measure of freedom to the humble and the oppressed masses. Oh, I realize all the big noises will just call it 'agitation' and so on. Well, let them say what they like! As long as my conscience is clear . . .

DR. STOCKMANN. Absolutely! Absolutely, my dear Mr. Hovstad. All the same . . . damn it . . . ! [*There is a knock at the door.*] Come in!

[ASLAKSEN, *the printer, appears at the hall door. He is poorly but decently dressed in a black suit, with a slightly crumpled white necktie; he carries in his hand a felt hat and gloves.*]

ASLAKSEN [*bows*]. Excuse me, Doctor, intruding like this . . .

DR. STOCKMANN [*rises*]. Well, well, here's Mr. Aslaksen!

ASLAKSEN. Yes, Doctor.

HOVSTAD [*stands*]. Is it me you're looking for, Aslaksen?

ASLAKSEN. No, it isn't. I didn't know I'd be seeing you here. No, actually it was the Doctor himself. . . .

DR. STOCKMANN. Well, and what can I do for you?

ASLAKSEN. Is it true what Mr. Billing tells me—that you are thinking of trying to get the water-supply improved?

DR. STOCKMANN. Yes, for the Baths.

ASLAKSEN. Well then, I've just called to say that I am ready to give every support to a thing like that.

HOVSTAD [*to the* DOCTOR]. There you are, you see!

DR. STOCKMANN. That's extremely kind of you, thank you very much; but . . .

ASLAKSEN. Because you might easily find you need some middle-class support to back you up. We now form what you might call a compact majority here in town—when we really *want* to, that is. And it's always a good thing to have the majority on your side, Dr. Stockmann.

DR. STOCKMANN. That is undoubtedly true. It's just that I don't quite understand why it should be necessary to take any special measures of that kind here. When it's such an ordinary straightforward thing, it seems to me . . .

ASLAKSEN. Ah, you never know but what it mightn't be a good thing anyway. I know well enough what the local authorities are like. Those in charge are never very keen on any kind of proposal that *other* people put forward. And that's why I think it wouldn't be a bad thing if we made a bit of a demonstration.

HOVSTAD. Yes, exactly.

DR. STOCKMANN. Demonstration, do you say? Well, what way did you think of demonstrating?

ASLAKSEN. Well, with great moderation, of course, Doctor. I try for moderation, in all things. For moderation is the first attribute of a good citizen . . . in my own opinion, that is.

DR. STOCKMANN. That's something that you yourself are well-known for, too, Mr. Aslaksen.

ASLAKSEN. Yes, I think I may say it is. And this matter of the water-supply is an extremely important one for us of the middle classes. The Baths show every sign of becoming a little goldmine for the town, as you might say; it's to them that many of us are looking for a means of livelihood, especially those of us who are house-holders. That's why we want to give the Baths all the support we can. And I happen to be the chairman of the Ratepayers Associ-ation . . .

DR. STOCKMANN. Yes?

ASLAKSEN. . . . and as I am moreover the local representative of the Temperance Society—you know, of course, that I take an active part in Temperance affairs?

DR. STOCKMANN. Yes, of course, of course.

ASLAKSEN. Well . . . you can see I meet quite a lot of people one way and another. And as I have the reputation of being a prudent and law-abiding citizen, as the Doctor himself said, it means that I have a certain influence in the town—a kind of little position of power, even though I say it myself.

DR. STOCKMANN. That I know very well, Mr. Aslaksen.

ASLAKSEN. And so, you see, it would be quite a simple matter for me to prepare an address, if such appeared necessary.

DR. STOCKMANN. An address?

ASLAKSEN. Yes, a kind of vote of thanks from the townspeople in appreciation of the way you have dealt with this matter of public interest. It goes without saying that the address would have to be drafted with proper moderation so as not to give offence to the authorities and those in power. And as long as we are careful about *that*, I don't really see that anybody can object, do you?

HOVSTAD. Well, even if they didn't like it very much . . .

ASLAKSEN. No, no, no! Nothing to give offence to the authorities, Mr. Hovstad. Nothing that might antagonize people with so much say in things. I've had quite enough of that sort of thing in my time, and no good ever comes of it, either. But the honest expression of a man's considered opinion surely cannot offend anybody.

DR. STOCKMANN [*shaking his hand*]. I just can't tell you, my dear Mr. Aslaksen, how delighted I am to find this support among my fellow citizens. It gives me great pleasure . . . great pleasure! I tell you what! What about a little glass of sherry, eh?

ASLAKSEN. No, thank you very much. I never touch spirits.

DR. STOCKMANN. What do you say to a glass of beer, then?

ASLAKSEN. No thank you again, Doctor. I never take anything as early in the day as this. I am going into town now to talk to some of the ratepayers to see if I can prepare public opinion.

DR. STOCKMANN. Well, it really is extremely kind of you, Mr. Aslaksen. But I just cannot see all these arrangements being necessary. I think surely this matter can be managed on its own.

ASLAKSEN. The authorities sometimes take a bit of moving, Dr. Stockmann. Not that I'm trying to blame anybody, of course! Dear me, no!

HOVSTAD. We'll have a go at them in the paper tomorrow, Aslaksen.

ASLAKSEN. Please, Mr. Hovstad, no violence. Proceed with moderation, otherwise you'll get nowhere. You can take my word for it, because my experience was acquired in the school of life.—Well, I'll say goodbye now, Doctor. You now know that we of the middle classes stand solidly behind you. You have the compact majority on your side, Dr. Stockmann.

DR. STOCKMANN. Thank you very much, my dear Mr. Aslaksen. [*Holds out his hand.*] Goodbye, goodbye!

ASLAKSEN. Are you coming with me as far as the office, Mr. Hovstad?

HOVSTAD. I'll be along soon. I still have one or two things to see to.

ASLAKSEN. Very good.

[*He bows and goes.* DR. STOCKMANN *accompanies him out into the hall.*]

HOVSTAD [*as the* DOCTOR *returns*]. Well, Doctor, what d'you think of that? Don't you think it's about time we did a bit of shaking up and clearing out of all this weary, cowardly fiddle-faddle?

DR. STOCKMANN. Are you referring to Mr. Aslaksen?

HOVSTAD. Yes, I am. He's one of the ones in the swamp—decent enough sort though he may be in other ways. Most of them are like that round here, teetering along, wobbling one way then the other; they are so damned cautious and scrupulous that they never dare commit themselves to any proper step forward.

DR. STOCKMANN. Yes, but Aslaksen seemed so genuinely anxious to help.

HOVSTAD. There's something I value more than that; and that is to stand firm, like a man with confidence in himself.

DR. STOCKMANN. Yes, I think you are absolutely right there.

HOVSTAD. That's why I'm going to take this opportunity to see if I can't get these well-intentioned people to show a bit of backbone. This worship of authority must be wiped out in this town. The real significance of this tremendous and unforgivable blunder about the water-supply must be brought home to every single person with a vote.

DR. STOCKMANN. Very well. If you think it is for the public good, so be it. But not till I've had a word with my brother about it.

HOVSTAD. In the meantime I'll be drafting a leading article. And if the Mayor refuses to go on with things . . .

DR. STOCKMANN. Oh, but how could you possibly think that?

HOVSTAD. It's not impossible. And if so . . . ?

DR. STOCKMANN. In that case, I promise you. . . . Listen, in that case you can print my article; every word of it.

HOVSTAD. May I? Is that a promise?

DR. STOCKMANN [*hands him the manuscript*]. Here it is, take it with you. There's no harm in your reading it through; you can give it back to me afterwards.

HOVSTAD. Good! I'll do that. Well then goodbye, Doctor!

DR. STOCKMANN. Goodbye, goodbye! You'll see, Mr. Hovstad, it'll be all plain sailing . . . nothing but plain sailing!

HOVSTAD. Hm! We'll see.

[*He bows and goes out through the door.*]

DR. STOCKMANN [*crosses and looks into the dining-room*]. Katherine . . . ! Ah, are you back, Petra?

PETRA [*comes in*]. Yes, I've just come from school.

MRS. STOCKMANN [*comes in*]. Hasn't he been yet?

DR. STOCKMANN. Peter? No. But I've had a long talk with Hovstad. He's quite worked up about this discovery I've made. It seems there's more in it than I'd first imagined, you know. He's put his paper at my disposal, if it's ever needed.

MRS. STOCKMANN. Do you think it will be needed?

DR. STOCKMANN. No, of course not. But it makes one very proud to think that one has the progressive and independent press on one's side. And what else do you think! I've also had the chairman of the Ratepayers Association here to see me.

MRS. STOCKMANN. Really? What did he want?

DR. STOCKMANN. Also to offer his support. They are all going to support me, if need be. Katherine—do you know what I've got backing me?

MRS. STOCKMANN. Backing you? No. What?

DR. STOCKMANN. The compact majority.

MRS. STOCKMANN. Oh, have you! And is that a good thing, then, Thomas?

DR. STOCKMANN. I should jolly well think it is! [*He walks up and down, rubbing his hands.*] Lord! How wonderful it is to stand, as it were, shoulder to shoulder in the brotherhood of one's fellow citizens!

PETRA. And to be doing such good and useful work, Father!

DR. STOCKMANN. Yes, not to mention that it's for one's own birth-place, too.

MRS. STOCKMANN. There's the bell.

DR. STOCKMANN. That must be him. [*There is a knock on the door.*] Come in!

MAYOR [*comes from the hall*]. Good morning.

DR. STOCKMANN. Glad to see you, Peter!

MRS. STOCKMANN. Good morning, Peter! How are things with you?

MAYOR. Oh, so-so, thank you. [*To the* DOCTOR.] I received from you yesterday, after office hours, a report concerning the state of the water at the Baths.

DR. STOCKMANN. Yes. Have you read it?

MAYOR. Yes, I have.

DR. STOCKMANN. And what have you got to say about it?

MAYOR [*with a sidelong glance*]. Hm . . .

MRS. STOCKMANN. Come along, Petra.

[MRS. STOCKMANN *and* PETRA *go into the room on the left.*]

MAYOR [*after a pause*]. Was it necessary to make all these investigations behind my back?

DR. STOCKMANN. Yes, because until I knew with absolute certainty . . .

MAYOR. And now you do, you mean?

DR. STOCKMANN. Yes. Surely you are also convinced yourself by now!

MAYOR. Is it your intention to present this document to the Board as an official report?

DR. STOCKMANN. Of course. Something will have to be done about this thing. And quick.

MAYOR. As usual, you use some rather emphatic expressions in your report. Among other things, you say that what we offer our summer visitors is sheer poison.

DR. STOCKMANN. Well, Peter, what else can you call it? Just think! That water's poison whether you drink it or bathe in it! And this is what we offer those poor invalids who come to us in good faith and pay good money hoping to get their health back!

MAYOR. And then you conclude by stating we must build a sewer to deal with these alleged impurities from Mölledal, and that the present water pipes must be re-laid.

DR. STOCKMANN. Well, can you suggest any other solution? I can't.

MAYOR. This morning I made it my business to look in on the town engineer. And—half as a joke, as it might be—I brought up these measures as something we might give consideration to at some future date.

DR. STOCKMANN. Some future date!

MAYOR. He smiled at what he took to be my extravagance—of course. Have you taken the trouble to think what these proposed alterations would cost? According to the information I received, the cost would very probably be several hundred thousand crowns.

DR. STOCKMANN. As much as that?

MAYOR. Yes. But that's not the worst. The work would take at least two years.

DR. STOCKMANN. Two years, eh? Two whole years?

MAYOR. At least. And what's to be done with the Baths in the meantime? Shall we shut them? We'll have to. You don't think people are going to come all the way here if the rumour got about that the water was polluted?

DR. STOCKMANN. But, Peter, that's just what it is.

MAYOR. And all this has to come out just when the Baths were beginning to pay their way. A lot of other places in the district could equally well develop into health resorts. Can't you see they would set to work at once to divert all our tourist traffic to themselves. Of course they would; no doubt whatever. And we'd be left sitting there with all that expensive plant on our hands; we'd probably have to abandon the entire project. The whole town would be ruined, thanks to you!

DR. STOCKMANN. Me. . . ? Ruined. . . ?

MAYOR. The whole future prosperity of the town is tied up with the Baths. You can see that as well as I can.

DR. STOCKMANN. Then what should be done, do you think?

MAYOR. I am not entirely convinced by your report that the state of the Baths is as serious as you make out.

DR. STOCKMANN. If anything it is worse. At least, it will be in the summer, when the warm weather comes.

MAYOR. As I said before, I think you exaggerate considerably. Any competent doctor would surely be able to meet this situation . . . take some suitable precautionary measures and treat any noticeable injurious effects, if there actually turned out to be any.

DR. STOCKMANN. Well? And what then?

MAYOR. The existing water-supply for the Baths is now an established fact, and must be treated as such. But it is reasonable to suppose that in time the Directors might not be disinclined to consider how far, in the light of the prevailing financial situation, it would be possible to initiate certain improvements.

DR. STOCKMANN. Do you honestly think I would lend myself to that sort of sharp practice?

MAYOR. Sharp practice?

DR. STOCKMANN. Sharp practice, yes! That's what it would be. A swindle, a fraud, an absolute crime against the public and against society!

MAYOR. As I remarked earlier, I have not been able to persuade myself that there is any actual imminent danger.

DR. STOCKMANN. Oh yes, you have! You couldn't help it. My report is absolutely correct and clear, I know that! And you know it too, Peter, but you won't admit it. You were the one responsible for having the Baths and the water-supply sited where they are now. And it's *this*—this damned blunder of yours—that you won't admit. Puh! Do you think I can't see right through you?

MAYOR. And even if that were so? Even if I may seem to guard my reputation somewhat jealously, it's all for the good of the town. Without some measure of moral authority, I should not be able to guide and direct public affairs in the way I consider best serves the common weal. Therefore—and for various other reasons—I consider it imperative that your report should not be presented to the Board. In the public interest, it must be withheld. Then I shall bring the matter up later, and we'll do all we can privately. But nothing, not a single word, of this disastrous business must be made public.

DR. STOCKMANN. My dear Peter, I doubt if we can prevent that now.

MAYOR. It must and shall be prevented.

DR. STOCKMANN. It's no use, I tell you. Too many people know about it already.

MAYOR. Know about it already! Who? I only hope it's not those people on the *Herald*. . . ?

DR. STOCKMANN. Oh yes, they know already. The progressive and independent press will see to it that you do your duty.

MAYOR [*after a short pause*]. You are an astonishingly indiscreet man, Thomas! Did you never think what consequences this might have for you personally?

DR. STOCKMANN. Consequences? For me?

MAYOR. For you and your family.

DR. STOCKMANN. What the devil do you mean by *that*?

MAYOR. Would you agree I've always been a decent brother to you, always ready to help?

DR. STOCKMANN. Yes, you have. And I'm grateful to you for it.

MAYOR. There's no need to be. In a way I had to be . . . in my own interests. It was always my hope that, by helping to improve your position economically, I might be able to some extent to hold you in check.

DR. STOCKMANN. What's that? It was only in your own interests . . . !

MAYOR. In a way, I said. It is distressing for a public figure to have his nearest relative for ever compromising himself.

DR. STOCKMANN. You mean that's what I do?

MAYOR. Yes, I'm afraid you do, without realizing it. You have a restless, pugnacious, aggressive temperament. And then there's this unfortunate habit of yours of rushing into print about everything under the sun. No sooner do you get some idea or other into your head than you've got to write an article for the papers about it . . . or even a whole pamphlet.

DR. STOCKMANN. But don't you think if a man's got hold of some new idea he has a duty to bring it to the notice of the public?

MAYOR. Oh, the public doesn't need new ideas. The public is best served by the good old, accepted ideas it already has.

DR. STOCKMANN. That's putting it pretty bluntly, anyway!

MAYOR. Yes, for once I'm going to be blunt with you. I've always tried to avoid that hitherto, knowing how irritable you are. But now, Thomas, I'm going to tell you the truth. You have no idea what harm you do yourself by this recklessness of yours. You complain about the authorities . . . about the government, even . . . you are always going on about them. Then you try to insist that you've been passed over, or been badly treated. But what do you expect, when you are so difficult?

DR. STOCKMANN. So I'm difficult too, am I?

MAYOR. Yes, Thomas, you are an extremely difficult man to work with, as I know from experience. You show absolutely no consideration. You seem to forget that it's me you have to thank for your appointment here as medical officer to the Baths. . . .

DR. STOCKMANN. I was the only possible man for the job! I, and nobody else! Wasn't I the first to see that the town could be made into a flourishing health resort? And wasn't I the only one to realize it at the time? Alone and single-handed I fought for the idea, year after year, writing and writing. . . .

MAYOR. Undoubtedly. But the time wasn't ripe for it then. Of course, you couldn't very well be any judge of that, living up there at the back of beyond. But when a more appropriate time came, then I— and some of the others—took the matter in hand. . . .

DR. STOCKMANN. Yes, and messed up the whole issue! My lovely plans! Oh yes, it's clear enough now all right what a brainy lot you turned out to be!

MAYOR. The only thing that's clear in my opinion is that you are simply trying to pick a quarrel again. You must find some outlet, so you go for your superiors—that's an old habit of yours. You just can't bear to submit to authority; you take a jaundiced view of anybody holding a superior appointment, regard him as a personal enemy. And straightway any weapon that happens to come to hand is good enough to attack him with. But now I've made it clear to you what other interests are at stake for the town as a whole—and consequently also for me personally. And that's why I'm telling you, Thomas, that I intend to be quite ruthless in demanding of you certain things.

DR. STOCKMANN. And what is it you demand?

MAYOR. Since you have been so indiscreet as to discuss this delicate matter with certain unauthorized persons—despite the fact that it should have been treated as a matter confidential to the Board— things can of course no longer be hushed up. All sorts of rumours will spread, and the more spiteful ones among us can be relied on to embellish them with all sorts of extras. It will therefore be necessary for you to make a public denial of these rumours.

DR. STOCKMANN. For me! How? I don't understand you.

MAYOR. We shall expect you, after making further investigations, to come to the conclusion that the matter is not by any means as dangerous or as serious as you in the first instance imagined it to be.

DR. STOCKMANN. Aha! So that's what you expect, is it?

MAYOR. Furthermore we shall expect you to make public declaration of your confidence in the Board, in its efficiency and its integrity, and in its readiness to take all necessary steps to remedy such defects as may arise.

DR. STOCKMANN. Yes, but don't you see, you'll never do anything just by fiddling with the problem, hoping to patch things up. I'm telling you straight, Peter, and I'm absolutely and utterly convinced . . .

MAYOR. As an employee you have no right to any private opinion.

DR. STOCKMANN [*falters*]. No right. . . ?

MAYOR. As an employee, I mean. As a private individual—good Lord, yes, that's quite different. But as a subordinate member of the staff of the Baths, you have no right to express any opinion that conflicts with that of your superiors.

DR. STOCKMANN. That's going too far! Are you trying to say that a doctor, a man of science, has no right . . . !

MAYOR. The matter in this instance is by no means a purely scientific one; it is a combination of technical and economic factors.

DR. STOCKMANN. It can be what the hell it likes, as far as I'm concerned. What matters to me is the right to speak my mind about any damn' thing under the sun.

MAYOR. Certainly! Anything at all—except the Baths. That we forbid.

DR. STOCKMANN [*shouts*]. Forbid! You lot!

MAYOR. *I* forbid you. I personally, your superior. And when I give you an order, it's up to you to obey.

DR. STOCKMANN [*controlling himself*]. Peter . . . if it wasn't that you were my brother . . . !

PETRA [*flings the door open*]. Don't stand for it, Father!

MRS. STOCKMANN [*following her*]. Petra! Petra!

MAYOR. Aha! You've been listening!

MRS. STOCKMANN. You were talking so loud, we just couldn't help . . .

PETRA. No! I stood there and listened.

MAYOR. Actually, I'm just as well pleased . . .

DR. STOCKMANN [*approaches him*]. You were saying something to me about ordering and obeying. . . ?

MAYOR. You compelled me to speak to you like that.

DR. STOCKMANN. And you expect me to get up in public and eat my own words?

MAYOR. We consider it absolutely necessary that you issue some sort of statement along the lines I laid down.

DR. STOCKMANN. And supposing I don't . . . obey?

MAYOR. Then we shall ourselves issue a statement to reassure the public.

DR. STOCKMANN. Indeed. Well, then I shall contradict you in the newspapers. I shall stand up for myself. I shall prove that I'm right and you're wrong. And then what will you do?

MAYOR. Then I shall not be able to prevent you from being dismissed.

DR. STOCKMANN. What!

PETRA. Father! Dismissed!

MRS. STOCKMANN. Dismissed!

MAYOR. Dismissed from the Baths. I shall be obliged to arrange for you to be given notice and to see that you sever all connection with the Baths.

DR. STOCKMANN. You wouldn't dare!

MAYOR. Blame your own recklessness.

PETRA. Uncle, this is a disgraceful way to treat a man like Father!

MRS. STOCKMANN. Do be quiet, Petra!

MAYOR [*looks at* PETRA]. Ah! So we can't wait to express our opinions, eh? Naturally. [*To* MRS. STOCKMANN.] Katherine, you are probably the most sensible one in this house. Please use whatever influence you have with your husband. Get him to see what this will mean both for his family . . .

DR. STOCKMANN. My family's got nothing to do with anybody but me!

MAYOR. . . . as I was saying, both for his family, and for the town he lives in.

DR. STOCKMANN. I'm the one with the real welfare of the town at heart. All I want to do is expose certain things that are bound to come out sooner or later anyway. Oh, I'll show them whether I love this town or not.

MAYOR. All you are really doing, by your sheer blind obstinacy, is cutting off the main source of the town's prosperity.

DR. STOCKMANN. That source is poisoned, man! Are you mad! We live by peddling filth and corruption! The whole of the town's prosperity is rooted in a lie!

MAYOR. Fantastic nonsense—or worse! Any man who can cast such aspersions against his own birthplace is nothing but a public enemy.

DR. STOCKMANN [*goes up to him*]. You dare . . . !

MRS. STOCKMANN [*throws herself between them*]. Thomas!

PETRA [*seizes her father by the arm*]. Steady, Father!

MAYOR. I am not going to wait to be assaulted. You've had your warning. Try to realize what you owe to yourself and to your family. Goodbye.

[*He goes.*]

DR. STOCKMANN [*walks up and down*]. Have I to stand for this? In my own house, Katherine! What do you think?

MRS. STOCKMANN. I agree it's shameful and disgraceful, Thomas. . . .

PETRA. If only I could get my hands on that uncle of mine. . . !

DR. STOCKMANN. It's my own fault, I should have had it out with them long ago . . . bared my teeth . . . bit back! Calling me a public enemy! Me! By God, I'm not going to stand for that!

MRS. STOCKMANN. But, Thomas my dear, your brother has a lot of power on his side. . . .

DR. STOCKMANN. Yes, but I have *right* on mine!

MRS. STOCKMANN. Right! Yes, of course. But what's the use of right without might?

PETRA. Oh, Mother! How can you say such a thing?

DR. STOCKMANN. So you think having right on your side in a free country doesn't count for anything? You are just being stupid, Katherine. And anyway, haven't I the progressive and independent press to look to, and the compact majority behind me. There's enough might there, surely, isn't there?

MRS. STOCKMANN. But heavens, Thomas! You surely aren't thinking of . . .

DR. STOCKMANN. Not thinking of what?

MRS. STOCKMANN. . . . of setting yourself up against your brother, I mean.

DR. STOCKMANN. What the devil do you expect me to do? What else is there if I'm going to hold to what's right and proper.

PETRA. Yes, that's what I'm wondering too.

MRS. STOCKMANN. But you know very well it won't do a scrap of good. If they won't, they won't.

DR. STOCKMANN. Aha, Katherine, just give me time. I'll fight this thing to a finish, you watch.

MRS. STOCKMANN. Yes, and while you are fighting, you'll lose your job, that's what!

DR. STOCKMANN. Then at least I shall have done my duty by the public . . . and by society. Calling me a public enemy, indeed!

MRS. STOCKMANN. But what about your family, Thomas? What about us at home? Will you be doing your duty by the ones you should provide for first?

PETRA. Oh, stop thinking always about us, Mother!

MRS. STOCKMANN. Yes, it's easy for *you* to talk. You can stand on your own feet, if need be. But don't forget the boys, Thomas. And think a little of yourself too, and of me. . . .

DR. STOCKMANN. You must be absolutely mad, Katherine! If I were to be such a miserable coward as to go grovelling to Peter and his blasted pals, do you think I'd ever be happy again as long as I lived?

MRS. STOCKMANN. I'm sure I don't know. But God preserve us from the kind of happiness we'll have if you insist on carrying on like this. We'll be just where we were before—no job, no regular income. I thought we had enough of that in the old days. Don't forget that, Thomas, and think what all this is going to lead to.

DR. STOCKMANN [*squirming and clenching his fists*]. Oh, the things that a free and decent man has to put up with at the hands of these damned bureaucrats! Isn't it terrible, Katherine?

MRS. STOCKMANN. Yes, they've treated you disgracefully, I will say that. But heavens! Once you start thinking of all the injustices in this world people have to put up with . . . ! There's the boys, Thomas! Look at them! What's going to become of them? Oh no, you'd never have the heart. . . .

[*Meanwhile* EJLIF *and* MORTEN *have come in, carrying their school-books.*]

DR. STOCKMANN. The boys . . . ! [*Suddenly stops with a determined look.*] No! Even if it meant the end of the world, I'm not knuckling under.

[*He walks over to his study.*]

MRS. STOCKMANN [*following him*]. Thomas! What are you going to do?

DR. STOCKMANN [*at the door*]. I want to be able to look my boys in the face when they grow up into free men.

[*He goes in.*]

MRS. STOCKMANN [*bursts into tears*]. Oh, God help us.

PETRA. Father's grand! He'll never give in.

[*The boys, in amazement, begin to ask what is happening;* PETRA *signs to them to be silent.*]

ACT THREE

The editorial office of the People's Herald. *The entrance door is on the back wall, left; on the same wall, right, is a glazed door, through which the printing shop can be seen. On the right wall is another door. A large table stands in the middle of the room covered with papers, newspapers, and books. Downstage, left, is a window, near which is a writing desk with high stool. A couple of armchairs by the table, other chairs along the walls. The room is gloomy and cheerless; the furniture is old, the armchairs dirty and torn. Within the printing shop, a few compositors are at work; further back a hand press is being worked.*

    HOVSTAD *is sitting at the desk, writing. After a moment or two,* BILLING *comes in from the right with the* DOCTOR'S *manuscript in his hand.*

BILLING. Well, I must say . . . !

HOVSTAD [*writing*]. Have you read it through ?

BILLING [*puts the manuscript on the desk*]. Yes, I have that.

HOVSTAD. Pretty scathing, isn't he?

BILLING. Scathing! Damn it, it's absolutely devastating! Every word lands—what shall I say?—like a blow from a sledge-hammer.

HOVSTAD. Yes, but they're not the sort you can knock down with one blow.

BILLING. That's true! But then we'll just keep on hitting them . . . time and time again until the whole set-up collapses. Sitting in there reading it, I just felt as though I could see the revolution coming.

HOVSTAD [*turning*]. Hush! Don't let Aslaksen hear that.

BILLING [*lowering his voice*]. Aslaksen is a chicken-hearted little coward. He's got no backbone. But I hope this time you're going to insist? Eh? The Doctor's article will go in?

HOVSTAD. Yes, as long as the Mayor doesn't give in without a fight. . . .

BILLING. Make things damned dull if he does.

HOVSTAD. Well, fortunately we can make something of the situation whatever happens. If the Mayor doesn't accept the Doctor's proposal, then he'll have all the middle class on to him . . . all the Ratepayers Association and the rest. And if he does accept it, then he's got to face a pack of the bigger shareholders in the Baths who have so far been his strongest supporters. . . .

BILLING. Yes, that's right. I dare say it'll cost them a pretty penny. . . .

HOVSTAD. You can be damn' sure it will. Then, you see, once the ring is broken, we can keep pegging away day after day in the paper, pointing out to the public how completely incompetent the Mayor is, and how all the positions of responsibility, in fact the whole council, ought to be handed over to the Liberals.

BILLING. By God, that's good, that is! I can see it . . . I can see it! We're on the brink of revolution!

[*There is a knock on the door.*]

HOVSTAD. Hush! [*Shouts*]. Come in!

[DR. STOCKMANN *comes through the entrance door, back, left.*]

HOVSTAD [*crosses to him*]. Ah, it's you, Doctor. Well?

DR. STOCKMANN. Print it, Mr. Hovstad!

HOVSTAD. Has it come to that?

BILLING. Hurrah!

DR. STOCKMANN. Print away, I tell you. Yes, it *has* come to that. Now they're going to get what's coming to them. This is war, Mr. Billing!

BILLING. War to the knife, I hope! Go ahead and slaughter them, Doctor!

DR. STOCKMANN. This article is only the beginning. Already I've got enough ideas for another four or five of them. Where's Aslaksen?

BILLING [*shouts into the printing shop*]. Can you come here a minute, Aslaksen?

HOVSTAD. Another four or five articles, d'you say? About the same thing?

DR. STOCKMANN. Oh, no! Far from it, my dear fellow. No, they're about quite different things. But they're all bound up with the question of the water-supply and the sewers. You know how one thing leads to another. It's just like what happens when you start tinkering with an old building—just like that.

BILLING. By God, that's true. You pretty soon realize it's all such a shambles that you'll never finish the job properly until you've pulled the whole thing down.

ASLAKSEN [*from the printing shop*]. Pulled the whole thing down! Surely, Doctor, you are not thinking of pulling the Baths down?

HOVSTAD. No, of course not! Don't get alarmed!

DR. STOCKMANN. No, we were referring to something quite different. Well, Mr. Hovstad, what have you got to say about my article?

HOVSTAD. I think it's an absolute masterpiece. . . .

DR. STOCKMANN. Yes, isn't it. . . ? Well, I'm very pleased, very pleased.

HOVSTAD. It's so clear and to the point. You don't need to be an expert to follow it; anybody can understand from it what it's all about. I bet you get every progressively-minded man on your side.

ASLAKSEN. And all the sensible ones as well, I hope.

BILLING. The sensible ones and the other sort too. . . . What I mean is, practically the whole town.

ASLAKSEN. In that case, I think we might venture to print it.

DR. STOCKMANN. I jolly well think so!

HOVSTAD. It will be in tomorrow morning.

DR. STOCKMANN. Yes, by heavens! We mustn't waste any time. By the way, Mr. Aslaksen, that was something I was going to ask you: you'll give the manuscript your own personal attention, won't you?

ASLAKSEN. I will indeed.

DR. STOCKMANN. Take care of it as though it were gold. No misprints, every word is important. I'll look in again later on; perhaps I could check some of the proofs.—Yes, I can't tell you how I'm longing to get this thing in print . . . slam it down . . .

BILLING. Slam it down, that's right! Like a thunderbolt!

DR. STOCKMANN. . . . to submit it to the scrutiny of every intelligent citizen. Oh, you can't imagine what I've had to put up with today. They've threatened me with all sorts of things; to deprive me of my most basic human rights . . .

BILLING. What! Your human rights!

DR. STOCKMANN. . . . They tried to degrade me, to rob me of my self-respect, tried to force me to put personal advantage before my most sacred convictions. . . .

BILLING. Damn it, that's going too far!

HOVSTAD. Ah, you can expect anything from that lot.

DR. STOCKMANN. But I'm not going to let them get away with it—I'll make that plain in black and white. Every blessed day I'll be in the *Herald*—lying at anchor, so to speak, and bombarding them with one high-explosive article after another . . .

ASLAKSEN. Oh but, come now. . . .

BILLING. Hurrah! It's war, it's war!

DR. STOCKMANN. . . . I'll batter them to the ground, I'll smash them, I'll blast their defences wide open for all right-thinking men to see! That's what I'll do!

ASLAKSEN. But you will act with moderation, Doctor! Shoot . . . but with moderation. . . .

BILLING. No, no! Don't spare the dynamite!

DR. STOCKMANN [*continues unbashed*]. Because, you see, it's no longer just the water-supply and the sewers now. No, the whole community needs cleaning up, disinfecting. . . .

BILLING. That's what I like to hear!

DR. STOCKMANN. All these dodderers have got to be chucked out! Wherever they are! My eyes have been opened to a lot of things today. I haven't quite got everything sorted out yet, but I will in time. My friends, what we must look for is young and vigorous men to be our standard-bearers. We must have new men in command in all our forward positions.

BILLING. Hear, hear!

DR. STOCKMANN. And if only we hold together, things can't help but go smoothly! We'll launch this whole revolution as smoothly as a ship off the stocks. Don't you think so?

HOVSTAD. For my own part, I think we now have every prospect of placing the control of the council in the proper hands.

ASLAKSEN. And as long as we proceed with moderation, I can't see that there should be any risk.

DR. STOCKMANN. Who the devil cares whether it's risky or not? What I do, I do in the name of truth and in obedience to my conscience.

HOVSTAD. You deserve every support, Doctor.

ASLAKSEN. Yes, it's quite obvious that the Doctor is a true benefactor to the town, a real benefactor to society.

BILLING. By God, Aslaksen, Dr. Stockmann is the people's friend!

ASLAKSEN. I rather think the Ratepayers Association might soon be wanting to use that phrase.

DR. STOCKMANN [*greatly moved, grasps their hands*]. Thank you, thank you, my good friends, for being so loyal. How gratifying it is to hear you say that. That brother of mine called me something quite different. Well, he'll get it all back again, with interest! Well, I must be off now to see a patient of mine, poor devil. But I'll be back, as I promised. Be sure you take good care of that manuscript, Mr. Aslaksen—and, whatever you do, don't go leaving out any of my exclamation marks! If anything, put a few more in! Well, well! Goodbye for now, goodbye!

[*As they show him out, they take leave of each other; he goes.*]

HOVSTAD. There's a man who could be extremely useful to us.

ASLAKSEN. Yes, as long as he keeps to this business of the Baths. But if he gets going on other things, it might not be very wise to follow him.

HOVSTAD. Hm! That all depends on . . .

BILLING. Don't be so damned frightened, Aslaksen.

ASLAKSEN. Frightened? Yes, Mr. Billing, I *am* frightened—when it's a question of local politics. That's something I've learnt in the hard school of experience, you see. But you just put me in high-level politics, even in opposition to the government itself, and you'll see then whether I'm frightened.

BILLING. No, I'm sure you wouldn't be. But that's just what makes you so inconsistent.

ASLAKSEN. It's because I'm a man with a conscience. That's what it is. You can attack the government without really doing society any harm, because you see people like that just don't take any notice— they stay in power as if nothing had happened. But the *local* leaders, they *can* be turned out; and then you might easily get a lot of inexperienced men at the helm, doing immense harm to the interests of the ratepayers and other people.

HOVSTAD. But what about self-government as a factor in the people's education—haven't you thought about *that*?

ASLAKSEN. When a man has acquired a vested interest in something, you can't always expect him to think of everything, Mr. Hovstad.

HOVSTAD. Then I hope to God I never have any vested interests.

BILLING. Hear, hear!

ASLAKSEN [*smiles*]. Hm! [*He points to the desk.*] Your predecessor in that editorial chair was Mr. Steensgaard. He used to be sheriff.

BILLING [*spits*]. Pah! That turncoat.

HOVSTAD. I'm no time-server—and never will be, either.

ASLAKSEN. A politician should never be too certain about anything, Mr. Hovstad. And you, Mr. Billing, hadn't you better draw your horns in just a little these days—seeing you've applied for the post of Secretary to the council?

BILLING. I . . . !

HOVSTAD. *Have* you, Billing?

BILLING. Well . . . Can't you see I'm only doing it to annoy our local bigwigs, damn them.

ASLAKSEN. Well, it's nothing whatever to do with me. But when people accuse me of being cowardly or inconsistent, there's one thing I want to stress: the political record of Aslaksen the printer is an open book. I haven't changed in any way except to become more moderate in my ways. My heart is still with the people. But I'll not deny that my head rather inclines me to support the authorities—the local ones, I mean.

[*He goes into the printing shop.*]

BILLING. Don't you think we'd better finish with him, Hovstad?

HOVSTAD. Do you know anybody else who'd agree to let us have our paper and printing on credit?

BILLING. It's a damned nuisance not having the necessary capital.

HOVSTAD [*sits down at the desk*]. Yes, if only we had *that*. . . !

BILLING. What about approaching Dr. Stockmann?

HOVSTAD [*turning over some papers*]. Oh, what's the use of that? He hasn't anything.

BILLING. No, but he's got a good man up his sleeve—Old Morten Kiil, 'the Badger', as he is called.

HOVSTAD [*writing*]. What makes you so sure *he's* got anything?

BILLING. By God, he's got money all right! And some of it is bound to come to the Stockmanns. Then he'll have to think of providing for . . . for the children, at any rate.

HOVSTAD [*half turning*]. Are you counting on *that*?

BILLING. Counting? I'm not counting on anything.

HOVSTAD. You're right there. And you'd better not count on that job with the council, either. Because I can tell you now—you won't get it.

BILLING. Do you think I don't know that? That's just what I want—not to get it. To be rejected like that is just like adding fuel to the flames —it's like getting a new supply of fresh gall, and you need something like that in a dump like this where nothing really stimulating ever happens.

HOVSTAD [*writing*]. Yes, yes, I know.

BILLING. Well . . . it won't be long now before they hear from me! Now I'm going to sit down and write that appeal to the Ratepayers.

[*He goes into the room, right.*]

HOVSTAD [*sits at his desk, bites his pen shank and says slowly*]. Hm! Aha, so that's it. . . . [*There is a knock at the door.*] Come in!

[*PETRA comes in by entrance door, back, left.*]

HOVSTAD [*rises*]. Well, look who it is! What are you doing here?

PETRA. You must excuse me, but . . .

HOVSTAD [*pulling an armchair forward*]. Won't you have a seat?

PETRA. No, thanks. I can't stay.

HOVSTAD. Is it something from your father, perhaps. . . ?

PETRA. No, it's something from me. [*She takes a book out of her coat pocket.*] Here's that English story.

HOVSTAD. Why have you brought it back?

PETRA. Because I'm not going to translate it.

HOVSTAD. But you promised me faithfully. . . .

PETRA. I hadn't read it then. And you haven't either, have you?

HOVSTAD. No, you know I don't know any English. But . . .

PETRA. Quite. That's why I wanted to tell you that you'll have to look round for something else. [*She puts the book on the table.*] You can never use a thing like this for the *Herald*.

HOVSTAD. Why not?

PETRA. Because it runs completely contrary to everything you believe in.

HOVSTAD. Well, what does that matter. . . ?

PETRA. You don't quite understand. It's all about some supernatural power that's supposed to watch over all the so-called good people, and how everything is for the best . . . and how all the so-called wicked people get punished in the end. . . .

HOVSTAD. Yes, but that's just fine. That's exactly what people want.

PETRA. Can you honestly put stuff like that in front of people? When you yourself don't believe a word of it? You know very well that's not what happens in reality.

HOVSTAD. You're absolutely right, of course. But an editor cannot always do what he wants. You often have to give way to public opinion, in minor things. After all, politics is the most important thing in life—at least, for a newspaper, it is. And if I want to win people over to certain liberal and progressive ideas, it's no good scaring them all off. If they find a nice moral story like this on the back pages of the paper, they are much more ready to accept what we print on the front page—it gives them a sort of feeling of security.

PETRA. Oh, no! Not you, surely! I just can't picture you as a spider spinning a kind of web to trap unwary readers.

HOVSTAD [*smiling*]. Thank you for those few kind words. No, in fact you are right—it was all Billing's idea, not mine.

PETRA. Billing's!

HOVSTAD. Yes, at least he was talking about it just the other day. Billing's really the one who is keen to get that story in. I don't know the book at all.

PETRA. Mr. Billing? A man with all his progressive ideas. . . ?

HOVSTAD. Oh, Billing is a man of parts. I've heard he's also applied for the post of Secretary to the council.

PETRA. I don't believe it, Mr. Hovstad. Whatever makes him think he could stand a job like that?

HOVSTAD. You'd better ask him yourself.

PETRA. I'd never have thought a thing like that of Mr. Billing.

HOVSTAD [*looks at her intently*]. Wouldn't you? Does it come as such a surprise to you?

PETRA. Yes. Or perhaps not. Oh, I don't really know. . . .

HOVSTAD. Journalists like us are not really up to much, Miss Stock-mann.

PETRA. Do you really mean that?

HOVSTAD. Now and again I think it.

PETRA. In the ordinary daily routine, perhaps; that I could understand. But when you've taken on something big . . .

HOVSTAD. You mean this business about your father?

PETRA. Yes, exactly. I imagine you must feel like a man with a more worthwhile job than most people.

HOVSTAD. Yes, I do feel a bit like that today.

PETRA. I'm sure you must! Oh, what a splendid calling you have chosen. Blazing a trail for the advancement of truth, and of new and bold ideas. . . ! Or even just to step up and give your support, without fear or favour, to a man who has suffered a great wrong. . . .

HOVSTAD. Especially when this unfortunate man happens to be . . . hm! . . . I don't really know how to put it. . . .

PETRA. Happens to be so decent and honest, you mean?

HOVSTAD [*quietly*]. Especially when he happens to be your father, is what I meant.

PETRA [*suddenly struck*]. What?

HOVSTAD. Yes, Petra—Miss Petra.

PETRA. Is *that* what you are thinking of first? You're not concerned about the thing itself? Not about truth? Not about Father's public-spirited action?

HOVSTAD. Oh yes, that too, naturally!

PETRA. No thank you, Mr. Hovstad! You have given yourself away this time. And I can never trust you again about anything.

HOVSTAD. I don't see why you want to take it like this when it was mainly for your sake . . . !

PETRA. What makes me cross is that you haven't played straight with Father. You talked to him as though all you cared about was truth and the common good. You made fools of us both. You are not the man you pretended to be. I'll never forgive you . . . never!

HOVSTAD. I shouldn't be too outspoken actually, Miss Petra. Especially not now.

PETRA. Why not now, particularly?

HOVSTAD. Because your father cannot manage without my help.

PETRA [*looking down at him*]. So you're one of those, are you? Pah!

HOVSTAD. No, no, I'm not. I don't know what came over me, saying a thing like that. You mustn't believe a word of it.

PETRA. I know what to believe. Goodbye!

ASLAKSEN [*comes in from the printing shop urgently and with an air of secrecy*]. In Heaven's name, Mr. Hovstad . . . [*He sees* PETRA.] Oh, I'm sorry. I shouldn't . . .

PETRA. There's the book. You'd better give it to somebody else.

[*She walks across to the main door.*]

HOVSTAD [*following her*]. But, Miss Petra . . .

PETRA. Goodbye.

[*She goes.*]

ASLAKSEN. I say, Mr. Hovstad!

HOVSTAD. Well, well . . . what is it?

ASLAKSEN. The Mayor's out there in the printing shop.

HOVSTAD. The Mayor, did you say?

ASLAKSEN. Yes, he wants a word with you. He came in the back way—didn't want to be seen, I suppose.

HOVSTAD. What does he want, I wonder? No, wait here, I'll go myself. . . .

[*He goes over to the door into the printing shop, opens it and invites the* MAYOR *in.*]

HOVSTAD. Aslaksen, keep an eye open to see that nobody . . .

ASLAKSEN. I understand.

[*He goes into the printing shop.*]

MAYOR. I don't suppose you were expecting me here, Mr. Hovstad.

HOVSTAD. No, as a matter of fact I wasn't.

MAYOR [*looking about him*]. You've settled yourself in here nice and comfortably. Very nice.

HOVSTAD. Oh . . .

MAYOR. And here I come without any appointment, and proceed to take up all your precious time.

HOVSTAD. *Please*, Mr. Mayor, I'm only too delighted to be of service. Let me take your things. [*He puts the* MAYOR's *hat and stick on a chair.*] Now, won't you sit down?

MAYOR [*sits at the table*]. Thank you.

[HOVSTAD *also sits down at the table.*]

MAYOR. I have had an extremely disagreeable matter to deal with today, Mr. Hovstad.

HOVSTAD. Really? Of course, with so many things to see to . . .

MAYOR. This particular matter has been raised by the Medical Officer of the Baths.

HOVSTAD. By the Doctor?

MAYOR. He's written a kind of report about a number of alleged shortcomings at the Baths, and sent it to the Board.

HOVSTAD. Has he?

MAYOR. Yes, hasn't he told you? I thought he said . . .

HOVSTAD. Oh yes, that's right! He did mention something about . . .

ASLAKSEN [*coming from the printing shop*]. I'd better have that manuscript. . . .

HOVSTAD [*angrily*]. It's on the desk there.

ASLAKSEN [*finds it*]. Good.

MAYOR. But I say, surely *that's* . . .

ASLAKSEN. Yes, that's the Doctor's article, Mr. Mayor.

HOVSTAD. Oh, is *that* what you were talking about?

MAYOR. Precisely. What do you think of it?

HOVSTAD. I'm no expert, of course, and I've only just glanced at it.

MAYOR. Yet you are printing it?

HOVSTAD. I can't very well refuse a man in his position. . . .

ASLAKSEN. I've got no say in what goes into the paper, Mr. Mayor. . . .

MAYOR. Of course not.

ASLAKSEN. I just print what I'm given.

MAYOR. Quite so.

ASLAKSEN. So if you'll excuse me . . .

[*He walks across towards the printing shop.*]

MAYOR. Just a moment, please, Mr. Aslaksen. With your permission, Mr. Hovstad . . .

HOVSTAD. Please.

MAYOR. Now you are a wise and sensible sort of man, Mr. Aslaksen.

ASLAKSEN. I am very pleased you should think so, Mr. Mayor.

MAYOR. And a man of considerable influence in some circles.

ASLAKSEN. Mainly among the people of moderate means.

MAYOR. The small ratepayers are in the majority—here as everywhere else.

ASLAKSEN. That's right.

MAYOR. And I've no doubt you know what most of them think about things in general. Isn't that so?

ASLAKSEN. Yes, I think I can safely say I do, Mr. Mayor.

MAYOR. Well . . . the fact that this admirable spirit of self-sacrifice is to be found in our town among its less well-endowed citizens . . .

ASLAKSEN. How do you mean?

HOVSTAD. Self-sacrifice?

MAYOR. ... This shows an admirable public spirit, most admirable. I almost said unexpected, too. But of course you know better than I what people's attitudes are.

ASLAKSEN. But, Mr. Mayor ...

MAYOR. And in fact it's no small sacrifice that the town will have to make.

HOVSTAD. The town?

ASLAKSEN. But I don't understand. . . . You mean the Baths, surely. . . .

MAYOR. At a rough estimate, the alterations which the Medical Officer considers desirable will come to something like a couple of hundred thousand crowns.

ASLAKSEN. That's a lot of money, but ...

MAYOR. Of course it will be necessary to raise a municipal loan.

HOVSTAD [*rises*]. Surely it's not the idea that the town ... ?

ASLAKSEN. It's not going to come out of the rates! Not out of the people's pockets!

MAYOR. My dear Mr. Aslaksen, where else do you see the money coming from?

ASLAKSEN. I think the owners ought to take care of that.

MAYOR. The owners do not see themselves in a position to provide any additional capital.

ASLAKSEN. Is that absolutely certain, Mr. Mayor?

MAYOR. I am assured on that point. If all these extensive alterations are considered desirable, the town itself must pay for them.

ASLAKSEN. But God damn it all—I beg your pardon!—but this puts a completely different light on things, Mr. Hovstad!

HOVSTAD. Yes, it does indeed.

MAYOR. The most ruinous thing is that we'll be forced to close the Baths for a couple of years.

HOVSTAD. Close them? Completely?

ASLAKSEN. For two years?

MAYOR. Yes, the work will take all that long—at least.

ASLAKSEN. Yes, but Heavens! We could never last out that long, Mr. Mayor. What would people like us live on in the meantime?

MAYOR. I regret to say that is an extremely difficult question to answer, Mr. Aslaksen. But what do you expect us to do? Do you think anybody is going to come here if you get people going round making up these stories about the water being polluted, and about the place being a cesspool, and the whole town . . .

ASLAKSEN. Do you think the whole thing might just be imagination?

MAYOR. With the best will in the world, I cannot come to any other conclusion.

ASLAKSEN. Then I must say Dr. Stockmann is being most irresponsible in all this. You must forgive me, Mr. Mayor, but . . .

MAYOR. I regret what you say is quite true, Mr. Aslaksen. My brother has always been rather impetuous, unfortunately.

ASLAKSEN. Are you still prepared to support him after this, Mr. Hovstad?

HOVSTAD. But who would have thought . . . ?

MAYOR. I have drawn up a short statement of the facts, putting a rather more sober interpretation on them; and in it I have suggested some ways in which such defects as may come to light could reasonably be dealt with without going beyond the present resources of the Baths.

HOVSTAD. Have you this statement with you, Mr. Mayor?

MAYOR [*fumbling in his pocket*]. Yes, I brought it with me on the off-chance that . . .

ASLAKSEN [*hastily*]. Heavens above, there he is!

MAYOR. Who? My brother?

HOVSTAD. Where?

ASLAKSEN. He's coming in through the printing shop.

MAYOR. It *would* happen. I don't want to bump into him here, and there was still a lot more I wanted to talk to you about.

HOVSTAD [*points to the door on the right*]. In there for the present.

MAYOR. But . . . !

HOVSTAD. There's only Billing in there.

ASLAKSEN. Quick, quick! He's coming now.

MAYOR. All right. But see if you can't get rid of him quickly.

[*He goes out through the door, right, which* ASLAKSEN *opens, and shuts again behind him.*]

HOVSTAD. Pretend you are doing something, Aslaksen.

[*He sits down and begins to write.* ASLAKSEN *rummages through a pile of newspapers on a chair, right.*]

DR. STOCKMANN [*entering from the printing shop*]. Back again!

[*He puts down his hat and stick.*]

HOVSTAD [*writing*]. Already, Doctor? Hurry up with what we were talking about, Aslaksen. We haven't got a lot of time to spare today.

DR. STOCKMANN. No proofs yet, they tell me.

ASLAKSEN [*without turning round*]. You could hardly expect them yet, Doctor.

DR. STOCKMANN. Well, well, it's just that I'm impatient—as you can well imagine. I can't settle to anything until I've seen the thing in print.

HOVSTAD. Hm! It'll be a good while yet, I fancy. Don't you think so, Aslaksen?

ASLAKSEN. Yes, I'm rather afraid so.

DR. STOCKMANN. Never mind, my dear fellows. I'll look in again. I don't mind coming twice if need be. An important thing like this . . . the welfare of the whole town . . . this is no time for dawdling on. [*About to go, but stops and comes back.*] Actually . . . there was something else I wanted to talk to you about.

HOVSTAD. Excuse me, but couldn't we perhaps make it some other time. . . ?

DR. STOCKMANN. It won't take a second. You see it's just that ... when people read my article in the paper tomorrow morning, and realize that all through the winter I have been quietly working away in the interests of the town ...

HOVSTAD. Yes, but Doctor ...

DR. STOCKMANN. I know what you are going to say. You think I was only damn' well doing my duty ... my simple duty as a citizen. Of course! I know that as well as you do. But my fellow citizens, you know. . . . Well, I mean, they think rather highly of me, actually, these good people. . . .

ASLAKSEN. Yes, the people have thought very highly of you up to now, Dr. Stockmann.

DR. STOCKMANN. Yes, and that's just what I'm a little bit afraid of. . . . What I mean is ... a thing like this comes along, and they—especially the underprivileged classes—take it as a rousing call to take the affairs of the town into their own hands in future.

HOVSTAD [*rising*]. Hm! Dr. Stockmann, I don't think I ought to conceal from you ...

DR. STOCKMANN. Aha! I might have guessed there'd be something in the wind. But I won't hear of it! If anybody's thinking of organizing anything like that ...

HOVSTAD. Like what?

DR. STOCKMANN. Well, anything at all—a parade or a banquet or a presentation—whatever it is, you must promise me faithfully to put a stop to it. And you too, Mr. Aslaksen! I insist!

HOVSTAD. Excuse me, Doctor, but sooner or later you've got to hear the real truth. . . .

[MRS. STOCKMANN, *in hat and coat, enters by the main door, back, left.*]

MRS. STOCKMANN [*sees the* DOCTOR]. Just as I thought!

HOVSTAD [*goes over to her*]. You here too, Mrs. Stockmann?

DR. STOCKMANN. What the devil do you want here, Katherine?

MRS. STOCKMANN. You know very well what I want.

HOVSTAD. Won't you take a seat? Or perhaps ...

MRS. STOCKMANN. Thanks, but don't you bother about me. And you must forgive me coming here to fetch my husband; for I'm the mother of three children, I'll have you know.

DR. STOCKMANN. What's all this rubbish! We all know that!

MRS. STOCKMANN. But it doesn't look as if you care very much these days about your wife and children; otherwise you wouldn't be carrying on as you are, bringing us all to rack and ruin.

DR. STOCKMANN. Have you gone stark, staring mad, Katherine? Are you trying to say a man with wife and children has no right to proclaim the truth—has no right to be a useful and active citizen— has no right to be of service to the town he lives in?

MRS. STOCKMANN. Do be reasonable, Thomas!

ASLAKSEN. Just what I say. Moderation in all things.

MRS. STOCKMANN. That's why it's very wrong of you, Mr. Hovstad, to lure my husband away from house and home and fool him into getting mixed up in all this.

HOVSTAD. I don't go about fooling people. . . .

DR. STOCKMANN. Fool me! Do you think I'd let anybody make a fool of *me*!

MRS. STOCKMANN. Yes, you would. I know, I know, you are the cleverest man in town. But you're too easily fooled, Thomas. [*To* HOVSTAD.] Remember, if you print what he's written he loses his job at the Baths. . . .

ASLAKSEN. What!

HOVSTAD. You know, Doctor . . .

DR. STOCKMANN [*laughs*]. Ha ha! Just let them try! Oh no, they wouldn't dare. You see, I have the compact majority behind me.

MRS. STOCKMANN. Yes, worse luck! Fancy having a nasty thing like that behind you.

DR. STOCKMANN. Fiddlesticks, Katherine! Go home and look to your house and let me look to society. Why should you be so afraid; I'm quite confident, and really rather pleased with things. [*Walks up and down, rubbing his hands.*] Truth and the People will prevail, you can take your oath on that. Oh, I see the massed ranks of a great citizen army marching on to victory. . . ! [*Stops by a chair.*] What the devil is *that*?

ASLAKSEN [*turns to look*]. Oh!

HOVSTAD [*similarly*]. Hm!

DR. STOCKMANN. There lies the highest mark of authority.

[*He picks the* MAYOR'S *hat up carefully by the tips of his fingers and holds it aloft.*]

MRS. STOCKMANN. The Mayor's hat!

DR. STOCKMANN. And here the baton of office, too. How in the name of glory . . . ?

HOVSTAD. Well . . .

DR. STOCKMANN. Ah, I see! He's been here trying to talk you over. Ha ha! Came to the right man, eh? Then he must have seen me in the printing shop. [*Bursts into laughter.*] Did he run away, Mr. Aslaksen?

ASLAKSEN [*hurriedly*]. Yes, Doctor, he ran away.

DR. STOCKMANN. Ran away without either his stick or . . . Rubbish, Peter never runs away from anything. But what the devil have you done with him? Ah . . . in there, of course. Now I'll show you something, Katherine!

MRS. STOCKMANN. Thomas . . . please!

ASLAKSEN. Have a care, Doctor!

[DR. STOCKMANN *puts the* MAYOR'S *hat on, takes his stick, walks over and throws open the door, and stands there saluting. The* MAYOR *comes in, red with anger; behind him comes* BILLING.]

MAYOR. What's the meaning of all this tomfoolery?

DR. STOCKMANN. Show some respect, my dear Peter. I'm the one in authority here now.

[*He walks up and down.*]

MRS. STOCKMANN [*near to tears*]. Oh, Thomas, really!

MAYOR [*following him about*]. Give me my hat and my stick!

DR. STOCKMANN [*as before*]. You might be chief constable, but I am the Mayor—I'm head of the whole town, can't you see!

MAYOR. Take that hat off, I tell you. Don't forget it's an official badge of office!

DR. STOCKMANN. Pooh! When a people rises from its slumber like a giant refreshed, do you think anybody's going to be scared by a hat? Because you might as well know, we are having a revolution in town tomorrow. You threatened to dismiss me; well now I'm dismissing you, relieving you of all your official positions. . . . Perhaps you think I can't? Oh yes, I can. Because I can bring irresistible social pressure to bear. Hovstad and Billing will put down a barrage in the *People's Herald*, and Aslaksen will sally forth at the head of the entire Ratepayers Association. . . .

ASLAKSEN. Not me, Doctor.

DR. STOCKMANN. Yes of course you will. . . .

MAYOR. Aha! Then perhaps Mr. Hovstad has decided to associate himself with this agitation after all?

HOVSTAD. No, Mr. Mayor.

ASLAKSEN. No, Mr. Hovstad is not so stupid as to go and ruin both the paper and himself for the sake of some wild idea.

DR. STOCKMANN [*looks round*]. What does this mean?

HOVSTAD. You have represented your case in a false light, Dr. Stockmann; consequently I cannot give it my support.

BILLING. And after what the Mayor was kind enough to tell me in there . . .

DR. STOCKMANN. A false light! You leave that side of things to me. You just print my article—I'm quite ready to stand by everything I say.

HOVSTAD. I'm not going to print it. I cannot and will not and dare not print it.

DR. STOCKMANN. Dare not? What sort of talk is that? You are the editor, aren't you? And it's the editors who control the press, surely?

ASLAKSEN. No, it's the readers.

MAYOR. Fortunately, yes.

ASLAKSEN. It's public opinion, the educated public, the ratepayers and all the others—these are the people who control the press.

DR. STOCKMANN [*calmly*]. And all these forces are against me?

ASLAKSEN. Yes, they are. It would mean total ruin for the town if your article were printed.

DR. STOCKMANN. Indeed.

MAYOR. My hat and my stick!

[DR. STOCKMANN *takes the hat off and puts it on the table, along with the stick.*]

MAYOR [*collecting them both*]. Your term as mayor has come to an abrupt end.

DR. STOCKMANN. This is not the end yet. [*To* HOVSTAD.] So it's quite impossible to get my article in the *Herald*?

HOVSTAD. Quite impossible. And I'm thinking partly also of your family. . . .

MRS. STOCKMANN. Oh, you needn't start worrying about his family, Mr. Hovstad.

MAYOR [*takes a sheet of paper out of his pocket*]. For the guidance of the public, it will be sufficient to print this. It is an official statement.

HOVSTAD [*takes it*]. Good. I'll see that it goes in.

DR. STOCKMANN. But not mine! You think you can gag me and silence the truth! You'll not get away with this so easily. Mr. Aslaksen, will you please take my manuscript and print it for me at once as a pamphlet—at my own expense, and on my authority. I want four hundred copies—no, five . . . six hundred, I want.

ASLAKSEN. Not if you offered me its weight in gold could I let my printing press be used for a thing like that. I daren't offend public opinion. You'll not get anybody in town to print it, I shouldn't think.

DR. STOCKMANN. Give it back to me then.

HOVSTAD [*hands him the manuscript*]. There you are.

DR. STOCKMANN [*takes his hat and stick*]. I'll get it out somehow. I'll call a mass meeting and read it out! All my fellow citizens shall hear the voice of truth!

MAYOR. You'll never get anybody to hire you a hall.

ASLAKSEN. Absolutely nobody, I'm quite certain.

BILLING. No, I'm damned if they will.

MRS. STOCKMANN. But that would be outrageous! Why is everybody against you all of a sudden?

DR. STOCKMANN [*angrily*]. I'll tell you why. It's because all the men in this town are nothing but a lot of old women—like you. All they can think about is their families; they never think about the rest of the community.

MRS. STOCKMANN [*taking his arm*]. Then I'll show them one . . . old woman at least who can be a man . . . for once. I'll stick by you, Thomas!

DR. STOCKMANN. Well said, Katherine. And I *will* have my say, by Heaven! If I can't book a hall, I'll hire a man with a drum to march round town with me, and I'll proclaim it at every street corner.

MAYOR. I can't believe you'd be so absolutely crazy.

DR. STOCKMANN. Oh yes, I would!

ASLAKSEN. You'll not get a single man in the whole of the town to go with you!

BILLING. No, I'm damned if you will!

MRS. STOCKMANN. Don't you give in now, Thomas. I'll get the boys to go with you.

DR. STOCKMANN. That's a wonderful idea!

MRS. STOCKMANN. Morten will love to go; and Ejlif's sure to come along as well.

DR. STOCKMANN. Yes, and then what about Petra! And you too, Katherine?

MRS. STOCKMANN. No, no, not me. But I'll stand in the window and watch, that's what I'll do.

DR. STOCKMANN [*puts his arms round her and kisses her*]. Thank you for that! And now, gentlemen, the gloves are off. We'll see whether you and your shabby tricks can stop an honest citizen who wants to clean up the town.

[*He and his wife go out through the door, back, left.*]

MAYOR [*shakes his head thoughtfully*]. Now he's sent her mad, too.

ACT FOUR

A large, old-fashioned room in the house of CAPTAIN HORSTER.
*At the back of the room, double doors open on to an anteroom. On
the wall, left, are three windows; against the opposite wall is a
dais, on which is a small table, and on it two candles, a water carafe,
a glass, and a bell.*

*The room is additionally lit by wall lamps between the windows.
Downstage left, a table with candles and a chair. Down right is a
door, and beside it a couple of chairs.*

*There is a big crowd of townspeople of all classes. A few women
and one or two schoolboys can be seen among them. More and more
people keep coming in through the door at the back, filling up the
room.*

FIRST MAN [*bumping into another man*]. Hello, Lamstad! You here as
well?

SECOND MAN. I never miss a public meeting.

THIRD MAN. I expect you've brought your whistle?

SECOND MAN. You bet I have. Haven't you?

THIRD MAN. I'll say I have. Skipper Evensen said he was going to
bring his great big cow-horn.

SECOND MAN. Good old Evensen!

[*Laughter in the group.*]

FOURTH MAN [*joining them*]. Here, I say, what's going on here tonight?

SECOND MAN. It's Dr. Stockmann. He's holding a protest meeting
against the Mayor.

FOURTH MAN. But the Mayor's his brother!

FIRST MAN. That doesn't matter. Dr. Stockmann's not frightened.

THIRD MAN. But he's got it all wrong. It said so in the *Herald*.

SECOND MAN. Yes, he must be wrong this time, because nobody would
let him have a hall for his meeting—Ratepayers Association, Men's
Club, nobody!

FIRST MAN. He couldn't even get the Baths Hall.

SECOND MAN. I should think not.

A MAN [*in another group*]. Whose side are we on here, eh?

A SECOND MAN [*in the same group*]. Just you keep an eye on Aslaksen, and do what *he* does.

BILLING [*with a briefcase under his arm, pushing his way through the crowd*]. Excuse me, gentlemen! May I come through, please? I'm reporting for the *Herald*. Thank you . . . thank you!

[*He sits at the table, left.*]

A WORKMAN. Who's he?

SECOND WORKMAN. Don't you know *him*? That's Billing, he's on Aslaksen's paper.

[CAPTAIN HORSTER *conducts* MRS. STOCKMANN *and* PETRA *in through the door, right front.* EJLIF *and* MORTEN *are with them.*]

HORSTER. I thought perhaps the family might like to sit here. You can easily slip out there if anything happens.

MRS. STOCKMANN. Do you really think things might get out of hand?

HORSTER. You never know . . . with all these people here. But you sit here, and don't worry.

MRS. STOCKMANN [*sits down.*] It was very kind of you to offer my husband this room.

HORSTER. Well, since nobody else would . . .

PETRA [*who has also sat down*]. And it was brave of you too, Captain Horster.

HORSTER. Oh, I can't see there was anything particularly brave about it.

[HOVSTAD *and* ASLAKSEN *arrive simultaneously but separately, and make their way through the crowd.*]

ASLAKSEN [*walks over to* HORSTER]. Hasn't Dr. Stockmann arrived yet?

HORSTER. He's waiting in there.

[*Movement in the crowd near the door at the back.*]

HOVSTAD [*to* BILLING]. Look! Here's the Mayor.

BILLING. Yes, damn me if he hasn't turned up after all!

[*The* MAYOR *eases his way through the crowd, bowing politely, and takes up a position by the wall, left. A moment later,* DR. STOCKMANN *enters by the door, right front. He wears a black frock coat and a white cravat. Some people clap uncertainly, which is met by subdued hissing. Then there is silence.*]

DR. STOCKMANN [*in an undertone*]. How do you feel, Katherine?

MRS. STOCKMANN. I'm all right, thanks. [*Lowers her voice.*] Try not to lose your temper, Thomas.

DR. STOCKMANN. Oh, I can control myself. [*Looks at his watch, steps up on the dais, and bows.*] It's now quarter past . . . so I think we can begin. . . .

[*He produces his manuscript.*]

ASLAKSEN. First I think we ought to elect a chairman.

DR. STOCKMANN. No. That's not necessary.

SEVERAL VOICES [*shouting*]. Yes, yes it is!

MAYOR. I should also have thought that we should elect a chairman.

DR. STOCKMANN. But I've called this meeting to deliver a lecture, Peter.

MAYOR. Your lecture might just possibly lead to divergent expressions of opinion.

MANY VOICES [*from the crowd*]. A chairman! A chairman!

HOVSTAD. The consensus of opinion seems to be that we should have a chairman.

DR. STOCKMANN [*controlling himself*]. Very well! Let the 'consensus of opinion' have its way.

ASLAKSEN. Wouldn't the Mayor accept nomination?

THREE MEN [*applauding*]. Bravo! Bravo!

MAYOR. For a number of obvious reasons, I must decline. But fortunately we have here with us a man whom I think we can all accept. I refer, of course, to the chairman of the Ratepayers Association, Mr. Aslaksen.

MANY VOICES. Yes, yes. Good old Aslaksen! Bravo!

[DR. STOCKMANN *gathers up his manuscript and steps down from the dais.*]

ASLAKSEN. If it is the wish of my fellow citizens, I can hardly refuse. . . .

[*Clapping and cheers.* ASLAKSEN *mounts the dais.*]

BILLING [*writing*]. Let's see—'Mr. Aslaksen elected by acclamation . . .'

ASLAKSEN. And now, perhaps I may be allowed, in this present capacity, to take the opportunity of saying a few brief words. I am a quiet and peace-loving man, who believes in discreet moderation and in . . . and in moderate discretion. Everyone who knows me is aware of that.

MANY VOICES. That's right! That's right, Aslaksen!

ASLAKSEN. I have learnt from long experience in the school of life that moderation is the quality that best befits a citizen . . .

MAYOR. Hear, hear!

ASLAKSEN. . . . and that discretion and moderation are the things whereby society is best served. I might perhaps, therefore, suggest to the honourable gentleman who has called this meeting that he endeavour to keep within the bounds of moderation.

A MAN [*near the door*]. Up the Moderates!

A VOICE. Shut up there!

MANY VOICES. Sh! Sh!

ASLAKSEN. No interruptions, gentlemen, please! Has anybody any comment to make?

MAYOR. Mr. Chairman!

ASLAKSEN. Yes, Mr. Mayor.

MAYOR. In view of the close relationship which, as is doubtless well known, exists between me and the present Medical Officer of the Baths, I should have much preferred not to speak this evening. But my connections with the Baths, to say nothing of my concern for the vital interests of the town, compel me to put forward some sort of proposal. I think I may safely assume that not a single one of us present here today wants to see irresponsible and exaggerated accounts put about concerning the sanitary conditions at the Baths and in the town generally.

MANY VOICES. No, no! Certainly not! We protest!

MAYOR. I should like to propose, therefore, that the Medical Officer be not permitted by this meeting to present his account of the matter.

DR. STOCKMANN [*flaring up*]. Not permitted! What is this . . .?

MRS. STOCKMANN [*coughing*]. Hm! hm!

DR. STOCKMANN [*composing himself*]. Ah! Not permitted, eh!

MAYOR. In my communication to the *People's Herald*, I acquainted the public with the relevant facts, and every right-thinking person can quite well form his own opinion. It clearly shows that the Doctor's proposal—apart from being a vote of censure on the leading citizens of the town—simply means saddling the ratepayers with an unnecessary expenditure of at least several hundred thousand crowns.

[*Cries of disapproval, and whistles.*]

ASLAKSEN [*ringing the bell*]. Order please, gentlemen! I should like to support the Mayor's proposal. I too believe there is some ulterior motive behind the Doctor's agitation. He talks about the Baths, but what he's really after is revolution. He wants to see the control of the council pass into other hands. Nobody doubts but what the Doctor is sincere in his intentions—nobody can be in two minds about that, surely. I too am in favour of self-government by the people, as long as it doesn't fall too heavily on the ratepayers. But that's just what *would* happen here. And that's why I'm damned . . . excuse me, gentlemen . . . why I just can't bring myself to agree with Dr. Stockmann this time. You can pay too dearly even for the best of things sometimes. That's *my* opinion.

[*Animated applause on all sides.*]

HOVSTAD. I feel I ought to make my position clear, too. Dr. Stockmann's agitation seemed in the early stages to be attracting a certain measure of approval and I supported it as impartially as I was able. But then we got wind of the fact that we had allowed ourselves to be misled by an incorrect account. . . .

DR. STOCKMANN. Incorrect. . . !

HOVSTAD. A not wholly reliable account, then. The Mayor's statement has proved that. I trust nobody here doubts my liberal convictions. The policy of the *People's Herald* on the more important political questions must surely be known to everybody. But I have profited from the advice of experienced and thoughtful men that, when it comes to local affairs, a paper should proceed with a certain caution.

ASLAKSEN. I entirely agree with the speaker.

HOVSTAD. And in the matter under discussion it is now undeniably true that Dr. Stockmann has public opinion against him. But what is the first and foremost duty of an editor, gentlemen? Is it not to work in harmony with his readers? Has he not been given, as it were, a tacit mandate to work loyally and unremittingly for the welfare of his fellows? Or am I perhaps mistaken?

MANY VOICES. No, no! Hovstad is right!

HOVSTAD. It has been a sad thing for me to break with a man in whose house I have of late been a frequent guest—a man who until today has enjoyed the undivided goodwill of his fellow citizens—a man whose only . . . or should we say, whose most characteristic failing is to be guided more by his heart than by his head.

A FEW SCATTERED VOICES. That's true! Good old Dr. Stockmann!

HOVSTAD. But my duty to the community compelled me to break with him. There is also one further consideration that impels me to oppose him and, if possible, to prevent him from going any further along this fateful course he has taken. And that is consideration for his family . . .

DR. STOCKMANN. You stick to the water-supply and the sewers!

HOVSTAD. . . . Consideration for his wife and his helpless children.

MORTEN. Is that us he means, Mother?

MRS. STOCKMANN. Hush!

ASLAKSEN. I shall now put the Mayor's proposal to the vote.

DR. STOCKMANN. You needn't bother! I don't intend speaking about all the dirty business at the Baths tonight. No! You are going to hear about something quite different.

MAYOR [*in an undertone*]. Now what's he up to?

A DRUNKEN MAN [*beside the entrance door*]. If I'm entitled to pay rates, I'm also entitled to my own opinion. And it's my entire . . . firm . . . incomprehensible opinion that . . .

SEVERAL VOICES. Be quiet over there!

OTHERS. He's drunk. Chuck him out.

[*The drunken man is put out.*]

DR. STOCKMANN. May I speak?

ASLAKSEN [*rings the bell*]. Dr. Stockmann has the floor!

DR. STOCKMANN. If anybody, even a few days ago, had tried gagging me as they've tried tonight . . . they'd have seen me leaping like a lion to the defence of my sacred rights as an individual. But that hardly matters to me now. Now I have more important things to speak about.

[*The crowd presses closer round him.* MORTEN KIIL *can be seen in the crowd.*]

DR. STOCKMANN [*continues*]. I've been doing a lot of thinking in the last few days . . . turning so many things over in my mind that in the end my head was buzzing . . .

MAYOR [*coughs*]. Hm!

DR. STOCKMANN. . . . but I sorted things out in the finish. Then I saw the whole situation very clearly. That's why I am here this evening. I am going to make a great exposure, gentlemen! And the revelation I am going to make to you is incomparably bigger than this petty business about the water-supply being polluted and the Baths standing over a cesspool.

SEVERAL VOICES [*shouting*]. Don't talk about the Baths! We don't want to hear it! None of that!

DR. STOCKMANN. I have said I am going to speak about the tremendous discovery I have made in the last few days . . . the discovery that all our *spiritual* sources are polluted and that our whole civic community is built over a cesspool of lies.

DISCONCERTED VOICES [*subdued*]. What's he saying?

MAYOR. Making insinuations. . . !

ASLAKSEN [*his hand on the bell*]. I call upon the speaker to moderate his language.

DR. STOCKMANN. I love my native town as much as ever a man can. I wasn't very old when I left here; and distance and longing and memory lent a kind of enchantment to both the place and the people. [*Some clapping and cheers.*] Then for many a long year I sat up there in the far North, in a miserable hole of a place. Coming across some of the people living here and there in that rocky wilderness, I often used to think they would have been better served, poor half-starved creatures that they were, if they had sent for a vet instead of somebody like me.

[*There is a murmuring in the room.*]

BILLING [*putting his pen down*]. Damn me if I've ever heard . . . !

HOVSTAD. That's a slander on a respectable people!

DR. STOCKMANN. Just be patient a little!—I don't think anybody would want to accuse me of having forgotten my home town up there. I sat brooding—rather like an eider duck—and the thing I hatched out . . . was the plan for the Baths. [*Applause and protests.*] And when fate at long last smiled on me, and it turned out I could come home again—yes, my friends, there didn't seem to be very much more I wanted from life. Just one thing I wanted: to be able to work—eagerly, tirelessly, ardently—for the common good and for the good of the town.

MAYOR [*looking away*]. You choose rather a peculiar way of . . . hm!

DR. STOCKMANN. So there I was—deliriously, blindly happy. Then, yesterday morning—no, actually, it was the evening before—my eyes were opened wide, and the first thing I saw was the colossal stupidity of the authorities. . . .

[*Noises, shouts and laughter.* MRS. STOCKMANN *coughs earnestly.*]

MAYOR. Mr. Chairman!

ASLAKSEN [*rings the bell*]. By virtue of my position . . . !

DR. STOCKMANN. Let's not be too fussy about a word here and there, Mr. Aslaksen! All I mean is I got wind of the colossal botch-up our so-called leaders had managed to make of things down at the Baths. If there's anything I just can't stand at any price—it's leaders! I've just about had enough of them. They are just like a lot of goats in a young forest—there's damage everywhere they go. Any decent man and they just get in his way, they're under his feet wherever he turns. If I had my way I'd like to see them exterminated like any other pest. . . .

[*Uproar in the room.*]

MAYOR. Mr. Chairman, is it in order to make remarks like this?

ASLAKSEN [*his hand on the bell*]. Dr. Stockmann . . . !

DR. STOCKMANN. I can't understand why it has taken me till now to wake up to what these gentlemen really are, when practically every day I've had a perfect specimen of them right in front of my very eyes—my brother Peter—slow on the uptake and set in his ideas. . . .

[*Laughter, noise and whistles.* MRS. STOCKMANN *sits coughing.* ASLAKSEN *rings his bell violently.*]

THE DRUNKEN MAN [*who has come in again*]. Are you referring to me? Because they do call me Petersen . . . but I'll be damned if . . .

ANGRY VOICES. Throw that drunk out! Get rid of him!

[*The man is again thrown out.*]

MAYOR. Who was that person?

A BYSTANDER. Don't know him, sir.

A SECOND MAN. He doesn't belong here.

A THIRD MAN. It must be that timber merchant over from . . . [*The rest is inaudible.*]

ASLAKSEN. The man had obviously had too much to drink. Proceed, Doctor, but do please remember—with moderation.

DR. STOCKMANN. Very well, gentlemen, I shall say no more about our leaders. If anyone imagines from what I've just said that I'm out after these gentlemen's blood this evening, then he's wrong—quite definitely wrong! Because I am happily convinced that all these old dodderers, these relics of a dying age, are managing very nicely to see themselves off—they don't need to call in a doctor to hasten the end. And besides they are not the people who constitute the greatest danger to society. *They* are not the ones who do most to pollute our spiritual life, or to infect the ground beneath us. *They* are not the ones who are the worst enemies of truth and freedom in our society.

SHOUTS FROM ALL SIDES. Who then? Who is, then? Name them!

DR. STOCKMANN. Yes, I'll name them, don't you fret! Because *that's* precisely the great discovery I made yesterday. [*Raises his voice.*] The worst enemy of truth and freedom in our society is the compact majority. Yes, the damned, compact, liberal majority. *That's* what! Now you know.

[*Tremendous commotion in the room. Most of the crowd are shouting, stamping and whistling. Some of the more elderly men exchange glances, and seem to be enjoying things.* MRS. STOCKMANN *anxiously gets to her feet.* EJLIF *and* MORTEN *advance threateningly on some schoolboys who are misbehaving.* ASLAKSEN *rings his bell and shouts for order.* HOVSTAD *and* BILLING *are both trying to speak, but cannot be heard above the noise. At last quiet is restored.*]

ASLAKSEN. As Chairman, I must request the speaker to withdraw his wild remarks.

DR. STOCKMANN. Not on your life, Mr. Aslaksen. It is that majority here which is robbing me of my freedom and is trying to prevent me from speaking the truth.

HOVSTAD. The majority is always right!

BILLING. And it damn' well always stands for the truth too!

DR. STOCKMANN. The majority is never right. Never, I tell you! That's one of these lies in society that no free and intelligent man can help rebelling against. Who are the people that make up the biggest proportion of the population—the intelligent ones or the fools? I think we can agree it's the fools, no matter where you go in this world, it's the fools that form the overwhelming majority. But I'll be damned if that means it's right that the fools should dominate the intelligent. [*Uproar and shouting.*] Yes, yes, shout me down if you like, but you can't deny it! The majority has the *might* —more's the pity—but it hasn't *right*. *I* am right—I and one or two other individuals like me. The minority is always right.

[*Renewed uproar.*]

HOVSTAD. Ha! ha! In the last day or two Dr. Stockmann has turned aristocrat!

DR. STOCKMANN. I've already said I'm not going to waste any words on that bunch of narrow-chested, short-winded old has-beens. They've no longer anything to give to the red-blooded life of today. I'm thinking of the few, the genuine individuals in our midst, with their new and vigorous ideas. These men stand in the very forefront of our advance, so far ahead that the compact majority hasn't even begun to approach them—and it's *there* they fight for truths too newly-born to have won any support from the majority.

HOVSTAD. Aha! So now he's a revolutionary.

DR. STOCKMANN. Yes, by God, I am, Mr. Hovstad! I'm plotting revolution against this lie that the majority has a monopoly of the truth. What are these truths that always bring the majority rallying round? Truths so elderly they are practically senile. And when a truth is as old as that, gentlemen, you can hardly tell it from a lie. [*Laughter and jeers.*] All right, believe it or not! But truths are not by any means the tough old Methuselahs people imagine. The life of a normally constituted truth is generally, say, about seventeen or eighteen years, at most twenty; rarely longer. But truths as elderly as that have always worn terribly thin. But it's only *then* that the majority will have anything to do with them; then it will recommend them as wholesome food for thought. But there's no great food-value in that sort of diet, I can tell you—as a doctor, I know what I'm talking about. All these majority truths are just like salt meat that's been kept too long and gone bad and mouldy. That's at the root of all this moral scurvy that's going about.

ASLAKSEN. It appears to me that the honourable gentleman is straying rather a long way from his subject.

MAYOR. I concur very much with what the Chairman says.

DR. STOCKMANN. You must be mad, Peter. I'm sticking as close to my subject as I can. For that's just what I'm trying to say: that the masses, this damned compact majority—*this* is the thing that's polluting the sources of our spiritual life and infecting the very ground we stand on.

HOVSTAD. And this is what happens, you say, just because the great majority of thinking people are sensible enough to keep their approval for recognized and well-founded truths?

DR. STOCKMANN. My dear Mr. Hovstad, don't talk to me about well-founded truths. The truths the masses recognize today are the same truths as were held by advanced thinkers in our grandfathers' day. We who man the advanced outposts today, we don't recognize them any more. In my opinion, only one thing is certain: and that is that no society can live a healthy life on the old dry bones of that kind of truth.

HOVSTAD. But instead of you standing there and giving us all this airy talk, it would be interesting to hear a bit more about these old, dry bones of truth we are supposed to be living on.

[*Approval from several quarters.*]

DR. STOCKMANN. Oh, I could draw up a whole list of these horrors. But for the moment I'll restrict myself to *one* recognized truth, which is actually a rotten lie but which nevertheless Mr. Hovstad and the *People's Herald* and all the *Herald's* supporters live by.

HOVSTAD. And that is?

DR. STOCKMANN. A doctrine inherited from your forefathers which you fatuously go on spreading far and wide—the doctrine that the general public, the common herd, the masses are the very essence of the people—that they *are* the people—that the common man, and all the ignorant and immature elements in society have the same right to criticize and to approve, to govern and to counsel as the few intellectually distinguished people.

BILLING. Well I'll be damned. . . .

HOVSTAD [*shouting at the same time*]. Citizens, take note of this!

ANGRY VOICES. So we are not the people, eh? Only the top people are to have any say, eh?

A WORKMAN. Chuck him out, saying things like that!

OTHERS. Out with him!

A MAN [*shouting*]. Let's have a blast of it now, Evensen!

[*Great blasts on a horn, along with whistles and tremendous uproar.*]

DR. STOCKMANN [*after the noise has died down somewhat*]. Be reasonable! Can't you bear to hear the voice of truth just for once? I don't expect you all to agree with me straight off. But I must say I expected Mr. Hovstad to admit I was right when he'd got over his first shock. Mr. Hovstad claims to be a free-thinker. . . .

VOICES [*in astonished undertones*]. Free-thinker, did he say? What? Mr. Hovstad a free-thinker?

HOVSTAD [*shouting*]. Prove it, Dr. Stockmann! Have I ever said so in black and white?

DR. STOCKMANN [*reflectively*]. No, damn it, you are right. You've never had the guts. Well, I don't want to embarrass you, Mr. Hovstad. Let's say it's me who's the free-thinker, then. What I'm going to do is prove to you, scientifically, that when the *People's Herald* tells you that you—the general public, the masses—are the real essence of the people, it's just a lot of bunkum. Don't you see it's just a journalistic lie? The public is only the raw material from which a people is made. [*Murmurs, laughter and general disturbance in the room.*] Well, isn't that the way it is with life generally. Look at the difference between pedigree and cross-bred animals. Look at an ordinary barn-yard hen, for instance—fat lot of meat you get off a scraggy old thing like that! And what about the eggs it lays? Any decent, self-respecting crow could do as well. But take a pure-bred Spanish or Japanese hen, or take a pheasant or a turkey—ah! what a difference! Or I might mention dogs, which are so like humans in many ways. Think first of an ordinary mongrel—I mean one of those filthy, shaggy rough dogs that do nothing but run about the streets and cock their legs against all the walls. Compare a mongrel like that with a poodle whose pedigree goes back many generations, who has been properly fed and has grown up among quiet voices and soft music. Don't you think the poodle's brain will have developed quite differently from the mongrel's? You bet it will! That kind of pedigree dog can be trained to do the most fantastic tricks—things an ordinary mongrel could never learn even if it stood on its head.

[*Uproar and laughter.*]

A MAN [*shouts*]. Are you trying to make out we are dogs now?

ANOTHER MAN. We're not animals, Doctor!

DR. STOCKMANN. Ah, but that's just exactly what we *are*, my friend! We are as good animals as any man could wish for. But you don't find all that many really outstanding ones. Oh, there's a tremendous difference between the poodles and the mongrels amongst us men. And the funny thing is that Mr. Hovstad fully agrees with me as long as we are talking about four-footed animals. . . .

HOVSTAD. Yes, it's all right for *them*.

DR. STOCKMANN. All right. But as soon as I apply the principle to two-legged creatures, that's the end of it for Mr. Hovstad. He hasn't the courage of his convictions, he doesn't take things to their logical conclusion. So he turns the whole theory upside down and proclaims in the *Herald* that the barn-yard hen and the street-corner mongrel—that these are the finest exhibits in the menagerie. But that's always the way, and always will be as long as a man still remains infected by the mass mind, and hasn't worked his way free to some kind of intellectual distinction.

HOVSTAD. I make no claim to any kind of distinction. I came from simple peasant stock, and I am proud that my roots go deep into that common people he is insulting.

SOME WORKMEN. Good old Hovstad! Hurrah! Hurrah!

DR. STOCKMANN. The sort of common people I'm talking about are not found simply among the lower classes; they are crawling and swarming all round us—right up to the highest social level. You've only got to look at that nice, pretty Mayor of yours. My brother Peter is as mass-minded a person as anything you'll find on two legs. . . .

[*Laughter and hisses.*]

MAYOR. I must protest against these personal remarks.

DR. STOCKMANN [*imperturbably*]. . . . and that's not because he's descended, like me, from some awful old Pomeranian pirate or something—because that's what we are . . .

MAYOR. An absurd story. I deny it!

DR. STOCKMANN. . . . but because he thinks what his superiors think, and believes what his superiors believe. And anybody who does that is just one of the masses in spirit. You see, that's why my magnificent brother Peter is so terribly lacking in natural distinction—and consequently has so little independence of mind.

MAYOR. Mr. Chairman . . . !

HOVSTAD. So in this country it seems it's the distinguished people who are the liberals! That's a new one!

[*Laughter.*]

DR. STOCKMANN. Yes, that's another part of my discovery. And along with that goes the fact that free-thinking is almost exactly the same as morality. That's why I call it downright irresponsible of the *Herald* to keep putting out this distorted idea, day in day out, that it's the masses, the compact majority that has the monopoly of morality and liberal principles—and that vice and corruption and every kind of depraved idea are an overflow from culture, just as all the filth in our Baths is an overflow from the tannery up at Mölledal! [*Uproar and interruptions.* DR. STOCKMANN, *unperturbed, smiles in his eagerness.*] And yet this same *Herald* can preach about raising the standards of the masses! Good Lord, if what the *Herald* says is right, raising the level of the masses would amount precisely to toppling them straight over the edge to perdition. But fortunately it's just one of those old lies we've had handed down—this idea that culture is demoralizing. No, stupidity and poverty and ugliness are the things that do the devil's work! A house that isn't aired and swept every day—and my wife Katherine says it ought to be scrubbed as well, but that's a debatable point—anybody living for more than two or three years in *that* kind of house will end up by having no moral sense left whatsoever. No oxygen, no conscience! And there must be an awful lot of houses in this town short of oxygen, it seems, if the entire compact majority is so irresponsible as to want to build the prosperity of the town on a quagmire of lies and deceit.

ASLAKSEN. I cannot allow such abusive remarks to be directed at the entire community.

A MAN. I move that the Chairman rule the speaker out of order!

ANGRY VOICES. Yes, yes! That's right. Out of order!

DR. STOCKMANN [*flaring up*]. Then I'll shout the truth on every street corner! I'll write to all the other newspapers! I'll see that the whole country gets to know what's going on here!

HOVSTAD. It might almost seem that Dr. Stockmann is set on ruining the town.

DR. STOCKMANN. I love this town so much that I'd rather destroy it than see it prosper on a lie.

ASLAKSEN. That's putting it pretty strongly.

[*Uproar and whistles.* MRS. STOCKMANN *coughs in vain; the* DOCTOR *no longer hears her.*]

HOVSTAD [*shouting above the din*]. Any man who wants to destroy a whole community must be a public enemy.

DR. STOCKMANN [*with rising temper*]. When a place has become riddled with lies, who cares if it's destroyed? I say it should simply be razed to the ground! And all the people living by these lies should be wiped out, like vermin! You'll have the whole country infested in the end, so that eventually the whole country deserves to be destroyed. And if it ever comes to that, then I'd say with all my heart: let it all be destroyed, let all its people be wiped out!

A MAN [*in the crowd*]. That's the talk of an enemy of the people!

BILLING. That, God damn me, was the voice of the people!

THE WHOLE CROWD [*shouting*]. Yes! Yes! He's an enemy of the people. He hates his country. He hates his people.

ASLAKSEN. As a citizen of this country, and as an individual, I am profoundly shocked by what I have just had to listen to. Dr. Stockmann has betrayed himself in a way I should never have dreamt possible. I must therefore, with great regret, associate myself with the opinion that has just been expressed by my honourable fellow citizens, and I propose we embody that opinion in the form of a resolution. I suggest something like this: 'This meeting declares that it considers Dr. Thomas Stockmann, Medical Officer to the Baths, to be an enemy of the people.'

[*A storm of applause and cheers. A number of people crowd round* DR. STOCKMANN, *cat-calling.* MRS. STOCKMANN *and* PETRA *have risen.* MORTEN *and* EJLIF *fight with the other schoolboys who have also been booing. Some of the grown-ups separate them.*]

DR. STOCKMANN [*to those whistling*]. You fools! I tell you that . . .

ASLAKSEN [*ringing his bell*]. Dr. Stockmann is out of order. A formal vote must be taken; but so as not to hurt anybody's feelings, we will do it by secret ballot. Have you any paper, Mr. Billing?

BILLING. There's both blue and white. . . .

ASLAKSEN [*stepping down*]. That's fine. We can do it quicker that way. Cut it into strips . . . there we are, now. [*To the meeting.*] Blue means no, white means yes. I'll come round myself to collect the votes.

[*The* MAYOR *leaves the room.* ASLAKSEN *and one or two others carry round the slips of paper in their hats.*]

ONE MAN [*to* HOVSTAD]. What's come over the Doctor? What are you to make of it?

HOVSTAD. Well, you know how impetuous he is.

SECOND MAN [*to* BILLING]. Tell me—you've been in their house quite a bit. Does the man drink, have you noticed?

BILLING. I'm damned if I know really what to say. They always bring the toddy out when anybody calls.

THIRD MAN. No, I think it's more likely he's a bit crazy.

FIRST MAN. Ah, I wonder if there's any insanity in the family.

BILLING. Could very well be.

FOURTH MAN. No, it's just spite, that's what it is. Wants to get his own back about something.

BILLING. He did say something secretly about wanting a rise; but he didn't get it.

ALL THE MEN TOGETHER. Well, there you are then!

THE DRUNKEN MAN [*in the crowd*]. I want a blue one. And I want a white one an' all.

VOICES. Is that that drunk again? Chuck him out!

MORTEN KIIL [*approaches the* DOCTOR]. Well, Stockmann, now you see where these monkey tricks of yours have landed you!

DR. STOCKMANN. I have simply done my duty.

KIIL. What was that you said about the tanneries at Mölledal?

DR. STOCKMANN. You heard. I said that was where all the muck came from.

KIIL. From *my* tannery as well?

DR. STOCKMANN. I'm afraid so. Yours is the worst.

KIIL. Are you going to print *that* in the papers?

DR. STOCKMANN. I'm not hiding anything.

KIIL. You might find that costly, Stockmann.

[*He leaves.*]

A FAT MAN [*goes up to* HORSTER, *ignoring the ladies*]. So, Captain Horster, so you lend your house to enemies of the people, eh?

HORSTER. I think I can do what I like with my own property, Mr. Vik.

THE FAT MAN. So you won't mind if I do the same with mine.

HORSTER. What do you mean?

THE FAT MAN. You'll hear from me in the morning.

[*He turns and goes.*]

PETRA. Isn't he the owner of your ship, Captain Horster?

HORSTER. Yes, that's Mr. Vik.

ASLAKSEN [*mounts the platform with the ballot papers; he rings the bell*]. Gentlemen, let me announce the result. With only one vote to the contrary . . .

A YOUNG MAN. That's the drunk!

ASLAKSEN. With only one drunken man's vote to the contrary, the resolution of this meeting was carried unanimously: that Dr. Thomas Stockmann is an enemy of the people. [*Shouting and applause.*] Three cheers for our ancient and honourable community! [*More cheers.*] Three cheers for our able and efficient Mayor, for putting duty before family! [*Cheers.*] The meeting is adjourned.

[*He steps down.*]

BILLING. Three cheers for the chairman!

THE WHOLE CROWD. Good old Aslaksen!

DR. STOCKMANN. My hat and coat, Petra! Captain, have you any room aboard for passengers for the New World?

HORSTER. For you and your family we'll make room, Doctor.

DR. STOCKMANN [*as* PETRA *helps him on with his coat*]. Good! Come on, Katherine! Come along, lads!

[*He takes his wife by the arm.*]

MRS. STOCKMANN [*in a low voice*]. Thomas dear, let's go out by the back way.

DR. STOCKMANN. No back way for me, Katherine. [*Raises his voice.*] You'll hear again from this enemy of the people before he shakes the dust off his feet. I'm not as sweet-tempered as a certain person I could mention. I'm not saying: 'I forgive you, for you know not what you do.'

ASLAKSEN [*shouts*]. That comparison is blasphemous, Dr. Stockmann!

BILLING. Well I'll be . . . ! What dreadful things to say in the presence of decent people.

A COARSE VOICE. And what about those threats he made!

ANGRY SHOUTS. Let's go and break his windows! Duck him in the fjord!

A MAN [*in the crowd*]. Give us another blast, Evensen! Blow! Blow!

[*The sound of a horn and whistles and wild shouts. The* DOCTOR *and his family make for the exit, and* HORSTER *clears a way for them.*]

THE WHOLE CROWD [*howling after them*]. Enemy of the people! Enemy of the people! Enemy of the people!

BILLING [*tidying his papers*]. Well I'm damned if I would want to drink toddy at the Stockmanns' tonight!

[*The crowd makes for the exit; the noise is continued outside; shouts from the street of 'Enemy of the people! Enemy of the people!'*]

ACT FIVE

DR. STOCKMANN'S *study. Along the walls are bookcases and medicine cupboards. On the back wall is the door to the hall; left front is the door to the living-room. On the right wall are two windows, all the glass panes of which are smashed. In the centre of the room is the* DOCTOR'S *desk, covered with books and papers. The room is in disorder. It is morning.*

    DR. STOCKMANN, *in dressing-gown, slippers and skull-cap, is bending down and raking under one of the cupboards with an umbrella. Finally he manages to rake out a stone.*

DR. STOCKMANN [*calling through the open door into the sitting-room*]. I've found another one, Katherine.

MRS. STOCKMANN [*from the living-room*]. Oh, you'll find a lot more yet, I'm sure.

DR. STOCKMANN [*adding the stone to a pile of others on the table*]. I'm going to keep these stones—like relics. Ejlif and Morten must see them every day, and when they grow up, they'll inherit them. [*Rakes under a bookcase.*] Hasn't—what the devil's her name again— you know, that girl—hasn't she gone for the glazier yet?

MRS. STOCKMANN [*comes in*]. Yes, but he said he didn't know if he could come today.

DR. STOCKMANN. He daren't—you'll see.

MRS. STOCKMANN. Yes, that's what Randina thought too—he was afraid of what the neighbours might say. [*Calls into the living-room.*] What's that you want, Randina? I see. [*She goes out and comes back at once.*] It's a letter for you, Thomas.

DR. STOCKMANN. Let me see. [*He opens it and reads.*] Aha!

MRS. STOCKMANN. Who's it from?

DR. STOCKMANN. From the landlord. He's given us notice.

MRS. STOCKMANN. Has he really? But he was such a nice man. . . .

DR. STOCKMANN [*looking at the letter*]. He daren't do anything else, he says. He's very sorry, but he daren't do anything else . . . because of the others . . . public opinion . . . not his own master . . . dare not risk putting certain people's backs up. . . .

MRS. STOCKMANN. There you see, Thomas.

DR. STOCKMANN. Yes, yes, I see all right. They are all cowards, the whole lot of them here. Nobody dares do anything because of all the others. [*Flings the letter on the table.*] But that doesn't make any difference to us, Katherine. We are leaving for the New World, and then . . .

MRS. STOCKMANN. But, Thomas, have you really thought about it properly, this business about leaving. . . ?

DR. STOCKMANN. You wouldn't want me to stay here, would you? Not after the way they've taken it out of me, branding me as an enemy of the people, and smashing all my windows! And look here, Katherine! I've even got a tear in my black trousers through them.

MRS. STOCKMANN. So you have! And they are the best pair you've got!

DR. STOCKMANN. You should never have your best trousers on when you turn out to fight for freedom and truth. Well, it's not that I care all that much about the trousers—you can always put a stitch in them for me. But what gets me is the idea of that mob going for me as though they were my equals—*that's* what I can't stomach, damn it!

MRS. STOCKMANN. Yes, they've really been horrid to you here, Thomas. But do we have to go so far as to leave the country for *that*?

DR. STOCKMANN. Don't you think you would get the same insolence from the masses in the other towns as you do here? Of course you would! They're all the same! Oh, to hell! Let them yap! That's not the worst; the worst thing is that all over the country everybody's got to toe the party line. Not that it's likely to be very much better out West either; it will be the same there too, with your liberal public opinions and your compact majorities and all the rest of the rigmarole. But things are on a bigger scale there, you see. They might kill, but they don't torture. They don't take a free man and put the screws on his soul, as they do here. And if the worst comes to the worst, you can get away from it all. [*Walks up and down.*] If only I knew where there was a primeval forest or a little South Sea island going cheap. . . .

MRS. STOCKMANN. But, Thomas, what about the boys?

DR. STOCKMANN [*halts*]. You are funny, Katherine! Would you rather the boys grew up in a society like this? You saw yourself last night how half the population is absolutely mad; and if the other half haven't lost their wits, it's only because they are such thickheads they haven't any wits to lose.

MRS. STOCKMANN. Now then, Thomas dear, you ought to watch what you are saying.

DR. STOCKMANN. Hah! You don't think I'm telling you the truth? Don't they turn every single idea upside down? Don't they make a complete hotch-potch of what's right and what's wrong? Don't they go and call lies what I know perfectly well is the truth? But the craziest thing of the lot is to see all these grown-up men going round calling themselves liberals and imagining they are men of independent minds! Have you ever heard anything like it, Katherine?

MRS. STOCKMANN. Yes, yes, of course that's quite stupid, but . . . [PETRA *comes in from the living-room.*] Back from school already?

PETRA. Yes. I've been given my notice.

MRS. STOCKMANN. Your notice?

DR. STOCKMANN. You too!

PETRA. Mrs. Busk gave me notice. And I thought it was better to leave at once.

DR. STOCKMANN. How right you were!

MRS. STOCKMANN. Who would have thought Mrs. Busk was that sort!

PETRA. Oh, Mother, Mrs. Busk isn't bad, really. I could see quite well she didn't like doing it. But she daren't do anything else, she said. So I have to leave.

DR. STOCKMANN [*laughs and rubs his hands*]. So she didn't dare do anything else, either! That's great!

MRS. STOCKMANN. Oh well, I dare say after that awful scene last night . . .

PETRA. It wasn't just *that*. Listen, Father!

DR. STOCKMANN. Well?

PETRA. Mrs. Busk showed me no less than three letters she'd had this morning. . . .

DR. STOCKMANN. Anonymous, of course?

PETRA. Yes.

DR. STOCKMANN. You see they *daren't* put their names to them, Katherine!

PETRA. And in two of them it said that a certain gentleman, who has been a frequent visitor here, had been talking in the club last night and saying that I had extremely advanced ideas about all sorts of things. . . .

DR. STOCKMANN. Which I hope you didn't deny?

PETRA. You know very well I wouldn't. Mrs. Busk has got one or two pretty advanced ideas herself, when she talks to me privately. But now that this has come out about me, she daren't keep me.

MRS. STOCKMANN. Fancy! A frequent visitor here! You see what you get for your hospitality, Thomas.

DR. STOCKMANN. We are not going to live in this stinking hole any longer. Pack up as quick as you can, Katherine. The sooner we get away the better.

MRS. STOCKMANN. Be quiet—I think there's somebody in the hall. Go and see, Petra.

PETRA [*opens the door*]. Oh, it's you, Captain Horster? Do come in.

HORSTER [*from the hall*]. Good morning. I thought I'd just look in to see how things were.

DR. STOCKMANN [*shaking his hand*]. Thank you. That's very kind of you.

MRS. STOCKMANN. And thank you for your help last night, Captain Horster.

PETRA. But how did you get back home again?

HORSTER. Oh, I managed. I'm pretty tough, you know. The only thing those people are good for is shooting off their mouths.

DR. STOCKMANN. Yes, isn't it astonishing, this sickening cowardice? Here, I want to show you something! Look, here are all the stones they chucked at us last night. Just look at them! Not more than a couple of honest-to-goodness lumps in the whole lot—the rest are just pebbles, bits of gravel! And yet they went on standing out there, shouting and yelling and swearing they were going to beat me up. But as for *doing* anything—no, there isn't much of that in this town.

HORSTER. It was just as well this time, Doctor.

DR. STOCKMANN. I dare say you're right. But it makes you angry all the same. Because if it ever comes to the point where the country really *has* to fight in earnest, then you'll see how public opinion is all for clearing out fast, and the whole of the compact majority will make for the woods like a great flock of sheep, Captain Horster. That's the saddening thing; that's what really upsets me. . . . Oh, what the hell . . . it's all just a lot of nonsense, really. If they've called me an enemy of the people, I might as well be an enemy of the people.

MRS. STOCKMANN. That's something you'll never be, Thomas.

DR. STOCKMANN. I shouldn't bet on it if I were you, Katherine. To be called some nasty name is just like getting a pinprick in the lung. And this blasted name they've called me—it's lodged here under the heart, embedded deep, griping me as if it were acid. And it's no use taking magnesia for *that*!

PETRA. Puh! I should just laugh at them, Father!

HORSTER. They'll come round to other ways of thinking in time, Doctor.

MRS. STOCKMANN. They will, you know, Thomas, as sure as you're standing here.

DR. STOCKMANN. When it's too late, perhaps. Well, serve them right! Then, as they wallow in their filth, they'll wish they hadn't been so ready to drive a patriot into exile. When do you sail, Captain Horster?

HORSTER. Well, actually that was what I came to talk to you about. . . .

DR. STOCKMANN. Well? Something wrong with the ship?

HORSTER. No, only that I'm not sailing with her.

PETRA. Surely you haven't been given notice?

HORSTER [*smiles*]. Yes, I have.

PETRA. You too.

MRS. STOCKMANN. There you are, you see, Thomas.

DR. STOCKMANN. And all in the cause of truth! Oh, if I'd thought for one moment that . . .

HORSTER. Don't you worry about that! I'll get a job all right with some company away from here.

DR. STOCKMANN. So that's our Mr. Vik . . . a man of means, beholden to nobody. . . ! It's a damned shame!

HORSTER. He's very decent otherwise. And he said himself he would have liked to keep me on, if only he dared. . . .

DR. STOCKMANN. But he didn't dare? No, of course not.

HORSTER. He said it wasn't so easy when you belonged to a party. . . .

DR. STOCKMANN. He never spoke a truer word, that fine friend of ours! A party's just like a mincing machine, grinding people's brains up into a kind of hash, and churning out a lot of thickheaded clots.

MRS. STOCKMANN. Oh, Thomas, really!

PETRA [*to* HORSTER]. If only you hadn't walked home with us, things might not have gone so far.

HORSTER. I don't regret it.

PETRA [*holds out her hand*]. Thank you!

HORSTER [*to the* DOCTOR]. What I really wanted to say was this: that if you are set on leaving, I've another idea. . . .

DR. STOCKMANN. Fine! As long as we can get away quickly.

MRS. STOCKMANN. Hush! Wasn't that a knock?

PETRA. That'll be Uncle, for sure.

DR. STOCKMANN. Aha! [*Shouts.*] Come in!

MRS. STOCKMANN. Thomas, dear, promise me . . .

[*The* MAYOR *comes in from the hall.*]

MAYOR [*in the doorway*]. Oh, you are busy. In that case I'd better . . .

DR. STOCKMANN. No, no! Come in.

MAYOR. But I wanted to speak to you alone.

MRS. STOCKMANN. We'll go into the living-room for the time being.

HORSTER. And I'll look in again later.

DR. STOCKMANN. No, you just go next door with them, Captain Horster. I want to know a bit more about . . .

HORSTER. Very well, I'll wait then.

[*He goes with* MRS. STOCKMANN *and* PETRA *into the living-room. The* MAYOR *says nothing but glances at the windows.*]

DR. STOCKMANN. Perhaps it's a bit draughty for you in here today. Put your hat on.

MAYOR. Thank you, if I may. [*Does so.*] I think I must have caught a cold yesterday. I stood there shivering. . . .

DR. STOCKMANN. Really? Things seemed warm enough to me.

MAYOR. I regret I was unable to prevent the excesses of last night.

DR. STOCKMANN. Is there anything particular you want to tell me besides that?

MAYOR [*produces a big envelope*]. I have this document for you, from the directors.

DR. STOCKMANN. My notice?

MAYOR. Yes, from today. [*Lays the letter on the table.*] We don't like doing this, but—to be perfectly frank—we daren't do anything else, in the light of public opinion.

DR. STOCKMANN [*smiles*]. Daren't? I seem to have heard that word before, today.

MAYOR. I want you to realize your position. You can't count on any kind of practice in this town in future.

DR. STOCKMANN. To hell with the practice! But what makes you so certain?

MAYOR. The Ratepayers Association is circulating a list, urging all respectable citizens to have nothing to do with you. And I am pretty confident that not a single man will dare refuse to sign it. They simply wouldn't *dare*.

DR. STOCKMANN. I don't doubt. But what then?

MAYOR. If I may give you some advice, it's this: go away for a while....

DR. STOCKMANN. Yes, I had actually been thinking of going away.

MAYOR. Good. And after you'd had six months or so to think things over, and if after mature consideration you then felt you were ready to write a few words of apology, admitting your mistake ...

DR. STOCKMANN. Then I might perhaps get my job back again, you mean?

MAYOR. Perhaps. It's not altogether impossible.

DR. STOCKMANN. But what about public opinion? Surely you won't dare, in the light of public opinion.

MAYOR. Opinion is an extremely variable thing. And, in point of fact, it's rather important that we get some sort of admission from you along those lines.

DR. STOCKMANN. Yes, I can see how you'd come slobbering after that. But, by God, surely you haven't forgotten already what I've told you before about dirty tricks like this!

MAYOR. At that time your position was quite different. At that time you had reason to suppose you had the whole town at your back....

DR. STOCKMANN. Yes, and now I'm supposed to feel as though I had the whole town *on* my back.... [*Flares up.*] I wouldn't care if I had the devil himself *and* his old woman on my back.... Never, I tell you! Never!

MAYOR. A man with a family has no right to be carrying on as you are. You have no right, Thomas.

DR. STOCKMANN. Haven't I? There's only one thing in this world a free man has no right to do. Do you know what that is?

MAYOR. No.

DR. STOCKMANN. Of course not. But *I'll* tell you. A free man has no right to get messed up with filth; things should never reach the stage where he feels like spitting in his own eye.

MAYOR. This all sounds extremely plausible. And if there weren't some other explanation for your obstinacy . . . But then, of course, there is. . . .

DR. STOCKMANN. What do you mean by *that*?

MAYOR. You know perfectly well what I mean. Speaking as your brother and as one who understands these things, let me give you some advice: don't build too much on certain expectations or prospects that might so terribly easily fall through.

DR. STOCKMANN. What on earth are you getting at?

MAYOR. You don't really expect me to believe that you are ignorant of the terms of Morten Kiil's will?

DR. STOCKMANN. I know that what little he has is to go to an Old People's Home. But what's that got to do with me?

MAYOR. In the first place, it's not so little. Morten Kiil is a pretty wealthy man.

DR. STOCKMANN. I had absolutely no idea . . .

MAYOR. Hm . . . really? And you have no idea, I suppose, that a not inconsiderable part of his fortune is to be left to your children, and that you and your wife are to have the interest on this money during your lifetime? Did he never tell you that?

DR. STOCKMANN. Blessed if he did! On the contrary, he's done nothing the whole time but grouse about the impossibly high taxes he had to pay. Are you quite sure about this, Peter?

MAYOR. I have it from a completely reliable source.

DR. STOCKMANN. But, Heavens, that means Katherine's taken care of —and the children too! I must tell them. . . . [*Shouts.*] Katherine, Katherine!

MAYOR [*holds him back*]. Hush! Don't say anything yet!

MRS. STOCKMANN [*opens the door*]. What is the matter?

DR. STOCKMANN. Nothing, my dear. Just go back in again. [MRS. STOCKMANN *shuts the door; he walks up and down.*] Provided for! To think they're all provided for! And for life! It's a wonderful feeling to know that one has that security!

MAYOR. Yes, but that's just it! You can't be sure. Morten Kiil can alter his will any time he likes.

DR. STOCKMANN. But he won't, my dear Peter. The old boy is tickled to death at the way I've gone for you and your precious friends.

MAYOR [*starts, and looks intently at him*]. Aha, that puts a lot of things in a different light.

DR. STOCKMANN. What things?

MAYOR. So the whole thing has been a combined operation. These violent, ruthless attacks you have made—all in the name of truth— against the leading men of the town. . . .

DR. STOCKMANN. What about them?

MAYOR. Just your part of the bargain in exchange for being included in that vindictive old man's will.

DR. STOCKMANN [*almost speechless*]. Peter . . . of all the scum I ever met, you are the worst.

MAYOR. Things are finished now between us. Your dismissal is final . . . for now we have a weapon against you.

[*He goes.*]

DR. STOCKMANN. Well I'll be . . . ! Of all the . . . ! [*Shouts.*] Katherine! I want the floor swilled down after him. Get her to bring her bucket in . . . what's her name . . . damn it, you know . . . that girl who's always got a dirty nose. . . .

MRS. STOCKMANN [*in the living-room doorway*]. Hush, Thomas, please!

PETRA [*also in the doorway*]. Father, Grandfather's here. He wants to know if he can have a word with you alone.

DR. STOCKMANN. Yes, of course he can. [*At the door.*] Come in, Father-in-law. [MORTEN KIIL *comes in; the* DOCTOR *shuts the door after him.*] Well now, what can I do for you? Do sit down.

MORTEN KIIL. I won't sit. [*Looks round him.*] It's looking very nice in here today, Stockmann.

DR. STOCKMANN. It is, isn't it?

KIIL. Very nice indeed it looks. And lots of fresh air too; plenty of that oxygen stuff you were talking about yesterday. Your conscience must be in pretty good shape today, I imagine.

DR. STOCKMANN. Yes, it is.

KIIL. I imagined it would be. [*Tapping his breast pocket.*] Do you know what I've got here?

DR. STOCKMANN. A good conscience too, I should hope.

KIIL. Puh! Something much better than that.

[*He brings out a fat wallet, opens it, and produces a bundle of papers.*]

DR. STOCKMANN [*looks at him in amazement*]. Shares in the Baths?

KIIL. They weren't difficult to come by today.

DR. STOCKMANN. You mean to say you've gone and bought . . . ?

KIIL. As many as I could afford.

DR. STOCKMANN. But, my dear Father-in-law—with things at the Baths in the state they are in now . . . !

KIIL. If only you behave like a sensible man, you'll soon have the place on its feet again.

DR. STOCKMANN. Well, you can see for yourself, I'm doing all I can, but . . . The people in this town are mad!

KIIL. You said yesterday that the worst of the filth came from my works. But if this happened to be true, then my grandfather, and my father before me, to say nothing of myself, have been slowly poisoning the town all these years—like three unclean spirits. You don't think I'm going to take this lying down, do you?

DR. STOCKMANN. I'm afraid you can't help it.

KIIL. No thank you. My good name means a lot to me. I'm told people call me an old badger; and a badger's a kind of pig, isn't it? But I'm not going to let them say 'I told you so'. I want to live and die with my reputation clear.

DR. STOCKMANN. And how are you going to manage that?

KIIL. You are going to clear me, Stockmann.

DR. STOCKMANN. *I* am!

KIIL. Do you know where I got the money to buy all these shares? No, how could you? But I'll tell you. This is the money that Katherine and Petra and the boys are to inherit from me. Because, you see, I've managed to put quite a bit aside, after all.

DR. STOCKMANN [*flaring up*]. You mean you've gone and taken Katherine's money for *this*?

KIIL. Yes, every bit of the money is tied up now in the Baths. And I just want to see now if you really are completely and absolutely stark raving mad, Stockmann. If you are still going to have it that creepy, crawly things are coming from my works, you might as well be flaying Katherine alive, for all the difference it makes—*and* Petra, *and* the boys as well. But then no decent father would do that—not unless he was a madman.

DR. STOCKMANN [*pacing up and down.*] But I *am* a madman! I *am* a madman!

KIIL. But you couldn't be so stark, staring mad as all that, not when it affects your wife and children.

DR. STOCKMANN [*halts in front of him*]. Why couldn't you have talked to me first before going and buying all that trash!

KIIL. What's done can't be undone—it's got to be faced.

DR. STOCKMANN [*walks about restlessly*]. If only I wasn't so certain . . . ! But I'm absolutely convinced I'm right.

KIIL [*weighing his wallet in his hand*]. If you persist with these stupid ideas, then these things will not be worth much, you know.

[*He puts his wallet in his pocket.*]

DR. STOCKMANN. Damn it, surely science could find *some* sort of prophylactic, some preventive or other. . . .

KIIL. You mean something to kill off the animals?

DR. STOCKMANN. Yes, or to render them harmless, at least.

KIIL. Couldn't you try with a bit of rat poison?

DR. STOCKMANN. Oh, don't talk rubbish! But then everybody keeps telling me it's just my imagination. Well, let's make it that then! Let them have it the way they want it! These ignorant little mongrels—calling me an enemy of the people! And tearing the very clothes off my back!

KIIL. And smashing all your windows!

DR. STOCKMANN. And then there's this business of my duty towards my family. I'll have to talk to Katherine about it. She's better than I am at things like that.

KIIL. Fine! She's a sensible woman—and just you pay attention to what she says.

DR. STOCKMANN [*turning on him*]. You're a fine one, too, behaving in this stupid way! Fancy gambling with Katherine's money—and putting me in this dreadful dilemma! When I look at you, it's just like looking at the devil himself. . . !

KIIL. I think I'd better go. But I want to hear from you by two o'clock at the latest. Yes or no. If it's no, the shares go to charity—this very day.

DR. STOCKMANN. And what does Katherine get then?

KIIL. Not a penny. [*The hall door opens;* HOVSTAD *and* ASLAKSEN *can be seen outside.*] Well, look who's here!

DR. STOCKMANN [*stares at them*]. What's this! You dare come to my house?

HOVSTAD. Yes, we do.

ASLAKSEN. You see, we want to talk to you about something.

KIIL [*whispers*]. Yes or no—by two o'clock.

ASLAKSEN [*with a glance at* HOVSTAD]. Aha!

[MORTEN KIIL *leaves.*]

DR. STOCKMANN. Well! What do you want with me? Make it snappy!

HOVSTAD. I can well understand that you are not very well disposed towards us as a result of our attitude at the meeting yesterday. . . .

DR. STOCKMANN. Attitude, you call it! A fine attitude that was! Of all the spineless exhibitions . . . ! Like a couple of old women! God damn it!

HOVSTAD. Call it what you like; but we *couldn't* do anything else.

DR. STOCKMANN. You daren't do anything else, you mean! Well?

HOVSTAD. Yes, if you like.

ASLAKSEN. But why didn't you drop us a hint beforehand? All it needed was a word to Mr. Hovstad or me.

DR. STOCKMANN. A hint? What about?

ASLAKSEN. About what was behind it all.

DR. STOCKMANN. I don't understand you at all.

ASLAKSEN [*nods confidentially*]. Oh yes you do, Dr. Stockmann.

HOVSTAD. There's no need to make a mystery of it any longer.

DR. STOCKMANN [*looks from one to the other*]. For God's sake, won't somebody tell me. . . !

ASLAKSEN. If you don't mind my asking—isn't it true that your father-in-law is going round town buying up all the shares in the Baths.

DR. STOCKMANN. Yes, he's been and bought some shares today. But . . . ?

ASLAKSEN. It might have been wiser if you had picked somebody else to do that—somebody not quite so closely related.

HOVSTAD. And you shouldn't have done all this in your own name, either. There wasn't any need for people to know that the attack on the Baths came from you. You should have approached me, Dr. Stockmann.

DR. STOCKMANN [*looks fixedly ahead; the truth seems to dawn on him, and he says as though thunderstruck*]. But this is incredible! Are such things possible?

ASLAKSEN [*smiles*]. Evidently they are. But they ought preferably to be done with finesse, you know.

HOVSTAD. And it's best to have one or two others in on it, too. Because then the individual responsibility is always reduced if there are several people.

DR. STOCKMANN [*composedly*]. Come to the point, gentlemen. What is it you want?

ASLAKSEN. Perhaps Mr. Hovstad had better . . .

HOVSTAD. No, you do it, Aslaksen.

ASLAKSEN. Well, the thing is that—now that we know how things really are—we think we might venture to put the *People's Herald* at your disposal.

DR. STOCKMANN. So *now* you dare do it? But what about public opinion? Aren't you afraid of having to face a storm of protest.

HOVSTAD. We must try to ride that storm.

ASLAKSEN. And then you must be ready to change your tack quickly, Doctor. As soon as your campaign has had its effect. . . .

DR. STOCKMANN. You mean as soon as my father-in-law and I have bought the shares up cheap . . . ?

HOVSTAD. I suppose it's mainly for research purposes you are anxious to get control of the Baths.

DR. STOCKMANN. Of course. It was with an eye on my research that I managed to get the old Badger to come in on it with me. Then we'll patch up the pipes a bit, and dig up a bit of the beach, and it won't cost the town a penny. Don't you think that'll work? Eh?

HOVSTAD. I think so—if you've got the *Herald* with you.

ASLAKSEN. In a free society, the press has great power, you know, Doctor.

DR. STOCKMANN. Yes, indeed. And so has public opinion. And you, Mr. Aslaksen, will take responsibility for the Ratepayers Association, I suppose?

ASLAKSEN. The Ratepayers Association *and* the Temperance Society. You may depend on that.

DR. STOCKMANN. But, gentlemen—I feel ashamed putting a question like this—but . . . what do *you* get out of this. . . ?

HOVSTAD. Actually, we'd rather not take anything at all for our help, really. But in fact the *Herald* is a bit shaky at the moment; it just can't quite make ends meet, and I should be most reluctant to wind the paper up now, just when there's such a lot of political work to be done.

DR. STOCKMANN. Of course. That would be a sad blow for a friend of the people like yourself. [*Flares up.*] But *I* am an enemy of the people. [*Rushes about the room.*] Where's my stick? Where the devil's my stick?

HOVSTAD. What does this mean?

ASLAKSEN. Surely you don't . . . !

DR. STOCKMANN [*stops*]. And what if I didn't give you a single brass farthing out of all my shares? It's not easy to get money out of us rich people, don't forget.

HOVSTAD. And *you* mustn't forget that this business about the shares can be presented in two very different ways.

DR. STOCKMANN. Yes, and you are just the man to do it. If I don't come to the aid of the *Herald*, then you'll take a pretty poor view of things. The hunt will be up, I dare say. . . . You'll be after my blood . . . you'll be on to me like a dog on to a hare!

HOVSTAD. That's the law of nature. Every animal must fight for survival.

ASLAKSEN. You've got to take your food where you find it, you know.

DR. STOCKMANN. Then let's see if you can find anything out in the gutter. [*Rushes about the room.*] Because now we are damned well going to see who is the strongest animal amongst us three. [*Finds his umbrella and waves it.*] Now, watch out. . . !

HOVSTAD. You wouldn't dare attack us!

ASLAKSEN. Watch what you are doing with that umbrella!

DR. STOCKMANN. Out of the window with you, Mr. Hovstad.

HOVSTAD [*near the hall door*]. Have you gone completely mad?

DR. STOCKMANN. Out of the window, Mr. Aslaksen! Jump, I tell you. And quick about it!

ASLAKSEN [*running round the desk*]. Moderation, Dr. Stockmann! I'm not very strong, I can't stand very much of this. . . . [*Shouts.*] Help! Help!

[MRS. STOCKMANN, PETRA *and* HORSTER *come in from the living-room.*]

MRS. STOCKMANN. Heavens above, Thomas, what's going on?

DR. STOCKMANN [*swinging the umbrella*]. Jump! Down into the gutter!

HOVSTAD. Unprovoked assault! You're a witness of this, Captain Horster.

[*He hurries out through the hall.*]

ASLAKSEN [*bewildered*]. Anybody who knew the lie of the land about here . . .

[*He slinks out through the living-room.*]

MRS. STOCKMANN [*clinging to her husband*]. Control yourself, Thomas!

DR. STOCKMANN [*throws the umbrella down*]. Damn them, they got away after all.

MRS. STOCKMANN. But what did they want with you?

DR. STOCKMANN. I'll tell you later. I've got other things to think about now. [*He goes to his desk and writes on a visiting card.*] Look, Katherine, what does this say?

MRS. STOCKMANN. 'No', three times. What's that for?

DR. STOCKMANN. That's something else I'll tell you later. [*Hands the card to* PETRA.] *There*, Petra. Get little dirty-face to run over to the Badger's with it, as quick as she can. Hurry! [PETRA *takes the card and goes out through the hall.*] Well, if this hasn't been a hell of a day for callers, I don't know what is. But now I'm going to sharpen up my pen; I'll impale them on it; I'll dip it in venom and gall; I'll chuck the inkpot right in their faces!

MRS. STOCKMANN. Yes, but we're leaving, aren't we, Thomas?

[PETRA *comes back.*]

DR. STOCKMANN. Well?

PETRA. She's taken it.

DR. STOCKMANN. Good! Leaving, did you say? No, I'm damned if we are. We're staying where we are, Katherine!

PETRA. We're staying?

MRS. STOCKMANN. In this town?

DR. STOCKMANN. Yes, just here. The battlefield is here; here the fight will be fought and here I shall triumph! As soon as I've had my trousers stitched, I'm off to town to look for somewhere to live. We've got to have a roof over our heads this winter.

HORSTER. You are welcome to share my house.

DR. STOCKMANN. Can I?

HORSTER. Yes, of course you can. I've plenty of room, and I'm hardly ever at home.

MRS. STOCKMANN. How very kind of you, Captain Horster.

PETRA. Thank you!

DR. STOCKMANN [*shaking his hand*]. Thank you! Thank you! That's that worry off my mind. Now I can get straight down to work in real earnest. Oh, there's no end to the things here that need going into, Katherine! But it's grand that I can give all my time to this now. Because—I was going to tell you—I've got my notice from the Baths, you know. . . .

MRS. STOCKMANN [*sighing*]. Yes, I was expecting that.

DR. STOCKMANN. . . . And they want to take my practice away as well. Well, let them! I won't lose the poor people anyway—those who don't pay anything. And, heavens, they are the ones who need me most. But, by God, they are going to listen to what I have to say. I'll read them a lesson, both in and out of season, as it says somewhere.

MRS. STOCKMANN. But, Thomas dear, surely you've seen now that reading them a lesson doesn't do much good.

DR. STOCKMANN. Don't be so ridiculous, Katherine. D'you think I'm going to let public opinion and the compact majority and all that rigmarole get the better of me? No, thank you! And anyway, what I want to do is so simple and clear and straightforward. I just want to take these mongrels and knock it into their heads that the Liberals are the worst enemies of freedom . . . that the party programmes grab hold of every young and promising idea and wring its neck . . . and that policies of expediency are turning all our standards of morality and justice upside down, so that life's just not going to be worth living. Surely I can make people understand that, Captain Horster? Don't you think so?

HORSTER. Very likely. I don't know very much about these things myself.

DR. STOCKMANN. Well, look here—I'll tell you what I mean! It's the party bosses you've got to get rid of. A party boss is just like a wolf, you see . . . a ravenous wolf who needs so and so many victims every year to keep him going. Just look at Hovstad and Aslaksen! How many do you think *they* haven't seen off in their time? Or else they worry them and maul them about so badly that they are no use for anything except to join the Ratepayers Association and subscribe to the *Herald*! [*Sits on the edge of the table.*] Come over here, Katherine . . . look how beautifully the sun is shining in here today. And this glorious, fresh, spring air that's been let in.

MRS. STOCKMANN. If only we could live on sun and fresh air, Thomas.

DR. STOCKMANN. Well, you'll just have to skimp and scrape a bit on the side—we'll manage all right. That's my least worry. No, the worst thing is this: I don't know of anybody with enough independence of mind to feel like taking on my work after me.

PETRA. Oh, you mustn't think about that, Father. You've plenty of time yet.—Why, here are the boys already.

[EJLIF *and* MORTEN *come in from the living-room.*]

MRS. STOCKMANN. Have you got a holiday today?

MORTEN. No, but we went for the others at playtime. . . .

EJLIF. That's not true. They started fighting us.

MORTEN. And then Mr. Rörlund said we'd better stay away for a few days.

DR. STOCKMANN [*snaps his fingers and jumps down from the table*]. I've got it! I've got it, by Heaven! You are not going to set foot in that school again!

THE BOYS. No more school!

MRS. STOCKMANN. Thomas, really . . . !

DR. STOCKMANN. Never, I say! I'll teach you myself—what I mean is, you'll not learn a blessed thing. . . .

MORTEN. Hurrah!

DR. STOCKMANN. . . . but I'll make decent and independent-minded men of you both. . . . And you must help me, Petra.

PETRA. You can count on me, Father.

DR. STOCKMANN. And we'll have the school in the very room where they called me an enemy of the people. But there ought to be a few more of us. I must have at least a dozen boys to start with.

MRS. STOCKMANN. You're not likely to get them here, not in this town.

DR. STOCKMANN. We'll see about that. [*To the boys.*] What about some of the street-corner lads . . . the real guttersnipes. . . ?

MORTEN. Yes, Father. I know plenty of them!

DR. STOCKMANN. That's fine! Get hold of one or two for me, will you? Just for once, I'm going to try an experiment on these mongrels. You never know what you might find amongst them.

MORTEN. But what are you going to do, when we've grown up into decent and independent-minded men?

DR. STOCKMANN. Then you can drive all the wolves out, lads—make sure that they all go west!

[EJLIF *looks rather doubtful;* MORTEN *jumps and shouts for joy.*]

MRS. STOCKMANN. Oh, just so long as it isn't the wolves who go chasing you, Thomas.

DR. STOCKMANN. You must be mad, Katherine! Chase *me! Now!* When I'm the strongest man in the town!

MRS. STOCKMANN. The strongest. . . ? *Now?*

DR. STOCKMANN. Yes, and I could even go so far as to say that *now* I'm one of the strongest men in the whole world.

MORTEN. Honestly?

DR. STOCKMANN [*dropping his voice*]. Sh! You mustn't say anything about it yet. But I've made a great discovery.

MRS. STOCKMANN. What, again?

DR. STOCKMANN. Yes I have. [*He gathers them about him and says confidentially.*] The thing is, you see, that the strongest man in the world is the man who stands alone.

MRS. STOCKMANN [*smiles and shakes her head*]. Oh, Thomas, Thomas. . . !

PETRA [*bravely, grasping his hands*]. Father!

THE WILD DUCK
[*Vildanden*]

PLAY IN FIVE ACTS
(1884)

CHARACTERS

HAAKON WERLE, businessman, industrialist, etc.

GREGERS WERLE, his son

OLD EKDAL

HJALMAR EKDAL, his son, a photographer

GINA EKDAL, Hjalmar's wife

HEDVIG, their fourteen-year-old daughter

MRS. SÖRBY, housekeeper to Haakon Werle

RELLING, a doctor

MOLVIK, a one-time theological student

PETTERSEN, Haakon Werle's servant

GRAABERG, the book-keeper

JENSEN, a hired waiter

A fat gentleman

A balding gentleman

A short-sighted gentleman

Six other gentlemen, Haakon Werle's guests

Several hired servants

The first act is at the home of Haakon Werle, and the four following acts at Hjalmar Ekdal's

ACT ONE

At HAAKON WERLE'S *house. The study, expensively and comfortably appointed, with bookcases and upholstered furniture; in the middle of the room a desk with papers and documents; the room is softly lit by green-shaded lamps. Folding doors at the back of the room are standing open, and the curtains are drawn back. The sitting-room, spacious and elegant, can be seen within, brilliantly lit by lamps and candelabra. In the study, right front, a baize-covered door leads to the offices. Left front, a fireplace with a glowing coal fire; and further back, a double door into the dining-room.*

PETTERSEN, WERLE'S servant, in livery, and JENSEN, the hired waiter in black, are putting the study in order. In the sitting-room, two or three other hired servants are busy arranging the room and lighting candles. A buzz of conversation can be heard from the dining-room, and the laughter of many voices; somebody taps a knife on a glass; silence follows and a toast is proposed; cheers, and again the buzz of conversation.

PETTERSEN [*lights a lamp on the mantelpiece and puts on the shade*]. Aye, just listen to them, Jensen. There's the old man at it now, off on a long toast to Mrs. Sörby.

JENSEN [*moving an armchair forward*]. Is it right what people say—that there's something between them?

PETTERSEN. God knows.

JENSEN. 'Cos he's been a bit of a lad in his day, hasn't he?

PETTERSEN. Maybe.

JENSEN. They say he's giving this dinner for his son.

PETTERSEN. Yes. His son came home yesterday.

JENSEN. I never knew old Werle had a son.

PETTERSEN. Oh, he's got a son, all right. But you could never get him to leave the works up at Höidal. In all the years I've worked in this house, he's never once been to town.

A HIRED WAITER [*at the door into the sitting-room*]. Here, Pettersen, there's an old fellow here who . . .

PETTERSEN [*muttering*]. Oh, damn. Who wants to come here at *this* time!

[OLD EKDAL *appears in the sitting-room from the right. He is wearing a shabby greatcoat with a high collar, and woollen mittens. He is carrying in his hand a stick and a fur cap, and under his arm a brown-paper parcel. He is wearing a dirty auburn wig and has a little grey moustache.*]

PETTERSEN [*goes towards him*]. Good Lord! What are *you* doing in here?

EKDAL [*in the doorway*]. I just *have* to get into the office, Pettersen.

PETTERSEN. The office shut an hour ago, and . . .

EKDAL. That's what they told me round at the gates, old man. But Graaberg's still in there. Be a good sort, Pettersen, and let me in *this* way. [*He points to the baize door.*] I've been this way before.

PETTERSEN. All right, then, you might as well. [*Opens the door.*] But mind you don't forget to go the proper way out. We've got company.

EKDAL. I can see that . . . hm! Thanks Pettersen, old man. Good old friend. Thanks! [*Mutters to himself.*] Silly old fool! [*He goes into the office;* PETTERSEN *shuts the door after him.*]

JENSEN. Does *he* work in the office as well.

PETTERSEN. No, they just farm some of the copying out to him at rush times. Not but what he hasn't been somebody in his time, Old Ekdal.

JENSEN. Yes, he seemed to have something about him.

PETTERSEN. You're right there. What would you say if I told you that he'd been a lieutenant!

JENSEN. Get away—him a lieutenant!

PETTERSEN. So help me, he was. But then he switched over to the timber business or whatever it was. Supposed to have done the dirty on Old Werle once, or so they say. They were both in on the Höidal works together, you see. Oh, I know Old Ekdal well enough, I do! Many's the time we have had a nip and a bottle of beer together down at Ma Eriksen's.

JENSEN. I don't suppose he's got much money to throw about, has he?

PETTERSEN. Good Lord, man, it's me that does the paying, believe you me. I think people ought to show a bit of respect to those who have known better days.

JENSEN. Did he go bankrupt, then?

PETTERSEN. No, it was worse than that. He was given hard labour.

JENSEN. Hard labour?

PETTERSEN. Or imprisonment, anyway—[*Listens.*] Hush! They are leaving the table now.

[*A couple of servants open the dining-room doors from within.* MRS. SÖRBY *comes out, in conversation with two gentlemen, followed gradually by all the other guests and* HAAKON WERLE. HJALMAR EKDAL *and* GREGERS WERLE *come last.*]

MRS. SÖRBY [*to the servant, in passing*]. Pettersen, will you have coffee served in the music room, please.

PETTERSEN. Very good, Mrs. Sörby.

[*She and the two gentlemen go into the sitting-room and out of it to the right.* PETTERSEN *and* JENSEN *go out the same way.*]

A FAT GUEST [*to a* BALDING GUEST]. Whew! What a dinner! Took a bit of getting through!

THE BALDING GUEST. Oh, if you put your mind to it, it's incredible what you can manage in three hours.

THE FAT GUEST. Yes, but afterwards, my dear sir, afterwards!

A THIRD GUEST. I hear they are serving coffee and liqueurs in the music room.

THE FAT GUEST. Splendid! And perhaps Mrs. Sörby will play something for us.

THE BALDING GUEST [*in a low voice*]. As long as she doesn't try playing anything *on* us.

THE FAT GUEST. Oh, I hardly think so. Bertha isn't the sort to go back on her old friends. [*They laugh and go into the sitting-room.*]

WERLE [*in a low, irritable voice*]. I don't think anybody noticed, Gregers.

GREGERS [*looks at him*]. Noticed what?

WERLE. Didn't you notice either?

GREGERS. What was there for me to notice?

WERLE. There were thirteen of us at table.

GREGERS. Really? Were there thirteen?

WERLE [*with a glance towards* HJALMAR EKDAL]. There are twelve of us as a rule. [*To the rest.*] Come along in here, gentlemen. [*He and the rest of the guests, except* HJALMAR *and* GREGERS, *go out at the back to the right.*]

HJALMAR [*who has heard what was said*]. You shouldn't have sent me that invitation, Gregers.

GREGERS. What! They say the party's for me. Am I not allowed to invite my best and only friend. . . .

HJALMAR. But I don't think your father is very pleased. I never come near the house any other time.

GREGERS. So I hear. But I had to see you and have a talk, because I dare say I'll be leaving again soon.—Yes, here we are, two old school friends, and drifted far, far apart, haven't we? We can't have seen each other now for sixteen or seventeen years.

HJALMAR. Is it as long as all that?

GREGERS. It is indeed. Well now, how are you getting along? You are looking well. You've put on a bit of weight, I might almost call you stout.

HJALMAR. Well, I don't know that I would call it stout exactly; but I dare say I look a bit more of a man now than I did then.

GREGERS. Yes, you do. Outwardly you don't seem to have suffered much harm.

HJALMAR [*in a rather gloomy voice*]. Ah, but inwardly, Gregers. It's different there, I can tell you. Of course, you know about the terrible things that have happened to me and my family since we last saw each other.

GREGERS [*softer*]. How are things now with your father?

HJALMAR. My dear fellow, don't let's talk about *that*. My poor unfortunate father is of course living in with me. He has nobody else in the whole world to turn to. But it's so desperately hard for me to talk about all this, you know.—Tell me instead how you have been getting on up at the works.

GREGERS. Delightfully lonely, that's how I've been. Plenty of opportunity to think about all sorts of things. Come over here; let's make ourselves comfortable. [*He sits down in an armchair by the fire and draws* HJALMAR *down into another beside him.*]

HJALMAR [*with feeling*]. Thank you all the same, Gregers, for asking me to your father's dinner-party. For now I can see that you don't hold anything against me any more.

GREGERS [*in surprise*]. What made you think I had anything against you?

HJALMAR. You did have the first few years.

GREGERS. What first few years?

HJALMAR. After the big crash came. And it was only natural you should. It was only by a hair's breadth that your own father missed being dragged into all that . . . that dreadful affair.

GREGERS. And you think I should have held that against you? Whoever gave you that idea?

HJALMAR. I know you *did*, Gregers. Your father told me himself.

GREGERS [*amazed*]. My father! Indeed. Hm! Was that the reason I never heard from you . . . not a single word?

HJALMAR. Yes.

GREGERS. Not even when you went and became a photographer?

HJALMAR. Your father said there was no point in writing to you about anything.

GREGERS [*absently*]. Well, well . . . perhaps he was right. But now Hjalmar, tell me . . . are you reasonably satisfied with things as they are now?

HJALMAR [*with a gentle sigh*]. Oh yes, I think so, pretty well. Can't really complain. As you might expect, it was a bit strange for me, in a way, to begin with. The circumstances I found myself in were so completely changed, of course; but then everything else was completely changed as well. The terrible calamity to Father ... the shame and the disgrace, Gregers. . . .

GREGERS [*feelingly*]. Yes, indeed, indeed.

HJALMAR. I couldn't possibly think of continuing my studies; there wasn't a penny left, if anything just the opposite, in fact. There were debts. Mostly to your father, I think.

GREGERS. Hm!

HJALMAR. Well, I thought it best to make a clean break, you know ... leave all the old life and its ways behind. Your father in particular advised me to do that. And since he had put himself out to be so helpful to me . . .

GREGERS. My father?

HJALMAR. Yes, surely you know that? Where could I have found the money to learn photography and set up a studio and establish myself? That sort of thing costs money, I can tell you.

GREGERS. And my father paid for all that?

HJALMAR. Yes, Gregers, didn't you know? I understood from him he had written and told you.

GREGERS. Not a word that it was *him*. He must have forgotten. We have never exchanged anything but business letters. So it was my father, was it!

HJALMAR. Yes, it was him all right. He never wanted anybody to know. But it *was* him. And it was him, too, who made it possible for me to get married. But maybe you didn't know anything about that either?

GREGERS. No, I certainly didn't. [*Clapping him on the arm.*] But my dear Hjalmar, I can't tell you how delighted I am to hear all this ... yet a bit worried as well. Perhaps I *have* been rather unjust to my father about certain things. For this does reveal a certain kindness of heart, doesn't it? Almost in a way as though he had a conscience. . . .

HJALMAR. Conscience!

GREGERS. Well, well, whatever you care to call it then. No, I can't tell you how glad I am to hear this about my father.—So you are married, then, Hjalmar! That's more than I'm ever likely to be. Well then, I hope you find married life suits you?

HJALMAR. Yes, I do. She's as good and capable a wife as ever a man could wish for. Nor is she altogether without education.

GREGERS [*a little surprised*]. No, I don't suppose she is.

HJALMAR. Life is a great teacher, you see. Contact with me every day . . . and then we have pretty regular visits from one or two most intelligent people. You wouldn't know Gina again, I assure you.

GREGERS. Gina?

HJALMAR. Yes, my dear Gregers, don't you remember she was called Gina?

GREGERS. Who was called Gina? I haven't the slightest idea what . . .

HJALMAR. But don't you remember her being in service in this house for a time.

GREGERS [*looks at him*]. Is it Gina Hansen?

HJALMAR. Yes, of course it's Gina Hansen.

GREGERS. . . . who kept house for us in the last year of Mother's illness?

HJALMAR. That's right. But my dear friend, I know for certain your father wrote and told you I had got married.

GREGERS [*who has risen*]. Yes, he did actually; but he didn't say . . . [*Walks up and down.*] But wait a minute . . . perhaps after all he did . . . now that I think about it. But my father always writes me such short letters. [*Sits on the arm of the chair.*] Listen, Hjalmar, tell me— this is really rather amusing—how did you happen to meet Gina . . . meet your wife?

HJALMAR. Oh, it was quite straightforward. Gina didn't stay very long here in the house. There was a lot of upset here at the time, what with your mother's illness. . . . Gina couldn't put up with it all, so she gave notice and left. That was the year before your mother died . . . or it might have been the same year.

GREGERS. It was the same year. I was up at the works at the time. But what about afterwards?

HJALMAR. Well, Gina went to live at home with her mother, a Mrs. Hansen, a very capable and hard-working woman who ran a little café. She also had a room to let, as well, a really nice, comfortable room.

GREGERS. And you, I take it, were lucky enough to land it?

HJALMAR. Yes. Actually it was your father who put me on to it. And it was *there*, you see, that I really got to know Gina.

GREGERS. So you got engaged?

HJALMAR. Yes. You know how it is with young people, they very soon get attached to each other. Hm. . . .

GREGERS [*rises and walks about*]. Tell me . . . when you got engaged . . . was it then that my father got you to . . . I mean, was it then that you began to take up photography?

HJALMAR. That's right. Because I was very keen on settling down to something, and the quicker the better. And both your father and I felt that this idea of photography was the best. And Gina thought the same. Besides, there was another reason as well, you see; it just so happened that Gina had taken up retouching.

GREGERS. That fitted in extraordinarily well.

HJALMAR [*pleased, rises*]. Yes, didn't it Gregers! It *did* fit in extraordinarily well, don't you think?

GREGERS. Yes it did, I must say. My father seems almost to have acted the part of Providence for you.

HJALMAR [*moved*]. He did not forsake his old friend's son in the hour of need. For he *is* good-hearted, you see.

MRS. SÖRBY [*enters, arm in arm with* HAAKON WERLE]. Now, my dear Mr. Werle, please don't argue. You mustn't stay in there any longer staring at all those lights. It's not good for you.

WERLE [*letting go her arm and running his hand over his eyes*]. I rather believe you are right.

[PETTERSEN *and* JENSEN, *the hired waiter, enter with trays.*]

MRS. SÖRBY [*to the guests in the other room*]. Punch is served, gentlemen; if anybody wants any, he'll have to come in here and get it.

THE FAT GUEST [*walks over to* MRS. SÖRBY]. But, I say, is it true you have abolished our precious freedom to smoke?

MRS. SÖRBY. Yes, my dear sir. Here, in Mr. Werle's private domain, it is forbidden.

THE BALDING GUEST. And when did you introduce this harsh clause into our smoking regulations, Mrs. Sörby?

MRS. SÖRBY. After the previous dinner-party, my dear sir. For there were certain people who over-stepped the mark.

THE BALDING GUEST. And is one not allowed to overstep the mark just the tiniest bit, Bertha? Seriously?

MRS. SÖRBY. Not in any circumstances, Mr. Balle.

[*Most of the guests are now assembled in* WERLE's *room; the servants hand round punch.*]

WERLE [*to* HJALMAR, *who is standing over at table*]. What are *you* standing there looking at, Ekdal?

HJALMAR. It's just an album, Mr. Werle.

THE BALDING GUEST [*strolling about*]. Ah! Photographs! That's obviously something for you.

THE FAT GUEST [*in an armchair*]. Haven't you brought along any of your own?

HJALMAR. No, I haven't.

THE FAT GUEST. You should have done. It's good for the digestion to sit and look at pictures.

THE BALDING GUEST. And it always adds something to the general entertainment, don't you know!

A SHORT-SIGHTED GUEST. All contributions gratefully received.

MRS. SÖRBY. What they mean is that, if you are invited out, you are expected to work for your supper, Mr. Ekdal.

THE FAT GUEST. And *that*, where the food is good, is just sheer pleasure, of course!

THE BALDING GUEST. Good Lord, if it's a matter of keeping body and soul together, I must say . . .

MRS. SÖRBY. You are right there!

[*They continue laughing and joking.*]

GREGERS [*quietly*]. You must join in, Hjalmar.

HJALMAR [*with a shrug*]. What do you expect me to say?

THE FAT GUEST. Don't you think, Mr. Werle, that Tokay can be regarded as relatively kind to the stomach?

WERLE [*by the fireplace*]. I can certainly vouch for the Tokay you had today, at any rate; it was one of the very finest vintages. Of course you must have seen that yourself.

THE FAT GUEST. Yes, it had a wonderfully delicate bouquet.

HJALMAR [*uncertainly*]. Does the vintage make any difference?

THE FAT GUEST [*laughing*]. By Heavens, that's good!

WERLE [*smiling*]. There's obviously not much point in putting good wine in front of *you*.

THE BALDING GUEST. It's the same with Tokay as with photographs, Mr. Ekdal. There has to be sunlight. Or am I wrong?

HJALMAR. No, indeed. Sunlight certainly plays a part.

MRS. SÖRBY. Well then it's exactly the same with you court officials. You have got to have a place in the sun as well, as the saying goes.

THE BALDING GUEST. Come, come, that joke's a bit ancient.

THE SHORT-SIGHTED GUEST. Mrs. Sörby is showing her paces. . . .

THE FAT GUEST. . . . And at our expense. [*Threateningly.*] Bertha! Bertha!

MRS. SÖRBY. Well, but it's perfectly true that the different vintages can vary enormously. The old vintages are the best.

THE SHORT-SIGHTED GUEST. Do you reckon *me* among the old ones?

MRS. SÖRBY. Oh, far from it.

THE BALDING GUEST. Listen to her! But what about *me* then, my dear Mrs. Sörby.

THE FAT GUEST. Yes, and me! What vintages do you class us among?

MRS. SÖRBY. I count you among the sweet vintages, gentlemen.

[*She sips a glass of punch; the guests laugh and joke with her.*]

WERLE. Mrs. Sörby always finds a way out . . . when she wants to. But you are not drinking, gentlemen. Pettersen, would you mind. . . ! Gregers, I think we might take a glass together. [GREGERS *does not move.*] Won't you join us, Ekdal? I didn't get a chance of drinking to you at table.

[GRAABERG, *the book-keeper, looks through the baize door.*]

GRAABERG. Excuse me, Mr. Werle, but I can't get out.

WERLE. What, you locked in again?

GRAABERG. Yes, and Flakstad's gone off with the keys. . . .

WERLE. Well, you had better come through this way.

GRAABERG. But there's somebody else as well. . . .

WERLE Come on, come on, both of you. Don't be shy.

[GRAABERG *and* OLD EKDAL *come out of the office.*]

WERLE [*involuntarily*]. Ah!

[*The laughter and chatter of the guests die away.* HJALMAR *starts up at the sight of his father, puts down his glass and turns towards the fireplace.*]

EKDAL [*without looking up, making a series of little bows to each side as he walks, mumbling*]. Excuse me. Came the wrong way. The gate's locked . . . gate's locked. Excuse me.

[*He and* GRAABERG *go out at the back, right.*]

WERLE [*with clenched teeth*]. Damn that Graaberg.

GREGERS [*staring open-mouthed, to* HJALMAR]. Surely that was never . . . !

THE FAT GUEST. What was that? Who was it?

GREGERS. Oh, nobody. Just the book-keeper and another man.

THE SHORT-SIGHTED GUEST [*to* HJALMAR]. Did you know the man?

HJALMAR. I don't know . . . I didn't notice. . . .

THE FAT GUEST [*rises*]. What the devil's wrong? [*He walks over to some of the others who are talking in lowered voices.*]

MRS. SÖRBY [*whispers to the servant*]. Slip him something outside, something really good.

PETTERSEN [*nodding*]. Certainly. [*Goes out.*]

GREGERS [*in a low, shocked, voice to* HJALMAR]. Then it really *was* him.

HJALMAR. Yes.

GREGERS. And yet you stood here and denied that you knew him!

HJALMAR [*in an urgent whisper*]. How could I . . . ?

GREGERS. . . . acknowledge your own father?

HJALMAR [*bitterly*]. Oh, if you were in my shoes, you . . .

[*The conversation among the guests, which has been conducted in low voices, now changes over to a forced conviviality.*]

THE BALDING GUEST [*approaching* HJALMAR *and* GREGERS *in friendly fashion*]. Ah! Standing here and reviving old student memories, eh? Don't you smoke, Mr. Ekdal? Want a light? Oh, no! That's right, we mustn't . . .

HJALMAR. No, thank you! I don't want . . .

THE FAT GUEST. Couldn't you recite us a nice piece of poetry, Mr. Ekdal? There was a time once when you used to do that so prettily.

HJALMAR. I'm afraid I can't remember any.

THE FAT GUEST. Oh, what a pity. Well, Balle, what do you think we had better do now?

[*The two guests walk across the room and out into another room.*]

HJALMAR [*gloomily*]. Gregers—I must go. When once a man has felt the crushing blows of fate, you know. . . . Say goodbye to your father for me.

GREGERS. Yes, of course. Are you going straight home?

HJALMAR. Yes. Why?

GREGERS. Nothing . . . just that I might drop in afterwards.

HJALMAR. No, don't do that. Not at my home. My house is a sad place, Gregers . . . especially after a brilliant banquet like this. We can always meet somewhere in town.

MRS. SÖRBY [*comes across and speaks in a low voice*]. Are you leaving, Mr. Ekdal?

HJALMAR. Yes.

MRS. SÖRBY. Give my regards to Gina.

HJALMAR. Thank you.

MRS. SÖRBY. And tell her I'll look in one of these days.

HJALMAR. Thanks, I will. [*To* GREGERS.] Stay here. I want to slip out unnoticed. [*He sidles across the room, into the next room, and out to the right.*]

MRS. SÖRBY [*softly, to the servant who has returned*]. Well, did the old fellow get anything?

PETTERSEN. Yes, I slipped him a bottle of brandy.

MRS. SÖRBY. Oh, you might have found him something a bit better than that.

PETTERSEN. Not at all, Mrs. Sörby. Brandy is the best thing he knows.

THE FAT GUEST [*in the doorway, with a sheet of music in his hands*]. Do you think we might play something together, Mrs. Sörby?

MRS. SÖRBY. Yes, let's do that.

THE GUESTS. Bravo, bravo!

[*She and all the guests go through the room and out to the right.* GREGERS *remains standing by the fire.* HAAKON WERLE *is searching for something in the writing-desk and seems to want* GREGERS *to leave. As the latter does not move,* WERLE *crosses to the doorway.*]

GREGERS. Just a moment, Father.

WERLE [*stops*]. What is it?

GREGERS. I want a word with you.

WERLE. Can't it wait till we are alone?

GREGERS. No, it can't. Because we might very easily never find ourselves alone.

WERLE [*approaching him*]. What do you mean by *that*?

[*During what follows, a piano is distantly heard from the music room.*]

GREGERS. How could people here let that family go to the dogs like that?

WERLE. I presume you mean the Ekdals?

GREGERS. Yes, I mean the Ekdals. Lieutenant Ekdal was such a close friend of yours once.

WERLE. Yes, he was a bit too close, I'm afraid. And I wasn't allowed to forget it either for years afterwards. He's the one I have to thank for the fact that *my* reputation also suffered.

GREGERS [*quietly*]. Was *he* in fact the only guilty one?

WERLE. Who else do you imagine there could be?

GREGERS. Well, the two of you were both in on the big timber deal together . . . weren't you?

WERLE. But was it not Ekdal who drew up the survey map of the area, that dubious map? He was the one who felled all that illegal timber on state land. It was he who was responsible for running the whole thing up there. I had no idea what Lieutenant Ekdal was up to.

GREGERS. Lieutenant Ekdal didn't seem to have much idea himself what he was up to.

WERLE. That might well be. But the fact remains he was found guilty and I was acquitted.

GREGERS. Yes, I know well enough there was no proof.

WERLE. Acquittal is acquittal. Why do you go raking up all these old and dreadful stories that turned my hair grey before its time? Are these the things you have been brooding about all these years up there? I can tell you one thing, Gregers: here in town all these stories have been forgotten long ago, as far as they concern *me*.

GREGERS. And the poor Ekdals?

WERLE. What do you really expect me to do for these people? When Ekdal was let out, he was a broken man, past helping. Some people in this world only need to get a couple of slugs in them and they go plunging right down to the depths, and they never come up again. You can take my word for it, Gregers, I have gone just as far as I ever could, short of laying myself open to all sorts of suspicion and gossip. . . .

GREGERS. Suspicion? Yes, indeed.

WERLE. I've put Ekdal on doing some copying for the office, and I pay him far, far more for his work than it is worth. . . .

GREGERS [*without looking at him*]. Hm! I don't doubt *that*.

WERLE. You smile? Perhaps you think I'm not telling you the truth? I admit there's nothing in my books to account for it; I never enter expenses of that kind.

GREGERS [*smiles coldly*]. No, there are some expenses better not accounted for.

WERLE [*startled*]. What do you mean by *that*?

GREGERS [*summoning up his courage*]. Have you accounted for what it cost to have Hjalmar Ekdal taught photography?

WERLE. I . . . Why should that be accounted for?

GREGERS. I know now that it was you who paid for it. And now I also know it was you who saw him so nicely settled.

WERLE. Well, and you still want to say I've done nothing for the Ekdals! Those people have involved me in quite enough expense, I can tell you.

GREGERS. Have you entered any of those expenses?

WERLE. What are you asking me about *that* for?

GREGERS. Oh, there are good reasons. Listen, tell me . . . that time you were ready to take such a warm interest in your old friend's son . . . wasn't that just when he was about to get married?

WERLE. Come now . . . how the devil do you expect me, after all these years . . . ?

GREGERS. You wrote me a letter at the time—a business letter, of course, and in the postscript it said, quite briefly, that Hjalmar Ekdal had married a Miss Hansen.

WERLE. Yes, and that was quite right. That's what she was called.

GREGERS. But what you didn't say was that Miss Hansen was Gina Hansen, our housekeeper as was.

WERLE [*with a scornful, but forced laugh*]. No, because it never struck me you were particularly interested in our one-time housekeeper.

GREGERS. No more I was. But . . . [*Lowers his voice.*] . . . there were others in this house who *were* particularly interested in her.

WERLE. What do you mean by *that*? [*Flaring up.*] You are not referring to me, I hope!

GREGERS [*quietly, but firmly*]. Yes, I am referring to you.

WERLE. You have the impertinence to . . . ! How dare you . . . ! And as for this . . . this photographer, the ungrateful . . . how dare he have the nerve to make accusations of this kind!

GREGERS. Hjalmar has never said a single word about this. I don't think he has the slightest suspicion of anything of the kind.

WERLE. Where have you got it from, then? Who could have said a thing like that?

GREGERS. My poor, unhappy mother said it. And that was the last time I saw her.

WERLE. Your mother! Yes, I might have known. The two of you were always pretty thick. She was the one who set you against me from the start.

GREGERS. No, it was all the things she had to put up with, till in the end she gave way and went completely to pieces.

WERLE. Oh, she hadn't anything to put up with at all, no more than plenty of other people, anyway. But what can you do with people that are sick and overwrought? That's something *I* found out. And then along you come harbouring suspicions like this, raking up all sorts of old rumours and nasty gossip about your own father. Listen now, Gregers, I honestly think that at your age you might find something a bit more useful to do.

GREGERS. Yes, perhaps the time has come.

WERLE. Then perhaps you wouldn't take things quite so seriously as you tend to do now. What's the point in you sitting up there at the works, year in and year out, slaving away like any ordinary clerk and not taking a penny more than the standard wage. It's sheer stupidity.

GREGERS. Oh, if only I were quite sure about that.

WERLE. I think I understand you. You want to be independent, don't want to be under any obligation to me. But now is just the opportunity for you to get your independence, be your own master.

GREGERS. Really? And in what way?

WERLE. When I wrote to you saying it was essential you came to town at once . . . hm . . .

GREGERS. Yes, what is it actually you wanted me for? I have been waiting all day to hear.

WERLE. I propose offering you a partnership in the firm.

GREGERS. Me? In your firm? As a partner?

WERLE. Yes. There would be no need for us always to be on top of each other. I thought you might take over the business here in town, and I should move up to the works.

GREGERS. *You* would?

WERLE. Yes. I haven't the capacity for work I once had, you know. And I have to watch my eyes, Gregers, they have started getting a bit weak.

GREGERS. They have always been that way.

WERLE. Not as bad as they are now. And besides—circumstances might make it desirable for me to live up there—at any rate for a time.

GREGERS. I had never imagined anything like that.

WERLE. Listen now, Gregers. There are many things where we don't exactly hit it off. But all the same we are father and son. I think we should be able to reach some kind of understanding between us.

GREGERS. To outward appearances, I suppose you mean?

WERLE. Well, at least that would be something. Think it over, Gregers. Don't you think something like that could be done? Eh?

GREGERS [*looking at him coldly*]. There's something behind all this.

WERLE. What do you mean?

GREGERS. There must be something you want to use me for.

WERLE. When two people are as closely connected as we are, one always has some use for the other, surely.

GREGERS. Yes, that's what they say.

WERLE. I should like to have you at home now for a while. I'm a lonely man, Gregers; I've always felt lonely, all my life; but especially now that I'm getting on a bit in years. I need somebody near me.

GREGERS. You've got Mrs. Sörby.

WERLE. Yes, I have. And she's become pretty nearly indispensable. She's bright, she's easy-going, she livens the place up. And that I can do with pretty badly.

GREGERS. Quite. But in that case you have got what you want.

WERLE. Yes, but I'm afraid it won't last. With a woman in a situation like this, it's so easy for the world to put a false interpretation on things. Indeed, you might say it doesn't do the man very much good, either.

GREGERS. Oh, when a man gives the sort of dinner-parties you give, he can risk a fair amount.

WERLE. Yes, but what about her, Gregers? I'm afraid she won't put up with it much longer. And even if she did—even if she disregarded all the gossip and the back-biting and things like that, out of devotion to me . . . ? Wouldn't you think, then, Gregers, you with your strong sense of justice . . .

GREGERS [*interrupts him*]. Without beating about the bush, tell me one thing. Are you thinking of marrying her?

WERLE. And if I were, what then?

GREGERS. Yes. That's what I'm asking, too. What then?

WERLE. Would you be so completely dead set against it?

GREGERS. No, not at all. By no means.

WERLE. I didn't know whether, perhaps out of respect for the memory of your late mother . . .

GREGERS. I am not neurotic.

WERLE. Well, whether you are or not, you have taken a great weight off my mind. I am delighted I can count on your support in this matter.

GREGERS [*looks steadily at him*]. Now I see what you want to use me for.

WERLE. Use you for? What an expression!

GREGERS. Oh, let's not be too particular in our choice of words—not when we are alone, at any rate. [*Laughs shortly.*] So that's it! That's why I damn' well had to turn up here in town in person. A bit of family life had to be organized in the house all for Mrs. Sörby's sake. A little tableau: father and son! That's something new, that is.

WERLE. How dare you speak like that!

GREGERS. When has there ever been any family life here? Never as long as I can remember! But now, if you please, there's a sudden need for something in that line. Think of the good impression it must create when it is known how the son hurried home—on wings of devotion—to his ageing father's wedding feast. What will be left then of all the stories about the things the poor dead wife had to put up with. Not a whisper! Her own son kills them all stone dead.

WERLE. Gregers, I don't think there's any man in the world you hate as much as me.

GREGERS [*quietly*]. I have seen you at too close quarters.

WERLE. You have seen me with your mother's eyes. [*Drops his voice a little.*] But you mustn't forget that those eyes were . . . clouded, now and again.

GREGERS [*trembling*]. I understand what you are getting at. But who bears the blame for my mother's unhappy disability. It's you, and all these. . . ! The last of them was this female who was palmed off on Hjalmar Ekdal when you no longer . . . ugh!

WERLE [*shrugging his shoulders*]. Word for word, as though I were listening to your mother.

GREGERS [*without paying any attention to him*]. . . . and now there he sits, so tremendously trusting and innocent, in the midst of deceit, living under the same roof with a woman like that and not knowing that what he calls his home is built on a lie. [*Comes a step nearer.*] When I look back on everything you've done, it's as if I looked out over a battlefield strewn with shattered lives.

WERLE. I almost think the gulf between us is too wide.

GREGERS [*with a stiff bow*]. So I have observed; I shall therefore take my hat and go.

WERLE. Go? Leave the house?

GREGERS. For now at last I see an objective I can live for.

WERLE. What sort of objective is that?

GREGERS. You would only laugh if I told you.

WERLE. Laughter doesn't come so easily to a lonely man, Gregers.

GREGERS [*pointing out to the back*]. Look, Father, your guests are playing Blind Man's Buff with Mrs. Sörby. Good night and goodbye.

[*He goes out at the back to the right. Laughter and banter are heard from the guests, who come into view in the outer room.*]

WERLE [*muttering scornfully after* GREGERS]. Huh! Poor fellow. And he says he's not neurotic!

ACT TWO

HJALMAR EKDAL'S *studio. The room, which is quite large, is recognizably an attic. On the right is a pitched roof with big skylights, half covered by a blue curtain. In the corner, top right, is the entrance-hall door; downstage, on the same side, a door leads into the living-room. Similarly there are two doors on the left wall, and between them an iron stove. On the rear wall are broad double sliding doors. The studio is cheaply but pleasantly furnished. Between the doors on the right, off the wall a little, stands a sofa, with a table and some chairs; on the table, a lighted lamp, shaded; in the corner by the stove, an old armchair. Various pieces of photographic apparatus and equipment are disposed about the room. On the rear wall, left of the double doors, is a bookcase containing a few books, some boxes and bottles of chemicals, various kinds of instruments, tools and other objects. Photographs and one or two little things like brushes, paper and so on are lying on the table.*

GINA EKDAL *is sitting at the table, sewing.* HEDVIG *is sitting reading a book on the sofa, shading her eyes with her hands, her thumbs in her ears.*

GINA [*after glancing several times at her, as though secretly worried*]. Hedvig!

[HEDVIG *does not hear.*]

GINA [*louder*]. Hedvig!

HEDVIG [*takes her hands away and looks up*]. Yes, Mother?

GINA. Hedvig dear, you mustn't sit reading any longer.

HEDVIG. Oh, but Mother, can't I read a little bit more? Just a little!

GINA. No, no, you must put the book away now. Your father doesn't like it; he never reads himself in the evenings.

HEDVIG [*shuts the book*]. No, Daddy isn't such a great one for reading.

GINA [*putting her sewing down and taking a pencil and a little note-book on the table*]. Can you remember what we paid for the butter today?

HEDVIG. It was one crown sixty-five.

GINA. That's right. [*Makes a note.*] The amount of butter we go through in this house! And then there was the salami and the cheese . . . let me see. . . . [*Notes it down.*] Then there was the ham . . . hm. . . . [*Adds it up.*] Yes, that already comes to . . .

HEDVIG. And then there was the beer.

GINA. Yes that's right. [*Notes it down.*] It soon mounts up. But there's nothing you can do about it.

HEDVIG. But then Daddy was going to be out, so there was no need to cook a dinner just for the two of us.

GINA. Yes, that was lucky. And then there was that eight crowns fifty I got for the photographs as well.

HEDVIG. Fancy! Was it as much as that?

GINA. Eight crowns fifty exactly.

[*Silence.* GINA *takes up her sewing again.* HEDVIG *takes paper and pencil and begins to draw, shading her eyes with her left hand.*]

HEDVIG. Isn't it lovely to think of Daddy being at a big dinner-party at Mr. Werle's!

GINA. You can't really say he's at Mr. Werle's. It was the son who asked him. [*After a pause.*] We've got nothing to do with Mr. Werle.

HEDVIG. I'm so terribly looking forward to Daddy coming home. Because he promised he'd ask Mrs. Sörby for something nice for me.

GINA. Aye, there's plenty of good things going in *that* house, believe you me.

HEDVIG [*goes on drawing*]. I think I might even be a little bit hungry.

[OLD EKDAL, *with the bundle of papers under his arm and another parcel in his coat pocket, enters by the hall door.*]

GINA. You're very late home today, Grandfather.

EKDAL. They had shut the office. Had to wait in Graaberg's room. And then I came out through . . . hm.

HEDVIG. Did they give you any more copying to do, Grandfather?

EKDAL. All this lot. Just look!

GINA. That was nice.

HEDVIG. And you've got another parcel in your pocket as well.

EKDAL. Eh? Nonsense! That isn't anything. [*Stands his walking stick in the corner.*] This will keep me busy for a long time, Gina, this will. [*Draws one of the sliding doors in the rear wall a little to one side.*] Hush! [*Peeps into the room for a moment or two and then carefully shuts the door again.*] Heh! heh! The whole lot's asleep. And *she's* gone to sleep in the basket. Heh! heh!

HEDVIG. Are you sure she'll not be cold in that basket, Grandfather?

EKDAL. Whatever gives you that idea! Cold? In all that straw? [*Walks over to the door, upper left.*] Are there any matches?

GINA. The matches are on the chest of drawers.

[EKDAL *goes into his room.*]

HEDVIG. It was jolly good, Grandfather getting all that copying to do.

GINA. Yes, poor old soul; now he can earn himself a bit of pocket-money.

HEDVIG. And besides, he'll not be able to sit all morning down at that horrid Ma Eriksen's place.

GINA. Yes, that's another thing.

[*Short silence.*]

HEDVIG. Do you think they'll still be having their dinner?

GINA. Lord knows. I dare say they could be.

HEDVIG. Think of all the lovely things Daddy will be getting to eat! I'm sure he'll be in a good mood when he comes home. Don't you think so, Mother?

GINA. Yes, I do. But just think, if only we could tell him we'd managed to let the room.

HEDVIG. But that's not necessary tonight.

GINA. Oh, it would come in very handy, you know. It's just standing there doing nothing.

HEDVIG. No, what I meant was we don't need it tonight because Daddy will be in a good temper anyway. It's better if we leave the business about the room for some other time.

GINA [*looks across at her*]. Do you like having something nice to tell your father when he comes home at night?

HEDVIG. Yes, because it makes things a bit more cheerful.

GINA [*thoughtfully*]. Oh yes, there's something in that.

[OLD EKDAL *comes in again and makes for the door, front left.*]

GINA [*half turning on her chair*]. Do you want something in the kitchen, Grandfather?

EKDAL. Yes, I do. Don't get up. [*Goes out.*]

GINA. I hope he isn't messing about with the fire in there! [*Waits a moment.*] Just go and see what he's up to, Hedvig.

[EKDAL *comes in again with a little jug of hot water.*]

HEDVIG. Have you been getting some hot water, Grandfather?

EKDAL. Yes, I have. I want it for something. I've got some writing to do, and the ink's gone all thick like porridge . . . heh!

GINA. But you ought to have your supper first, Grandfather. It's all set.

EKDAL. I can't be bothered with any supper, Gina. I'm terribly busy, I tell you. I don't want anybody coming into my room. Nobody at all . . . hm!

[*He goes into his room.* GINA *and* HEDVIG *look at each other.*]

GINA [*in a low voice*]. Where do you suppose he got the money from?

HEDVIG. He must have got it from Graaberg.

GINA. No, never. Graaberg always sends the money to me.

HEDVIG. Then he must have got a bottle on tick somewhere.

GINA. Nobody will give him anything on tick, poor old soul.

[HJALMAR EKDAL, *wearing a topcoat and a grey felt hat, enters right.*]

GINA [*throws down her sewing and gets up*]. Why, Hjalmar! Are you back already!

HEDVIG [*at the same time jumping up*]. Fancy coming now, Daddy!

HJALMAR [*putting down his hat*]. Well, most of them were coming away.

HEDVIG. So early?

HJALMAR. Yes, it was a dinner party, you know.

[*About to take off his topcoat.*]

GINA. Let me help you.

HEDVIG. And me.

[*They help him off with his coat,* GINA *hangs it up on the rear wall.*]

HEDVIG. Were there many there, Daddy?

HJALMAR. Oh no, not many. There were about twelve or fourteen of us when we sat down.

GINA. And did you manage to talk to them all?

HJALMAR. Oh yes, a little. But it was Gregers who monopolized me in the main.

GINA. Is Gregers still as awful as ever.

HJALMAR. Well, he's not particularly good-looking. Hasn't the old man come home?

HEDVIG. Yes, Grandfather's in there writing.

HJALMAR. Did he say anything?

GINA. No, what about?

HJALMAR. Didn't he say anything about . . . ? I thought I heard he'd been to see Graaberg. I'll look in on him for a minute.

GINA. No, no, it's hardly worth . . .

HJALMAR. Why not? Did he say he didn't want me to go in?

GINA. He didn't want *anybody* going in tonight. . . .

HEDVIG [*making signs*]. Sst! sst!

GINA [*does not notice*]. . . . he's been and got himself some hot water. . . .

HJALMAR. Ah! Is he sitting there. . . ?

GINA. Yes, that's just what he is doing.

HJALMAR. Ah, well . . . my poor, white-haired, old father. . . ! Yes, let him get what little pleasure he can out of life.

[OLD EKDAL, *in a dressing-gown, his pipe lit, comes in from his room.*]

EKDAL. You back? I thought it was you I heard talking.

HJALMAR. I've just this minute come.

EKDAL. You didn't see me, did you?

HJALMAR. No, but they said you'd gone through. And I thought I'd walk home with you.

EKDAL. Hm! Nice of you, Hjalmar! Who were all the people there?

HJALMAR. Oh, all sorts. There was Mr. Flor, he's something at Court, and Mr. Balle and Mr. Kaspersen and Mr. . . . What's-his-name. . . . I can't remember . . . all of them people in Court circles. . . .

EKDAL [*nods*]. Do you hear *that*, Gina? He's been mixing with high society.

GINA. Yes, things are pretty posh in that house now.

HEDVIG. Did any of them sing, Daddy? Or give a recitation?

HJALMAR. No, they just burbled on. They wanted to get me to recite to them, but I wasn't having any.

EKDAL. You weren't having any, eh?

GINA. You could easily have done it, if you wanted to.

HJALMAR. No. You haven't to be at everybody's beck and call. [*Walking up and down.*] I'm not, anyway.

EKDAL. No, no. You don't catch Hjalmar as easily as that.

HJALMAR. I don't see why *I* should be expected to provide the entertainment when I happen to have an evening out. Let the others put themselves out a little. That sort does nothing but go from one house to the next, eating and drinking, day in and day out. Let them jolly well do something in return for all the good food they get.

GINA. But I hope you didn't tell them that?

HJALMAR [*hums*]. Hm . . . hm . . . hm. They were told quite a number of things. . . .

EKDAL. What! All those Court people!

HJALMAR. That doesn't make them any different. [*Casually.*] After that we had a little argument about the Tokay.

EKDAL. Tokay, eh? That's a good wine, that!

HJALMAR [*pauses*]. It *can* be. But, you know, the different vintages are not always equally good; it all depends on how much sunshine the grapes have had.

GINA. Why, Hjalmar, the things you know!

EKDAL. And that's what they started arguing about?

HJALMAR. They tried it on; but then they were given to understand that it was exactly the same with Court officials. It was pointed out that not all *their* vintages were equally good either.

GINA. Really, the things you think of!

EKDAL. Heh, heh! So they had to put that in their pipes and smoke it!

HJALMAR. They got it, straight to their faces!

EKDAL. There you are, Gina. He let them have it straight to their faces, these people at Court.

GINA. Well, fancy! Straight to their faces.

HJALMAR. Yes, but I don't want it talked about. It's not the sort of thing to pass on. And it was all taken in good part, of course. They were nice, pleasant people. Why should I want to hurt them? No!

EKDAL. But straight to their faces . . .

HEDVIG [*ingratiatingly*]. What fun it is to see you in evening dress. You look so nice in evening dress, Daddy!

HJALMAR. Yes, I do, don't I! And this one is really an impeccable fit. Almost as though it had been made for me . . . a bit tight under the arms, perhaps. Help me off, Hedvig. [*Takes the coat off.*] I'll put my jacket on instead. Where have you put my jacket, Gina?

GINA. Here it is.

[*Brings the jacket and helps him on with it.*]

HJALMAR. There we are! Don't forget to let Molvik have the coat back first thing tomorrow morning.

GINA [*puts it aside*]. We'll see to that all right.

HJALMAR [*stretching himself*]. Ah, that feels a bit more like home. And I think it's rather more my line to wear a few casual things like this about the house. Don't you think so, Hedvig?

HEDVIG. Yes, Daddy, I do!

HJALMAR. And if I pull out my tie like this so that the ends can flap about. . . . Look! Eh?

HEDVIG. Yes, it goes well with your moustache and your curly hair.

HJALMAR. I wouldn't exactly call it curly; more wavy, you might say.

HEDVIG. Yes, because it has such soft curls.

HJALMAR. Waves, actually.

HEDVIG [*after a pause, tugs at his coat*]. Daddy!

HJALMAR. Well, what is it?

HEDVIG. Oh, you know as well as I do.

HJALMAR. No, honestly I don't.

HEDVIG [*laughing and crying*]. Oh yes you do, Daddy. You mustn't tease me any longer.

HJALMAR. But what is it?

HEDVIG [*shaking him*]. Oh, stop it now and come on, Daddy. You remember all those nice things you promised me.

HJALMAR. Oh, there now! Fancy me forgetting!

HEDVIG. Now you are just making fun of me, Daddy. Oh, it's horrid of you! Where have you put them?

HJALMAR. But just a minute! I've got something else for you, Hedvig.

[*Walks across and feels in the pockets of the coat.*]

HEDVIG [*jumping and clapping her hands*]. Oh, Mother, Mother!

GINA. Look, you see! Just give him time. . . .

HJALMAR [*with a piece of paper*]. Look, here it is.

HEDVIG. This thing? It's just a piece of paper.

HJALMAR. That's the menu, Hedvig, the complete menu. There it says 'Bill of fare', that means menu.

HEDVIG. Haven't you got anything else?

HJALMAR. I forgot the rest, I tell you. But believe me—it's no great treat having to eat all those things. Go and sit over at the table now, and read what it says on the card, and afterwards I'll tell you what the different courses taste like. There you are, Hedvig.

HEDVIG [*swallows her tears*]. Thanks.

[*She sits down, but does not read;* GINA *makes a sign to her, which* HJALMAR *notices.*]

HJALMAR [*pacing up and down*]. It's incredible all the things a man is supposed to think about; he's only to forget the slightest thing, and straight away all he gets is a lot of sour looks. Well, that's another thing you get used to. [*Pauses near the stove, beside the old man.*] Have you peeped in this evening, Father?

EKDAL. Yes, you bet I have. She's gone in the basket.

HJALMAR. Has she really? In the basket! She must be getting used to it.

EKDAL. Yes, I told you she would. But now, you know, there are still a few other things. . . .

HJALMAR. One or two improvements, you mean.

EKDAL. They've *got* to be done, you know.

HJALMAR. Yes, let's have a little chat about these improvements, Father. Come on, we'll sit on the sofa.

EKDAL. Yes, fine. Hm! Think I'll just fill my pipe first. . . . Must clean it out as well. Hm!

[*He goes into his room.*]

GINA [*smiles to* HJALMAR]. Cleaning his pipe!

HJALMAR. Well, well, Gina, just let him be . . . he's just a poor, old wreck of a man. . . . Yes, those improvements. . . . We'd best get them done tomorrow.

GINA. You'll not have any time tomorrow, Hjalmar.

HEDVIG [*breaking in*]. Yes he will, Mother!

GINA. . . . Don't forget those prints that need retouching; they've been asked for ever so many times.

HJALMAR. What! Those prints again? They'll be ready all right. Have there been any new orders?

GINA. No, worse luck. Tomorrow I've nothing but those two sittings, you know.

HJALMAR. Is that all? Oh well, if you are not ready to put yourself out, then . . .

GINA. But what more am I supposed to do? I'm putting as many adverts in the papers as we can afford, I reckon.

HJALMAR. Oh, the papers, the papers. You can see what use *that* is. And I suppose nobody's been to look at the room either?

GINA. No, not yet.

HJALMAR. Just what you might expect. If people don't show any initiative . . . well! We must pull ourselves together, Gina!

HEDVIG [*going over to him*]. Wouldn't you like me to fetch you your flute, Daddy?

HJALMAR. No, no flute, thank you. *I* don't need any of life's little pleasures! [*Paces about.*] Oh yes, I'll be working tomorrow all right, don't you fret. Working till I'm fit to drop. . . .

GINA. But, my dear Hjalmar, I didn't mean it that way.

HEDVIG. Daddy, what about bringing you a bottle of beer?

HJALMAR. No, certainly not. There's no need to bring out anything for me. . . . [*Pauses.*] Beer? Was it beer you said?

HEDVIG [*gaily*]. Yes, Daddy. Nice cool beer.

HJALMAR. Well . . . if you really want to, you might bring a bottle.

GINA. Yes, go on. It'll cheer things up a bit.

[HEDVIG *runs over towards the kitchen door.*]

HJALMAR [*stops her by the stove, looks at her, takes her head in his hands and draws her to him*]. Hedvig! Hedvig!

HEDVIG [*smiling through her tears*]. Daddy dear!

HJALMAR. No, don't call me that. There I've been sitting indulging myself at the rich man's table . . . stuffing myself at the festive board. . . ! And I couldn't even . . .

GINA [*sitting at the table*]. Oh, don't talk so silly, Hjalmar.

HJALMAR. It's true. But you mustn't think too badly of me. You know I love you, all the same.

HEDVIG [*throws her arms around him*]. And we love you so much, too, Daddy!

HJALMAR. And even if I am a bit unreasonable now and again, well . . . heavens above! You mustn't forget I'm a man beset by a whole host of troubles. Well, now! [*Dries his eyes.*] This is not the moment for beer. Bring me my flute.

[HEDVIG *runs to the shelves and gets it.*]

HJALMAR. Thanks! There we are. With flute in hand, and both of you close to me . . . ah!

[HEDVIG *sits down at the table beside* GINA; HJALMAR *walks up and down and begins resolutely on a rendering of a Bohemian folk dance, but in a slow elegiac tempo with much 'feeling'.*]

HJALMAR [*breaks off the tune, holds out his left hand to* GINA *and says with emotion*]. What though we have to pinch and scrape in this place, Gina! It's still our home. And this I will say: it is good to be here.

[*He starts to play again; at once there is a knock at the door.*]

GINA [*gets up*]. Hush, Hjalmar! I think somebody's coming.

HJALMAR [*placing the flute back on the shelf*]. Isn't that just like it!

[GINA *walks over and opens the door.*]

GREGERS WERLE [*outside in the passage*]. Excuse me, but . . .

GINA [*shrinking back*]. Oh!

GREGERS. . . . doesn't Mr. Ekdal the photographer live here?

GINA. Yes, he does.

HJALMAR [*walks over to the door*]. Gregers! Is that you again! Come along in.

GREGERS [*comes in*]. I told you I'd be looking in, didn't I?

HJALMAR. But tonight . . . ? Have you left the party?

GREGERS. Both the party and my father's house. Good evening, Mrs. Ekdal. I'm not sure if you recognize me again?

GINA. Oh yes. It's not difficult to recognize you again, Mr. Werle.

GREGERS. No, they say I take after my mother, and I expect you remember her all right.

HJALMAR. Did you say you've left the house?

GREGERS. Yes, I've moved to a hotel.

HJALMAR. Have you now! Well, now that you're here, you might as well take your things off and sit down.

GREGERS. Thanks.

[*Takes off his topcoat. He has changed into plain grey country tweeds.*]

HJALMAR. Here, on the sofa. Make yourself comfortable.

[GREGERS *sits down on the sofa,* HJALMAR *on a chair at the table.*]

GREGERS [*looking round*]. So this is your place, Hjalmar. This is where you live.

HJALMAR. This, as you see, is the studio. . . .

GINA. But it's a bit more roomy here, so we like being in here best.

HJALMAR. We had a nicer place before; but there's one great advantage about this flat, and that's all the extra space. . . .

GINA. And we've also got another room on the other side of the passage, and we can let that.

GREGERS [*to* HJALMAR]. Well, well . . . so you've got lodgers as well?

HJALMAR. No, not yet. It's not as easily done as all that, you know. It needs initiative. [*To* HEDVIG.] Now what about that beer!

[HEDVIG *nods and goes out to the kitchen.*]

GREGERS. So that's your daughter?

HJALMAR. Yes, that's Hedvig.

GREGERS. And she's an only child?

HJALMAR. She's the only one, yes. She's our greatest joy in life, and . . . [*Drops his voice.*] . . . she's also our deepest sorrow, Gregers.

GREGERS. What do you mean?

HJALMAR. Yes, Gregers. She is in grave danger of losing her sight.

GREGERS. Going blind!

HJALMAR. Yes. So far there's only been the first signs, and things might still be all right for quite some time yet. But the doctor has warned us. It's inevitable.

GREGERS. How terribly sad. How did she get like that?

HJALMAR [*sighs*]. Apparently, it's hereditary.

GREGERS [*with a start*]. Hereditary!

GINA. Hjalmar's mother also had poor sight.

HJALMAR. Yes, that's what Father says. I can't remember her myself.

GREGERS. The poor child. And how does she take it?

HJALMAR. Oh, can't you see we haven't the heart to tell her. She doesn't suspect anything. Happy and carefree, just like a little singing bird, there she goes fluttering into a life of eternal night. [*Overcome.*] Oh, it's quite heart-breaking for me, Gregers!

[HEDVIG *enters carrying a tray with beer and glasses which she puts on the table.*]

HJALMAR [*strokes her head*]. Thank you, Hedvig.

[HEDVIG *puts her arms round his neck and whispers in his ear.*]

HJALMAR. No, no sandwiches just now. [*Looks across.*] Unless perhaps Gregers would like some?

GREGERS [*declining*]. No, no thank you.

HJALMAR [*still sadly*]. Well, perhaps you might fetch a few, after all. If you've a crust, that would be all right. But mind you see there's plenty of butter on.

[HEDVIG *nods happily and goes out again into the kitchen.*]

GREGERS [*who has been following her with his eyes*]. She looks strong and healthy enough to me in other respects.

GINA. Yes, there's nothing much else wrong with her, thank God.

GREGERS. She's going to be like you in time, Mrs. Ekdal. How old might she be now?

GINA. Hedvig is just fourteen; it's her birthday the day after tomorrow.

GREGERS. She's a big girl for her age.

GINA. Yes, she's just shot up this last year.

GREGERS. It makes you realize your own age when you see all the young people growing up. How long is it you've been married now?

GINA. We've been married now . . . yes, close on fifteen years.

GREGERS. Fancy, is it so long?

GINA [*suddenly attentive, watching him*]. Yes, that's what it is all right.

HJALMAR. Yes, it must be all that. Fifteen years all but a few months. [*Changing the subject.*] It must have seemed a long time for *you*, Gregers, sitting up there at the works.

GREGERS. It seemed long at the time. But looking back now, I hardly know where it's all gone to.

[OLD EKDAL *comes out of his room, without his pipe, but wearing his old officer's cap; his gait is a bit unsteady.*]

EKDAL. Now then, Hjalmar, now we can sit down and talk about that . . . er . . . what was it again?

HJALMAR [*goes across to him*]. Father, there's somebody here, Gregers Werle . . . I don't know if you remember him.

EKDAL [*looks at* GREGERS, *who has risen*]. Werle? Is that the son? What does he want with me?

HJALMAR. Nothing. It's me he's come to see.

EKDAL. Ah! So there isn't anything the matter?

HJALMAR. No, nothing at all.

EKDAL [*waving his arms*]. Not that I care, you know; I'm not frightened, but . . .

GREGERS [*walks over to him*]. All I wanted was to bring greetings from your old hunting grounds, Lieutenant Ekdal.

EKDAL. Hunting grounds?

GREGERS. Yes, up there by the Höidal works.

EKDAL. Oh, there! They knew me well enough up there at one time.

GREGERS. You were a great one for shooting in those days.

EKDAL. Yes, I dare say you're right there. You are looking at my uniform. I don't have to ask anybody if I can wear it here in the house. So long as I don't go out in the street with it on . . .

[HEDVIG *brings in a plate of sandwiches which she puts on the table.*]

HJALMAR. Sit down now, Father, and have a glass of beer. Help yourself, Gregers.

[EKDAL *staggers mumbling over to the sofa.* GREGERS *sits on the chair nearest him,* HJALMAR *on the other side of* GREGERS. GINA *sits sewing a little way from the table;* HEDVIG *stands beside her father.*]

GREGERS. Can you remember, Lieutenant Ekdal, how Hjalmar and I used to come up in the summer and at Christmas to visit you?

EKDAL. Did you? No, no, no, I can't remember that. But I was a pretty crack shot, although I say it myself. I've even shot bears . . . nine of them, no less.

GREGERS [*looks sympathetically at him*]. And have you given up shooting now?

EKDAL. Oh no, I wouldn't say *that*, my dear sir. Still manage a bit of shooting now and again. Not *that* sort, of course. Because the forest, you know . . . the forest . . . the forest . . . ! [*Drinks.*] Is the forest in good shape up there now?

GREGERS. Not as fine as it was in your day. There's been a lot of felling.

EKDAL. Felling, eh? [*Lowers his voice, as if afraid.*] That's a dangerous business, that. That brings trouble. The forests avenge themselves.

HJALMAR [*fills up his glass*]. A little more, Father?

GREGERS. How is it possible for a man so fond of the outdoor life as you are to live cooped up here in town, hemmed in by these four walls?

EKDAL [*gives a short laugh and glances at* HJALMAR]. Oh, it's not bad here. Not bad at all.

GREGERS. But what about all those things that came to be so much a part of you at one time? The cool, caressing breezes, the open-air life in the forest and on the moors, among the beasts and the birds. . . .

EKDAL [*smiling*]. Hjalmar, shall we show him?

HJALMAR [*quickly, and a little embarrassed*]. Oh, no, no, Father. Not tonight.

GREGERS. What does he want to show me?

HJALMAR. Oh, it's only a sort of . . . You can see it another time.

GREGERS [*continues talking to the old man*]. Now what I had in mind, Lieutenant Ekdal, was that you ought to come back with me up to the works; I'll be returning there very soon. You could quite easily get copying to do up there as well. And there's really nothing here to keep you amused or liven things up for you.

EKDAL [*staring at him in astonishment*]. Me? Nothing here for *me*. . . ?

GREGERS. Oh yes, you have Hjalmar. But then he's got his own family. And a man like yourself who's always felt the call of the wild . . .

EKDAL [*strikes the table*]. Hjalmar, he *must* see it now.

HJALMAR. But, Father, is it worth it? It's dark. . . .

EKDAL. Nonsense! It's moonlight. [*Gets up.*] I tell you he *must* see it. Let me past. Come on and help me, Hjalmar!

HEDVIG. Oh yes, go on, Daddy.

HJALMAR [*gets up*]. Very well.

GREGERS [*to* GINA]. What is it?

GINA. Oh, you mustn't expect anything very special.

[EKDAL *and* HJALMAR *have gone to the back wall, and each pushes one of the sliding doors to one side;* HEDVIG *helps* OLD EKDAL; GREGERS *remains standing by the sofa;* GINA *sits unperturbed, sewing. Through the door can be seen a long irregularly shaped loft, with recesses and a couple of free-standing stove-pipes. There are skylights through which bright moonlight shines on some parts of the loft, leaving the rest in deep shadow.*]

EKDAL [*to* GREGERS]. You'd best come right over.

GREGERS [*walks over to them.*] But what *is* it, then?

EKDAL. Look and see. Hm!

HJALMAR [*rather embarrassed*]. All this belongs to Father, you understand.

GREGERS [*beside the door, looks into the loft*]. So you keep poultry, Lieutenant Ekdal!

EKDAL. I'll say we keep poultry. They've gone to roost now. But you should just see *this* poultry in daylight!

HEDVIG. And then there's . . .

EKDAL. Hush! hush! Don't say anything yet.

GREGERS. You've got pigeons as well, I see.

EKDAL. Oh yes! Sure, we have pigeons! They have their nesting boxes up under the eaves. Pigeons like best being up high, you know.

HJALMAR. They're not all ordinary pigeons, though.

EKDAL. Ordinary! No, I should just say not! We've got some tumblers, and we've also a pair of pouters. But come over here! Can you see that hutch over there by the wall?

GREGERS. Yes. What do you use that for?

EKDAL. That's where the rabbits sleep at night, my dear fellow.

GREGERS. Well! So you've got rabbits as well?

EKDAL. Yes, I should damn' well think we have got rabbits! He's asking if we've got rabbits, Hjalmar! Ha! But *now* we really do come to something! *Now* it comes! Out of the way, Hedvig! Come and stand here, that's right; now look down there. Can you see a basket with straw in?

GREGERS. Yes, I can. And I can see a bird sitting in the basket.

EKDAL. Ha! 'A bird!'

GREGERS. Isn't it a duck?

EKDAL [*hurt*]. Yes, obviously it's a duck.

HJALMAR. But what *kind* of duck do you think it is?

HEDVIG. It isn't an ordinary duck. . . .

EKDAL. Hush!

GREGERS. And it isn't one of those foreign breeds either.

EKDAL. No, Mr. . . . Werle; that's no foreign breed; that's a wild duck.

GREGERS. No, is it really? A wild duck?

EKDAL. Yes, that's just what it is. That 'bird' as you call it . . . that's a wild duck. Our wild duck, my dear sir.

HEDVIG. *My* wild duck. Because it belongs to *me*.

GREGERS. And can it really live up here in the loft? Does it get on all right here?

EKDAL. Of course she's got a trough of water to splash about in, you understand.

HJALMAR. Clean water every other day.

GINA [*turning to* HJALMAR]. Hjalmar, my dear, it's getting absolutely freezing in here now.

EKDAL. Hm, let's shut it up then. It's not good to disturb them when they're settled for the night, either. Go on, Hedvig, help!

[HJALMAR *and* HEDVIG *push the doors of the loft closed.*]

EKDAL. You can come and see her properly another time. [*Sits in the armchair by the stove.*] Oh, very remarkable birds, wild ducks are, I can tell you.

GREGERS. But how did you manage to catch it, Lieutenant Ekdal?

EKDAL. It wasn't me who caught it. There's a certain gentleman here in town whom we can thank for that.

GREGERS [*with a slight start*]. That gentleman wouldn't happen to be my father, would it?

EKDAL. You've got it! Precisely! Your father! Hm!

HJALMAR. Funny your guessing *that*, Gregers.

GREGERS. You told me before that you owed such a lot to my father, and so I thought . . .

GINA. But we didn't get the duck from Mr. Werle personally. . . .

EKDAL. It's Haakon Werle we have to thank for her just the same, Gina. [*To* GREGERS.] You see, he was out in a boat, and he let fly at her. But his sight isn't so good now, your father's isn't. Hm! So she was only winged.

GREGERS. Aha! She got a slug or two in her, did she!

HJALMAR. Yes, two or three maybe.

HEDVIG. It was in the wing, so she couldn't fly.

GREGERS. And then she dived right down to the bottom, eh!

EKDAL [*sleepily, his voice thick*]. She did that. Always do that, wild ducks do. Go plunging right to the bottom . . . as deep as they can get, my dear sir . . . hold on with their beaks to the weeds and stuff—and all the other mess you find down there. Then they never come up again.

GREGERS. But, Lieutenant Ekdal, *your* wild duck came up again.

EKDAL. He had such an absurdly clever dog, your father. . . . And that dog, he dived in and fetched the duck up again.

GREGERS [*turning to* HJALMAR]. And then you got it?

HJALMAR. Not straight away. First it was taken to your father's, but it didn't seem to thrive there; so Pettersen was told to do away with it. . . .

EKDAL [*half asleep*]. Ha! Pettersen! That old fool. . . .

HJALMAR [*in a lower voice*]. That was the way we got it, you see, with Father knowing Pettersen; when he heard all the business about the wild duck, he managed to get it turned over to him.

GREGERS. And now it's thriving perfectly well in the loft.

HJALMAR. Yes, incredibly so. It's got quite fat. Well, it's been so long there now it's forgotten what real wild life is like. And that's all that counts.

GREGERS. I'm sure you are right, Hjalmar. So long as it never catches sight of sea and sky. . . . But I mustn't stay any longer. I think your father's asleep.

HJALMAR. Oh, don't you worry about that. . . .

GREGERS. But, by the way . . . didn't you say you had a room to let . . . a vacant room?

HJALMAR. Yes, what of it? Perhaps you know somebody . . . ?

GREGERS. Can *I* have the room?

HJALMAR. You?

GINA. What, *you*, Mr. Werle. . . ?

GREGERS. Can I have the room? I'd move in first thing tomorrow morning.

HJALMAR. Yes, with the greatest pleasure. . . .

GINA. Oh, but Mr. Werle, that's not the sort of room for the likes of you, really.

HJALMAR. But, Gina, what are you saying?

GINA. Well, I mean, that room isn't big enough or light enough, and . . .

GREGERS. I'm not fussy about that, Mrs. Ekdal.

HJALMAR. Myself I'd have said it was rather a nice room; and not badly furnished either.

GINA. But don't forget about those two living underneath.

GREGERS. Who are they?

GINA. Oh, one of them's been a private tutor . . .

HJALMAR. That's Mr. Molvik.

GINA. . . . and then there's a doctor called Relling.

GREGERS. Relling? I know him slightly; he was in practice up in Höidal for a while.

GINA. They're a right pair of wasters, them two. As often as not they're off on a binge in the evenings, and they don't come back till late at night, and then they're not always quite . . .

GREGERS. You soon get used to things like that. I hope I shall be like the wild duck and . . .

GINA. Well, I think you'd better sleep on it first, all the same.

GREGERS. I don't think you're very keen on having me in the house, Mrs. Ekdal.

GINA. Heavens, whatever gives you that idea?

HJALMAR. Yes, really you are behaving very strangely, Gina. [*To* GREGERS.] But tell me, does this mean you are thinking of staying on in town for the time being?

GREGERS [*putting on his topcoat*]. Yes, now I'm thinking of staying.

HJALMAR. But not at your father's? What do you intend doing with yourself?

GREGERS. Ah, if only I knew *that*, my dear Hjalmar . . . it wouldn't be so bad. But when you are burdened with a name like 'Gregers'. . . ! 'Gregers!' And followed by 'Werle'! Have you ever heard anything so hideous?

HJALMAR. Oh, I don't know. . . .

GREGERS. Ugh! I feel I would want to spit at anybody with a name like that. But when once you have the burden of being 'Gregers . . . Werle' in this life, as I have . . .

HJALMAR [*laughs*]. Ha! ha! And if you weren't 'Gregers Werle', what would you want to be?

GREGERS. If I had the choice, I should like most of all to be a clever dog.

GINA. A dog!

HEDVIG [*involuntarily*]. Oh, no!

GREGERS. Yes, a really absurdly clever dog; the sort that goes in after wild ducks when they dive down and bite on to the weeds and tangle in the mud.

HJALMAR. You know, Gregers . . . I don't understand a word of what you are saying.

GREGERS. Oh, well, I dare say there's nothing much to it, anyway. Well then, first thing tomorrow . . . and I'll move in. [*To* GINA.] I'll not cause you much bother; I'll do for myself. [*To* HJALMAR.] We'll talk about the rest tomorrow. Good night, Mrs. Ekdal. [*Nods to* HEDVIG.] Good night!

GINA. Good night, Mr. Werle.

HEDVIG. Good night.

HJALMAR [*who has lit a candle*]. Just a minute, I'll bring a light. It's sure to be dark on the stairs.

[GREGERS *and* HJALMAR *leave by the hall door.*]

GINA [*staring vacantly, her sewing on her lap*]. Wasn't that funny, him talking about wanting to be a dog?

HEDVIG. I'll tell you what, Mother . . . I think he meant something else.

GINA. What else could he mean?

HEDVIG. I don't know. But all the time it was just as though he meant something different from what he was saying.

GINA. Do you think so? It was certainly very funny.

HJALMAR [*comes back*]. The lamp was still on. [*Snuffs the candle and puts it down.*] Ah, at last a man can get a bite to eat. [*Begins to eat a sandwich.*] There you are, you see, Gina . . . see what you can do with a bit of initiative. . . .

GINA. What do you mean 'initiative'?

HJALMAR. Well, wasn't it lucky getting the room let at last. And then imagine! . . . to somebody like Gregers . . . an old friend.

GINA. Really, I don't know what to say, I don't.

HEDVIG. Oh Mother, it'll be lovely, you'll see.

HJALMAR. You are funny, you know. First you were keen on getting it let, and now you don't like it.

GINA. Oh, yes, Hjalmar. If only it had been somebody else. . . . But what do you suppose Mr. Werle's going to say?

HJALMAR. Old Werle? It's no concern of his.

GINA. But you can see they've fallen out about something again, what with him moving out of the house. You know what those two are like with each other.

HJALMAR. Yes, that may be, but . . .

GINA. And now perhaps Mr. Werle will think you are behind it all. . . .

HJALMAR. Let him think! Good God, I admit Mr. Werle's done a great deal for me. But that doesn't mean I've got to go on for ever doing what he wants me to do.

GINA. But, Hjalmar dear, it might also affect Grandfather. Perhaps he'll lose the little bit of money he makes working for Graaberg.

HJALMAR. I could almost wish he would! Isn't it rather humiliating for a man like me to see his grey-haired father being treated like an outcast? But soon we shall know what time in its fullness will bring, I should think. [*Helps himself to another sandwich.*] As truly as I have a mission in life, so shall I fulfil it!

HEDVIG. Oh yes, Daddy, do!

GINA. Hush! Mind you don't wake him.

HJALMAR [*in a lower voice*]. I *will* fulfil it, I tell you. The day will come, when . . . And that's why it's a good thing we managed to let the room; it gives me a bit more independence. And *that's* something a man with a mission in life must have. [*Over by the armchair, greatly moved.*] My poor white-haired old father! Trust in your Hjalmar! He has broad shoulders . . . strong shoulders, anyway. One fine day you'll wake up and . . . [*To* GINA.] You believe that, don't you?

GINA [*getting up*]. Of course I believe it. But let's see about getting him to bed first.

HJALMAR. Yes, let's.

[*They lift the old man carefully.*]

ACT THREE

HJALMAR EKDAL's *studio. It is morning; the daylight comes through the big window in the sloping roof; the curtain is drawn back.*

HJALMAR is sitting at the table busy retouching a photograph; several other pictures are lying in front of him. After a while GINA comes in by the hall door, in her hat and coat, carrying on her arm a covered basket.

HJALMAR. Is that you back already, Gina?

GINA. Oh, yes. Have to look slippy. [*She puts the basket on a chair and takes off her things.*]

HJALMAR. Did you look in on Gregers?

GINA. Yes, I did. And a bonny sight it is in there. He's no sooner here but what he's got the whole room in a right rare state.

HJALMAR. Oh?

GINA. Yes, he wanted to manage for himself, he said. Decided to light the fire, so what did he do but screw the damper down so the whole room was filled with smoke. Ugh, the stink! Just like . . .

HJALMAR. Oh dear!

GINA. But you haven't heard the best bit. Because then he wanted to put it out, so he just took a whole jug of water off the washstand and poured it all into the stove, and now there's the most awful wet mess all over the floor.

HJALMAR. What a nuisance!

GINA. I've got the woman downstairs to come and clean up after him—the pig. But the place won't be fit to go into again until this afternoon.

HJALMAR. What's he doing with himself in the meantime?

GINA. He was going out for a bit, he said.

HJALMAR. I looked in on him as well for a minute. Just after you'd gone out.

GINA. So I heard. And you've asked him to lunch.

HJALMAR. Just for a bit of a bite of something, you know. Seeing it's his first day . . . we can't really get out of it. You've always got something in the house.

GINA. I'd better see what I can find.

HJALMAR. But let's not be too stingy about it. Because I think Relling and Molvik are also coming up. I happened to run into Relling on the stairs, you see, so I more or less had to . . .

GINA. So we're going to have them two an' all.

HJALMAR. Good Lord . . . one or two more or less . . . that's surely neither here nor there.

OLD EKDAL [*opens his door and looks out*]. I say, Hjalmar . . . ! [*Notices* GINA.] Oh . . . ah . . .

GINA. Is there something you want, Grandfather?

EKDAL. Oh no, it doesn't matter. Hm! [*Goes in again.*]

GINA [*takes the basket*]. Just keep an eye on him and see he doesn't go out.

HJALMAR. Yes, yes, I will. . . . I say, Gina, a little bit of herring salad would be nice. Because Relling and Molvik were out on the tiles last night.

GINA. As long as they don't land on me before . . .

HJALMAR. No, of course they won't. Take your time.

GINA. Yes, all right. And in the meantime you can get a bit of work done.

HJALMAR. I *am* working! I'm working as hard as I can.

GINA. Because then it means you'll have *that* off your hands, you see.

[*She takes the basket and goes out to the kitchen.* HJALMAR *sits a while working on the photograph with a brush, with obvious distaste and reluctance.*]

EKDAL [*peeps out, looks round the studio and says in a low voice*]. Busy, Hjalmar?

HJALMAR. Yes, can't you see I'm sitting here slaving away at these portraits. . . .

EKDAL. Oh well, of course, if you're all *that* busy. . . . Hm! [*Goes in again: the door remains standing open.*]

HJALMAR [*continues for a while in silence; then he puts down his brush and walks over to the door*]. Are you busy, Father?

EKDAL [*from within, grumbling*]. If *you're* so busy, then *I'm* busy too. Hm!

HJALMAR. All right.

[*Goes back to his work.*]

EKDAL [*after a short pause, appears again at his door*]. Hm! Look, Hjalmar, I'm not *really* as busy as all that.

HJALMAR. I thought you were busy with your copying.

EKDAL. Oh, hell! Surely Graaberg can wait a day or two, can't he? I don't suppose it's a matter of life and death.

HJALMAR. No, and besides you're no slave.

EKDAL. Then there was that thing, you know, for in there . . .

HJALMAR. Yes, precisely. Do you want to go in? Shall I open up for you?

EKDAL. That's maybe not such a bad idea.

HJALMAR [*getting up*]. And then we'd have *that* off our hands.

EKDAL. Exactly. It has to be ready for first thing tomorrow morning. It is tomorrow, isn't it? Eh?

HJALMAR. Yes, it's tomorrow all right.

[HJALMAR *and* EKDAL *take a door each and push; the morning sun is shining in through the skylights; a few pigeons are flying about, others sit cooing on the rafters; occasionally, hens can be heard cackling from further back in the loft.*]

HJALMAR. Well, you'd better get on with it now, Father.

EKDAL [*goes in*]. Aren't you coming?

HJALMAR. Yes, do you know . . . I rather think . . . [*Sees* GINA *at the kitchen door.*] Who me? No, I haven't time. I have to work. But what about our little gadget. . . ? [*He pulls a string and inside a curtain falls, the bottom part of which consists of a strip of old sail cloth, and the upper part of a piece of fishing net stretched taut. As a result the floor of the loft is no longer visible.*]

HJALMAR [*walks over to the table*]. There now! Perhaps I can get on in peace for a while now.

GINA. Is he fiddling about in there again?

HJALMAR. Would you rather see him running off to Ma Eriksen's? [*Sits down.*] Do you want something? You said . . .

GINA. I just wanted to ask if you thought we could lay the table in here?

HJALMAR. Yes. I take it we haven't got anybody booked for as early as that.

GINA. No, the only people I'm expecting are that couple that wanted to be taken together.

HJALMAR. Why the devil couldn't they have been taken together some other day!

GINA. Now, Hjalmar my dear, I booked them specially for after dinner when you are having your sleep.

HJALMAR. Oh well, that's all right then. Yes, we'll eat in here.

GINA. All right. But there's no hurry about laying the table. There's nothing to stop you from using it for a good while yet.

HJALMAR. Surely you can see I'm using the table just about as hard as I can go.

GINA. And then you'll be free later, won't you? [*Goes out into the kitchen again. Short pause.*]

EKDAL [*appears at the loft door, behind the net*]. Hjalmar!

HJALMAR. Well?

EKDAL. I'm afraid we'll have to move the water trough after all.

HJALMAR. Yes, that's just what I've been saying all along.

EKDAL. Hm, hm, hm!

[*Moves away from the door again.* HJALMAR *does a little work, glances over at the loft and half gets up.* HEDVIG *comes in from the kitchen.*]

HJALMAR [*sits down again quickly*]. What do you want?

HEDVIG. I just wanted to be beside you, Daddy.

HJALMAR [*after a moment*]. What do you want to come sniffing round like this for? Are you supposed to be keeping an eye on me, or something?

HEDVIG. No, of course not.

HJALMAR. What's your mother up to now out there?

HEDVIG. Oh, she's right in the middle of making herring salad. [*Walks over to the table.*] Isn't there anything I could help you with, Daddy?

HJALMAR. No, no. I'd best see to it all myself . . . as long as my strength lasts. There's no need, Hedvig; provided your father manages to keep his health. . . .

HEDVIG. Oh, no, Daddy! You mustn't say horrid things like that.

[*She wanders round, stops by the opening and looks into the loft.*]

HJALMAR. What's he doing, Hedvig?

HEDVIG. Looks like a new way up to the water trough.

HJALMAR. He'll never manage *that* by himself, never in this world! Yet here am I condemned to sit here. . . !

HEDVIG [*goes across to him*]. Let *me* have the brush, Daddy. I *can* do it, you know.

HJALMAR. Nonsense. You'll just ruin your eyes.

HEDVIG. Really I shan't. Come on, give me the brush.

HJALMAR [*gets up*]. Well, I don't suppose it'd take more than a minute or two.

HEDVIG. Pooh! What if it did! [*Takes the brush.*] There now. [*Sits down.*] And here's one I can copy from.

HJALMAR. But don't ruin your eyes! D'you hear? I'm not taking any responsibility; you have to take the responsibility yourself. Understand?

HEDVIG [*retouching*]. Yes, yes, I will.

HJALMAR. You are a clever little girl, Hedvig. Just for a couple of minutes, then.

[*He slips past the edge of the curtaining into the loft.* HEDVIG *sits at her work.* HJALMAR *and* EKDAL *can be heard discussing things inside.*]

HJALMAR [*appears behind the netting*]. Oh, Hedvig, hand me those pincers off the shelf, will you? And the chisel as well. [*Turns to face into the loft.*] Now I just want you to see something, Father. Just give me the chance to show you what I mean first.

[HEDVIG *fetches the tools he wanted from the shelf and hands them in to him.*]

HJALMAR. Thanks. Yes, it was a good thing I came, you know.

[*Moves away from the opening; hammering and talking are heard within.* HEDVIG *stands there watching them. A moment later there is a knock on the hall door which she does not notice.* GREGERS WERLE *comes in and stands near the door; he is bare-headed and without a topcoat.*]

GREGERS. Hm?

HEDVIG [*turns and walks over to him*]. Good morning! Please come in.

GREGERS. Thanks. [*Looks over at the loft.*] Sounds as though you've got workmen in the house.

HEDVIG. No, it's only Daddy and Grandfather. I'll go and tell them.

GREGERS. No, no, don't do that. I'll just wait a minute or two instead.

[*He sits down on the sofa.*]

HEDVIG. Everything's in such a mess. . . .

[*Begins to clear away the photographs.*]

GREGERS. Oh, just leave it. Are these photographs waiting to be finished?

HEDVIG. Yes, it's just a little job I was helping Daddy with.

GREGERS. Please don't let me disturb you.

HEDVIG. All right.

[*She arranges the things around her again and settles down to work;* GREGERS *watches her in silence.*]

GREGERS. Did the wild duck sleep well last night?

HEDVIG. Yes, thank you, I think so.

GREGERS [*turning towards the loft*]. It looks quite different in daylight from what it did last night by moonlight.

HEDVIG. Yes, it can change such a lot. In the mornings it looks different from in the afternoons; and when it's raining it looks different from when it's fine.

GREGERS. Have you noticed that?

HEDVIG. Yes, you can't help seeing it.

GREGERS. Do you like being in there too beside the wild duck.

HEDVIG. Yes, when it can be managed. . . .

GREGERS. But I dare say you haven't a great deal of spare time. You have to go to school, haven't you?

HEDVIG. No, I don't go now any more. Daddy is afraid I'll spoil my eyes.

GREGERS. So he probably helps you with your lessons himself.

HEDVIG. Daddy's promised to do some lessons with me, but he hasn't been able to find the time just yet.

GREGERS. But isn't there anybody else who could help you a little?

HEDVIG. Yes, there's Mr. Molvik; but he's not always quite . . . not properly . . . er . . .

GREGERS. You mean, he's drunk?

HEDVIG. Yes, he is.

GREGERS. Well then, you've got time for all sorts of things. And inside there, it must just be like a world of its own, I should think?

HEDVIG. Yes, all of its own. And such a lot of strange things, too.

GREGERS. Really?

HEDVIG. Yes, big cupboards with books in, and a lot of the books have pictures.

GREGERS. Aha!

HEDVIG. And then there's an old cabinet with drawers and compartments in, and a big clock with figures that are supposed to pop in and out. But the clock doesn't go any more.

GREGERS. So time stands still in there . . . beside the wild duck.

HEDVIG. Yes. And then there are old paint boxes and things like that. And all the books.

GREGERS. And do you read these books?

HEDVIG. Oh yes, when I can manage it. But most of them are in English, and I don't understand that. But then I look at the pictures. There's a great big book called *Harryson's History of London*—it must be easily a hundred years old—and that has an enormous number of pictures in. In the front there's a picture of Death with an hour glass, and a girl. I think that's awful. But then there's also all the other pictures of churches and palaces and streets and big ships sailing on the sea.

GREGERS. But tell me, where did you get all these rare things from?

HEDVIG. Oh, an old sea captain used to live here once, and he brought them back with him. They used to call him 'the Flying Dutchman'. That was funny, because he *wasn't* a Dutchman at all.

GREGERS. Wasn't he?

HEDVIG. No. But then in the end he never came back; and all these things were just left here.

GREGERS. Listen now, tell me—when you sit in there looking at the pictures, don't you ever feel you want to get out into the big wide world itself and see something of it?

HEDVIG. Not me! I'm always going to stay at home and help my father and mother.

GREGERS. Touching up photographs?

HEDVIG. No, not just that. Best of all I'd like to learn how to engrave pictures like those in the English books.

GREGERS. Hm! What does your father say to that?

HEDVIG. I don't think Daddy likes it; Daddy's funny that way. Just think, he keeps on at me about learning basket-weaving and wicker-work! But I can't see there can be anything much in *that*.

GREGERS. Oh, no! I don't think so either.

HEDVIG. But Daddy's right when he says if I'd learnt basket-work, I could have made the new basket for the wild duck.

GREGERS. Yes, you could; and you would have been the proper person to do it.

HEDVIG. Because it's my wild duck.

GREGERS. Of course, it is.

HEDVIG. Yes, it belongs to *me*. But Daddy and Grandfather can have the loan of it as often as they like.

GREGERS. Indeed, and what do they do with it?

HEDVIG. Oh, they look after it, and build things for it, and things like that.

GREGERS. I suppose they do; because the wild duck is the most important of all the things in there.

HEDVIG. Yes, she is; because she's a *real* wild bird. It's such a shame, poor thing, she hasn't anybody to keep her company.

GREGERS. No family, like the rabbits.

HEDVIG. No. There's plenty of hens too, and they have grown up together from being chickens. But she's completely cut off from her friends. And then everything about the wild duck is so mysterious. Nobody really knows her; and nobody knows where she's from either.

GREGERS. And the fact that she's been down in the briny deep.

HEDVIG [*glances quickly at him, suppresses a smile and asks*]. What makes you say 'the briny deep'?

GREGERS. What do you expect me to say?

HEDVIG. You could say 'the bottom of the sea' or 'the sea bed'.

GREGERS. But can't I just as well say 'the briny deep'?

HEDVIG. Yes. But it sounds so strange when I hear other people say 'briny deep'.

GREGERS. Why is that? Tell me.

HEDVIG. No, I don't want to. It's just silly.

GREGERS. Oh, I'm sure it isn't. Tell me why you smiled?

HEDVIG. It's because every time I catch myself wondering about things in there—suddenly, you know without thinking—it always strikes me that the whole room and everything in it should be called 'the briny deep'. But that's just silly.

GREGERS. No, you mustn't say that.

HEDVIG. Yes, of course, because it's really only a loft.

GREGERS [*looking hard at her*]. Are you so certain?

HEDVIG [*astonished*]. That it's a loft?

GREGERS. Yes. Do you know for sure?

[HEDVIG *looks at him, open-mouthed and silent.* GINA *enters from the kitchen with a tablecloth.*]

GREGERS [*gets up*]. I'm afraid I've come too early.

GINA. Oh, well, I suppose you've got to be somewhere. Anyway, it will soon be ready. Clear the table, Hedvig.

[HEDVIG *clears up; she and* GINA *lay the table during the following dialogue.* GREGERS *sits down in the easy-chair and glances through an album.*]

GREGERS. I hear you can do retouching, Mrs. Ekdal.

GINA [*with a sidelong glance*]. Yes, I can that.

GREGERS. That was very lucky.

GINA. What do you mean, 'lucky'?

GREGERS. After Hjalmar took up photography, I mean.

HEDVIG. Mother can do photography too.

GINA. Oh yes, I've managed to pick *that* up, all right.

GREGERS. I dare say you're the one that runs the business.

GINA. Yes, when Hjalmar hasn't the time himself. . . .

GREGERS. I imagine his time's pretty well taken up with his old father.

GINA. Yes. And besides it's no job for a man like Hjalmar taking pictures all day long.

GREGERS. I quite agree. But once he's gone in for that kind of thing . . .

GINA. Hjalmar's not like any of your ordinary photographers, Mr. Werle, I can tell you.

GREGERS. Quite. But all the same . . .

[*A shot is fired inside the loft.*]

GREGERS [*starts up*]. What's that!

GINA. Huh! They're shooting again!

GREGERS. Do they shoot, too?

HEDVIG. They go out hunting.

GREGERS. They what! [*Walks over to the loft door.*] Are you hunting, Hjalmar?

HJALMAR [*behind the netting*]. You here? I didn't know. I was so busy. . . . [*To* HEDVIG.] Why didn't you tell us? [*Comes into the studio.*]

GREGERS. Do you go shooting in the loft?

HJALMAR [*shows him a double-barrelled pistol*]. Oh, only with this.

GINA. Yes, and the two of you will finish up by having an accident one of these fine days with that gun.

HJALMAR [*irritated*]. How many times do I have to tell you a weapon like this is called a pistol.

GINA. Well, I can't see that's much better myself.

GREGERS. So you've taken up hunting too, Hjalmar?

HJALMAR. Just a bit of rabbit shooting, now and again. Mostly for Father's sake, you know.

GINA. Funny creatures, men! Always have to have something to deviate themselves with.

HJALMAR [*angrily*]. That's right, yes. We always have to have something to divert ourselves with.

GINA. Yes, *that's* what I said.

HJALMAR. Oh, well! [*To* GREGERS.] Yes, you see, we are lucky the loft is so placed that nobody can hear us when we shoot. [*Places the pistol on the top shelf.*] Don't touch the pistol, Hedvig! One of the barrels is loaded, don't forget.

GREGERS [*looks in through the netting*]. I see you've also got a sporting gun.

HJALMAR. That's Father's old gun. You can't fire it any more, there's something wrong with the lock. But it's fun to have it all the same, because we can take it to pieces and clean it every now and then and grease it and put it together again. . . . Of course, it's mainly my father who tinkers about with these things.

HEDVIG [*over beside* GREGERS]. Now you can see the wild duck properly.

GREGERS. I'm just looking at it now. She seems to be dragging one wing a bit, I think.

HJALMAR. Well, that's not surprising; after all, she's been wounded.

GREGERS. And she's trailing one foot too. Or am I mistaken?

HJALMAR. Perhaps ever so slightly.

HEDVIG. Well, that was the foot the dog bit.

HJALMAR. Otherwise there's absolutely nothing wrong with her; and that's really rather remarkable when you consider she's had a load of shot in her and been chewed about by a dog. . . .

GREGERS [*with a glance at* HEDVIG]. . . . and been down in the briny deep . . . for so long.

HEDVIG [*smiles*]. Yes.

GINA [*arranging the table*]. That blessed wild duck! All the carrying-on there is about that bird!

HJALMAR. Hm! . . . Will lunch soon be ready?

GINA. Any minute now. Hedvig, you must come and help me now.

[GINA *and* HEDVIG *go out into the kitchen.*]

HJALMAR [*in an undertone*]. I don't think there's any point in standing and watching Father. He doesn't like it.

[GREGERS *walks away from the loft door.*]

HJALMAR. And I'd better shut it up before the others arrive. [*Waving his hands to chase the birds away.*] Shoo! Shoo! Get away. [*Speaking as he draws up the curtaining, and pulls the doors together.*] These gadgets here are my own invention. Really it's great fun having something like this to look after, and mending it when it gets broken. And besides it's absolutely necessary, you know, because Gina doesn't like having the rabbits and hens in the studio.

GREGERS. Of course not. And I suppose it's your wife who has the running of it?

HJALMAR. The routine jobs I generally leave to her; then I can retire to the living-room and give my attention to more important things.

GREGERS. What sort of things, actually, Hjalmar?

HJALMAR. I'm surprised you haven't asked me about *that* before. Or perhaps you haven't heard about the invention?

GREGERS. Invention? No.

HJALMAR. Really? Haven't you? Oh, of course, being stuck out there in the wilds, up in the forest. . . .

GREGERS. So you've made an invention!

HJALMAR. Haven't quite managed it yet, but I'm busy on it. When I decided to devote myself to photography, you don't suppose it was with the idea of doing nothing but take pictures of anybody who happened to come along?

GREGERS. No, no, your wife's just been saying the same thing.

HJALMAR. I swore that if I was going to dedicate my powers to this calling, I would raise it to the level where it was both an art and a science. So I decided to make this remarkable invention.

GREGERS. And what does the invention consist of? What's the purpose of it?

HJALMAR. Ah, my dear Gregers, you mustn't ask for details yet. It all takes time, you know. And you mustn't think it's vanity that's urging me on. I'm not thinking of myself in the least. Oh no, night and day I see before me what must be my life's work.

GREGERS. What life's work?

HJALMAR. Have you forgotten that dear old, silver-haired man?

GREGERS. Your poor old father? Yes, but what can you in fact do for him?

HJALMAR. I can restore his own self-respect by raising once more the name of Ekdal to a place of honour and dignity.

GREGERS. So that is your life's work, then?

HJALMAR. Yes, I will rescue this poor castaway, shipwrecked as he was from the moment the storm broke over him. During that terrible inquiry he was no longer himself. That pistol over there, Gregers . . . the one we use to shoot rabbits with . . . it has played its role in the tragedy of the House of Ekdal.

GREGERS. The pistol? Really?

HJALMAR. When judgement had been pronounced and he was about to be sent to prison . . . he had the pistol in his hand. . . .

GREGERS. He had the . . . ?

HJALMAR. Yes, but he didn't dare. He was a coward. He was already so demoralized, so broken in spirit by then. Oh, can you imagine it? Him a soldier, a man who had shot no less than nine bears, who was descended from two lieutenant-colonels . . . not both at the same time of course. . . . Can you imagine it, Gregers?

GREGERS. Yes, I can imagine it very well.

HJALMAR. I can't. But then the pistol figured a second time in our family history. When they had taken him away, and he sat there under lock and key—oh, that was a terrible time for me, I can tell you. I kept the blinds lowered at both windows. When I looked out and saw the sun shining the same as usual, I couldn't understand it. I saw people walking about the streets, laughing and talking about things of no importance. I couldn't understand it. I felt that all creation ought to have come to a standstill, like an eclipse.

GREGERS. I felt just the same when Mother died.

HJALMAR. It was in such a moment that Hjalmar Ekdal held the pistol to his own breast.

GREGERS. You too thought of . . . !

HJALMAR. Yes.

GREGERS. But you didn't shoot?

HJALMAR. No. At the crucial moment I won a great victory over myself. I went on living. But as you can quite understand, it takes some courage to choose life on *those* terms.

GREGERS. Well, it depends how you look at it.

HJALMAR. No, my dear fellow, there's no doubt about it. But it was all for the best, because soon now I shall have my invention ready. And Dr. Relling thinks—as I do too—that Father will then be able to wear his uniform again. I ask for no other reward than that.

GREGERS. So *that's* how it is with the uniform he . . . ?

HJALMAR. Yes, *that's* what he longs and yearns for more than anything else. You have no idea how my heart bleeds for him. Every time we have a little family party—like Gina's and my wedding anniversary, or whatever it might be—in comes the old chap dressed in his lieutenant's uniform of happy memory. But if there's so much as a knock on the front door—because he daren't show himself in front of strangers—away he's off into his room again as fast as his poor old legs will carry him. It's heart-breaking for a son to have to see things like that, Gregers.

GREGERS. Roughly, when do you think the invention will be ready?

HJALMAR. Good Lord, you mustn't ask me about details like dates. An invention is something you can never be completely master of. It's largely a matter of inspiration . . . of intuition . . . and it's pretty nearly impossible to predict when that will come.

GREGERS. But it's making good progress?

HJALMAR. Certainly it's making good progress. Not a day goes by but what I do something on the invention; I'm absorbed in it. Every day after dinner I shut myself up in the living-room, where I can concentrate in peace. But it's no good people trying to rush me, that's no good. Relling says the same.

GREGERS. And you don't feel all these things going on in the loft take you away from your work . . . distract you too much?

HJALMAR. No, no. On the contrary. You mustn't get that idea at all. I can't always go on poring over the same old exhausting problems. I've got to have something else as well to keep me occupied. Inspiration, revelation, you know—when it comes, it comes, that's all.

GREGERS. My dear Hjalmar, I almost believe you've a bit of the wild duck about you.

HJALMAR. The wild duck? How do you make that out?

GREGERS. You have gone plunging down and bitten fast to the weeds.

HJALMAR. You are referring, I suppose, to the blow that crippled my father and very nearly killed him . . . and me too?

GREGERS. Not primarily to that. I wouldn't say you're lamed exactly; but you've landed up in a poison swamp, Hjalmar; you've picked up some insidious disease, and you've gone down to die in the dark.

HJALMAR. Me? Die in the dark? Look, Gregers, you really must stop this kind of talk.

GREGERS. But don't upset yourself. I'll see we get you up again. For now, you see, I too know what my life's work is to be. I found out yesterday.

HJALMAR. That's all very well; but will you please keep *me* out of it. I can assure you that, apart from feeling naturally rather depressed, I am as well as any man could wish.

GREGERS. The very fact that you are, also comes from the poison.

HJALMAR. Please now, my dear Gregers, let's have no more of this talk about diseases and poisons; I'm just not used to that kind of conversation; in my house people never talk to me about unpleasant things.

GREGERS. That's something I can well believe.

HJALMAR. No, it isn't good for me. And this place *doesn't* smell like a swamp, as you keep saying. I know it's only the humble home of a poor photographer of modest means . . . and the place is not very grand. But I am an inventor, you know . . . and a breadwinner too. That's what keeps me above all these petty things.—Ah! Here they are with the lunch!

[GINA *and* HEDVIG *carry in bottles of beer, a decanter of brandy, glasses and other things for the table; at the same time,* RELLING *and* MOLVIK *enter from the hallway; both are without hats or topcoats;* MOLVIK *is dressed in black.*]

GINA [*putting the things on the table*]. Trust them two to be here in time.

RELLING. Molvik got the idea he could smell herring salad, and then there was no holding him. Good morning for the second time, Ekdal.

HJALMAR. Gregers, may I introduce Mr. Molvik, and Doctor . . . ah, but of course you know Relling?

GREGERS. Yes, slightly.

RELLING. Oh, it's Mr. Werle, junior. Yes, we came up against each other once or twice up at the Höidal works. You've just moved in?

GREGERS. I moved in this morning.

RELLING. Molvik and I live just underneath, so if ever you need a doctor or a parson, you don't have far to go.

GREGERS. Thanks, it could happen. Yesterday there were thirteen of us at table.

HJALMAR. Oh, let's not get on to that horrid business again!

RELLING. You needn't worry, Ekdal, it's not going to affect you.

HJALMAR. I hope not, if only for my family's sake. But now let's sit down, and eat, drink and be merry.

GREGERS. Shouldn't we wait for your father?

HJALMAR. No, he'll have his in his room afterwards. Come along!

[*The men sit down at the table, and eat and drink.* GINA *and* HEDVIG *go in and out, waiting on them.*]

RELLING. Molvik was filthy drunk last night, Mrs. Ekdal.

GINA. What, again last night?

RELLING. Didn't you hear him when I brought him home during the night?

GINA. No, can't say I did.

RELLING. Just as well. Because last night Molvik was pretty dreadful.

GINA. Is this true, Mr. Molvik?

MOLVIK. Let us draw a veil over the events of last night. Such things bear no relation to my better self.

RELLING. It just comes over him like a sort of revelation, and then there's nothing for it but to take him out on a binge. Mr. Molvik, you see, is a demonic.

GREGERS. A demonic?

RELLING. Molvik is a demonic, yes.

GREGERS. Hm!

RELLING. And demonic natures are not made for the straight and narrow; they've got to kick over the traces now and then. . . . So you still manage to stick it up there at those nasty, filthy works?

GREGERS. I have until now.

RELLING. And did you get anywhere with that 'claim' you were always coming out with?

GREGERS. Claim? [*Understands him.*] Oh, that!

HJALMAR. What's all this about 'claims', Gregers?

GREGERS. Oh, it's nothing.

RELLING. Ah, but there *was* something. He used to go the rounds of all the labourers' cottages serving up what he called 'the claim of the ideal'.

GREGERS. I was young then.

RELLING. You're right there; you were very young. And this 'claim of the ideal'—you never got anybody to honour it as long as *I* was there.

GREGERS. Nor afterwards, either.

RELLING. Well, I suppose you've had the sense to mark the price down a bit.

GREGERS. Never when I'm dealing with a man who *is* a man.

HJALMAR. Well, that strikes me as being pretty reasonable.—Butter please, Gina.

RELLING. And a slice of pork for Molvik.

MOLVIK. Ugh, not pork!

[*There is a knock on the loft door.*]

HJALMAR. Open up, Hedvig. Father wants to be let out.

[HEDVIG *goes and opens the door a little;* OLD EKDAL *enters carrying a fresh rabbit skin; she shuts the door after him.*]

EKDAL. Good morning, gentlemen! Had some good hunting today. Bagged a big 'un.

HJALMAR. Have you gone and skinned it without *me*. . . !

EKDAL. Salted it, too. It's good tender meat, rabbit-meat. And sweet. Tastes like sugar. Enjoy your lunch, gentlemen!

[*Goes into his room.*]

MOLVIK [*rising*]. Excuse me . . . I can't . . . I must run downstairs at once. . . .

RELLING. Have some soda-water, man!

MOLVIK [*hurrying*]. Ugh! Ugh!

[*Leaves by the hall door.*]

RELLING [*to* HJALMAR]. Let's drink to the grand old sportsman.

HJALMAR [*touching glasses with him*]. Yes, to the sportsman, standing on the brink of the grave.

RELLING. To the grey-haired. . . . [*Drinks.*] But tell me, is it grey hair he has, or is it white?

HJALMAR. Actually, it's somewhere in between. As a matter of fact, he hasn't got all that much hair left.

RELLING. Ah well, people still manage to get by with a wig. Yes, Ekdal, you're really a very lucky man, devoting your life to this splendid mission.

HJALMAR. And I *do* devote myself to it, too, I can tell you.

RELLING. And then you've also got your clever little wife to look after you, pottering about in her slippers all nice and cuddlesome, and making the place all cosy.

HJALMAR. Yes, Gina. . . . [*Nods to her.*] You are a great helpmate to have on life's way, my dear.

GINA. Oh, I wish you wouldn't sit there weighing me up and down.

RELLING. Then what about your Hedvig, eh, Ekdal?

HJALMAR [*moved*]. The child, yes! More than anything else, the child. Come to me, Hedvig. [*Strokes her hair.*] What day is it tomorrow?

HEDVIG. Oh, no, you mustn't say anything, Daddy!

HJALMAR. It's like a knife plunged into my heart when I think how little there will be. Just a small party there in the loft. . . .

HEDVIG. Oh, but that will be simply lovely!

RELLING. Just you wait till this amazing invention sees the light of day, Hedvig.

HJALMAR. Ah yes, then you'll see! Hedvig, I've decided I must make your future secure. You shall not want for anything as long as you live. I shall insist on your having . . . something or other. That shall be the humble inventor's only reward.

HEDVIG [*with her arm round his neck, whispers*]. Oh, my dear, dear Daddy!

RELLING [*to* GREGERS]. Well now, don't you think *this* makes a nice change, to sit at a well-filled table in a happy family circle.

HJALMAR. Yes, I really appreciate these meal-times.

GREGERS. Personally I don't thrive in a poisoned atmosphere.

RELLING. Poisoned atmosphere?

HJALMAR. Oh, let's not have that nonsense all over again!

GINA. God knows there aren't any bad smells in here, Mr. Werle. I give the place a good airing every blessed day.

GREGERS [*rising from the table*]. No amount of airing will get rid of the stench *I* mean!

HJALMAR. Stench!

GINA. Well, what do you think of that, Hjalmar!

RELLING. Excuse me . . . I suppose *you* couldn't be the one who has brought the stench in, from the mines up there?

GREGERS. It's just like you to call what I bring into this house a stench.

RELLING [*walks across to him*]. Listen, Mr. Werle, junior! I strongly suspect you are still carrying this 'claim of the ideal' about with you in full, in your back pocket.

GREGERS. I carry it in my breast.

RELLING. Well, carry the thing where the devil you like; but I wouldn't advise you to try and cash in on it here as long as *I'm* about the place.

GREGERS. And if I do?

RELLING. Then you'll find yourself going head-first down the stairs. Now you know.

HJALMAR [*getting up*]. I say, Relling!

GREGERS. Yes, you just try throwing me out and . . .

GINA [*coming between them*]. You mustn't do that, Mr. Relling. But *this* I will say, Mr. Werle—anybody who can make such an awful mess as the one in your stove has no right coming to me and talking about smells.

[*There is a knock at the hall door.*]

HEDVIG. Mother, somebody's knocking.

HJALMAR. Oh, really! There's just no end to all these comings and goings.

GINA. Let me go. [*Walks over and opens the door, starts, shudders and draws back.*] Oh!

[HAAKON WERLE, *wearing a fur coat, takes a step into the room.*]

WERLE. I beg your pardon, but I believe my son is supposed to be living here.

GINA [*gulping*]. Yes.

HJALMAR [*coming forward*]. Won't you be so good, Mr. Werle, as to ...

WERLE. Thanks. All I want is to speak to my son.

GREGERS. Yes, what is it? Here I am.

WERLE. I wish to speak to you in your room.

GREGERS. In my room ... very well.

[*He turns to go.*]

GINA. Good Lord, no! It's in no state for ...

WERLE. Well, out in the passage, then; I wish to speak to you privately.

HJALMAR. You can do that here, Mr. Werle. Relling can come into the living-room.

[HJALMAR *and* RELLING *go out right;* GINA *leads* HEDVIG *out into the kitchen.*]

GREGERS [*after a short pause*]. Well, now we are alone.

WERLE. You passed a number of remarks last night. . . . And since you've now moved in on the Ekdals, I can only assume that you have in mind something against me.

GREGERS. What I have in mind is to open Hjalmar Ekdal's eyes. He shall see the situation as it is ... that's all.

WERLE. Is *this* the life's work you were talking about yesterday?

GREGERS. Yes. You haven't left me any other.

WERLE. Is it my fault, then, if your ideas are all mixed up, Gregers?

GREGERS. You've messed up my whole life. I'm not thinking of all the business with Mother. . . . But it's thanks to you that I now suffer the torment of a desperately guilty conscience.

WERLE. Aha! So it's your conscience that's a bit queer, eh?

GREGERS. I should have stood up to you at the time the trap was laid for Lieutenant Ekdal. I should have warned him. For I had a pretty good idea how things would turn out in the end.

WERLE. Yes, you really should have spoken out then.

GREGERS. I didn't dare. I was scared . . . too much of a coward. I can't tell you how frightened of you I was then and for a long time after, too.

WERLE. It would seem that that fear is past now.

GREGERS. Fortunately it is. The wrong that's been done to Old Ekdal, both by me and by . . . others, can never be put right. But what I can do now is free Hjalmar from all the lies and deceit that are causing his ruination.

WERLE. Do you think *that's* likely to do any good?

GREGERS. I'm convinced it will.

WERLE. Do you really think Hjalmar Ekdal is the sort of man who would thank you for that kind of favour?

GREGERS. Yes. He *is* that sort.

WERLE. Hm! We'll see.

GREGERS. And besides, if I'm to go on living, I must find something to cure my sick conscience.

WERLE. It will never recover. From being a child, you've always had a sickly conscience. It's a heritage from your mother, Gregers . . . one thing she did leave you.

GREGERS [*with a contemptuous smile*]. That must have been a bitter pill to swallow when you found you had miscalculated, after expecting her to bring you a fortune.

WERLE. Let us keep to the point.—Are you set on this scheme of putting Ekdal on what you imagine to be the right track?

GREGERS. Yes, I'm quite set on it.

WERLE. Well, in that case I might have saved myself a journey. For I suppose it's no use asking you now if you'll come home again?

GREGERS. No.

WERLE. And you won't come into the firm either?

GREGERS. No.

WERLE. Very well. But as I now intend to marry again, the estate will be divided between us.

GREGERS [*quickly*]. No. I don't want that.

WERLE. You don't want that?

GREGERS. No. My conscience won't let me.

WERLE [*after a pause*]. Are you going back up to the works again?

GREGERS. No. I regard myself as having left your service.

WERLE. But what will you do now?

GREGERS. I shall fulfil my mission, that's all.

WERLE. But what about afterwards? What are you going to live on?

GREGERS. I've saved a bit out of my pay.

WERLE. But how long will *that* last!

GREGERS. I think it will last my time out.

WERLE. What do you mean by that?

GREGERS. I'm not answering any more questions.

WERLE. Goodbye, then, Gregers.

GREGERS. Goodbye.

[HAAKON WERLE *goes.*]

HJALMAR [*peeps in*]. Has he gone?

GREGERS. Yes.

[HJALMAR *and* RELLING *enter;* GINA *and* HEDVIG *come in from the kitchen.*]

RELLING. That's put paid to *that* lunch.

GREGERS. Put your things on, Hjalmar. You are coming for a long walk with me.

HJALMAR. Yes, with pleasure. What did your father want? Anything to do with me?

GREGERS. Just come with me. We must have a little talk. I'll go and get my coat.

[*He goes out by the hall door.*]

GINA. I wouldn't go out with him if I was you, Hjalmar.

RELLING. No, don't do it, old man; stay where you are.

HJALMAR [*takes his hat and topcoat*]. What, when an old friend feels the need to open up his heart to me. . . !

RELLING. Damn it, man! Can't you see the man's mad, barmy, off his head!

GINA. There you are! Now just you be told! His mother sometimes used to have bouts just the same as that.

HJALMAR. All the more reason for him to need a friend's watchful eye. [*To* GINA.] See that dinner's ready in good time, won't you? Goodbye for now.

[*He leaves by the hall door.*]

RELLING. What a pity the man didn't get to hell out of it down one of those mines at Höidal.

GINA. Good Lord! Why d'you say that?

RELLING [*muttering*]. Oh, I've got my reasons.

GINA. D'you think young Werle is really mad?

RELLING. No, worse luck! He's no madder than most. But one kind of ailment he is suffering from, all the same.

GINA. What's wrong with him, then?

RELLING. I'll tell you, Mrs. Ekdal. He's an acute case of inflamed scruples.

GINA. Inflamed scruples?

HEDVIG. Is that a sort of illness?

RELLING. Yes. It's a national illness. But it only occurs sporadically. [*Nods to* GINA.] Thanks for lunch!

[*He goes out by the hall door.*]

GINA [*walking restlessly about the room*]. Ugh, that Gregers Werle. He's always been a queer fish.

HEDVIG [*stands by the table and looks inquiringly at her.*] I think this is all very strange.

ACT FOUR

HJALMAR EKDAL'S *studio. A photograph has obviously just been taken; a camera covered with a cloth, a stand, a few chairs, a whatnot and similar things are standing about the floor. Late afternoon light, with the sun about to set; after a little while it begins to get dark.*

GINA is standing at the open door, in her hand a little container and a wet photographic plate; she is speaking to somebody outside.

GINA. Yes, absolutely certain. I always keep my promises. The first dozen will be ready for Monday. Good afternoon, good afternoon!

[*Somebody can be heard going downstairs.* GINA *shuts the door, puts the plate into the container and puts that in the shrouded camera.*]

HEDVIG [*enters from the kitchen*]. Have they gone now?

GINA [*tidying up*]. Yes, thank heavens. I've got rid of them at last.

HEDVIG. I wonder why Daddy hasn't come back yet?

GINA. Are you sure he's not down at Relling's?

HEDVIG. No, he's not there. I slipped down the back stairs just now and asked.

GINA. And his dinner's standing here getting cold.

HEDVIG. Yes, fancy! And Daddy's generally home for his dinner on the dot.

GINA. Oh, don't fret, he'll be here soon.

HEDVIG. Oh, I do wish he'd come; because everything seems so strange now.

GINA [*calls out*]. There he is!

[HJALMAR EKDAL *comes in through the hall door.*]

HEDVIG [*going to meet him*]. Daddy! We've been waiting and waiting for you.

GINA [*glancing across*]. There's a long time you've been, Hjalmar.

HJALMAR [*without looking at her*]. Yes, I have, rather.

[*He takes off his topcoat;* GINA *and* HEDVIG *go to help him; he waves them away.*]

GINA. Have you had something to eat with Gregers Werle?

HJALMAR [*hangs up his coat*]. No.

GINA [*going towards the kitchen door*]. Then I'll bring your dinner in for you.

HJALMAR. No, don't bother about any dinner. I don't want anything to eat now.

HEDVIG [*going closer*]. Aren't you feeling well, Daddy?

HJALMAR. Feeling well? Oh yes, not so bad. We went for a rather tiring walk, Gregers and I.

GINA. You shouldn't have, Hjalmar; you're not used to it.

HJALMAR. Huh! There are many things a man's got to get used to in this world. [*Walks up and down.*] Has anybody been here while I've been out?

GINA. Only that engaged couple.

HJALMAR. No new orders?

GINA. No, not today.

HEDVIG. There'll be some more tomorrow all right, Daddy, you'll see.

HJALMAR. I hope you're right. Because tomorrow I'm going to get down to things in real earnest.

HEDVIG. Tomorrow! You haven't forgotten what day it is tomorrow?

HJALMAR. Oh, that's right. . . . Well, the day after, then. After this I'm doing everything myself; I want to do the work all on my own.

GINA. But, Hjalmar, what's the good of *that*? You'll only make your life a misery. I can still manage the photographing; and then you can get on with the invention.

HEDVIG. And then there's the wild duck, Daddy . . . and all the hens and rabbits. . . .

HJALMAR. Don't speak to me about all that nonsense! I'm never going to set foot in that loft again after today.

HEDVIG. But Daddy, you promised me there'd be a party tomorrow. . . .

HJALMAR. Hm, that's right. . . . Well, starting the day after tomorrow, then. That damned wild duck, I'd like to wring its neck.

HEDVIG [*with a scream*]. The wild duck!

GINA. Well, I never did!

HEDVIG [*shaking him*]. But Daddy . . . it's *my* wild duck!

HJALMAR. That's the only thing that's stopping me. I haven't the heart. . . . For your sake, Hedvig, I haven't the heart. But deep down inside me I ought to. I can't see why I should have any creature under my roof that's been in *that* man's hands.

GINA. But, good Lord, just because it was that rogue Pettersen Grandfather got it off, that's no . . .

HJALMAR [*walking about*]. There are certain demands . . . what should I call them? Let us say, demands of the ideal . . . certain claims that a man can't disregard without doing violence to his own soul.

HEDVIG [*following him about*]. But think of the wild duck . . . the poor little wild duck!

HJALMAR [*halts*]. I've told you I'm not going to touch it . . . for your sake. Not a hair of its . . . well, as I said, I'm not going to touch it. There are things of much greater importance to be undertaken. But it's time you had your evening walk, Hedvig; it's nicely dusk for you now.

HEDVIG. No, I can't be bothered to go out now.

HJALMAR. Yes, go on. You seem to be blinking a lot. It's not good for you, all these fumes in here. The air's thick here, under this roof.

HEDVIG. All right, I'll run down the back stairs and go for a little walk. Where's my hat and coat? Oh, they're in my room. But mind, Daddy . . . you mustn't do anything to the wild duck while I'm out.

HJALMAR. Not a feather of its head shall be touched. [*Hugging her.*] You and I, Hedvig . . . we two! Now, run along, my dear.

[HEDVIG *waves to her parents and goes out through the kitchen.*]

HJALMAR [*walks up and down without looking up*]. Gina.

GINA. Yes?

HJALMAR. As from tomorrow—or the day after, let us say—I think I would like to keep the household accounts myself.

GINA. You want to keep the accounts as well?

HJALMAR. Yes, or keep a check on what comes in, at any rate.

GINA. Oh, *that's* not a big job, so help me.

HJALMAR. Ah, I'm not so sure of *that*; you seem to make the money stretch a remarkably long way. [*Halts and looks at her.*] How does that happen?

GINA. It's because Hedvig and me don't need very much.

HJALMAR. Is it true Father gets paid pretty lavishly for the copying he does for Mr. Werle?

GINA. I don't know that it's *so* lavish. I don't know what the rates are for things like that.

HJALMAR. Well, roughly what does he get? Tell me!

GINA. It varies; roughly the cost of his board, and a bit extra for pocket money.

HJALMAR. The cost of his board! You never told me that before!

GINA. Well, really I couldn't. You liked to think he got everything from you.

HJALMAR. And instead he gets it all from Werle!

GINA. Oh well, he's not likely to miss it.

HJALMAR. Light the lamp!

GINA [*lights it*]. Besides, we don't really know if it actually comes from him. It might easily be Graaberg. . . .

HJALMAR. Why are you trying to shift things on to Graaberg?

GINA. Well, I don't know. I just thought . . .

HJALMAR. Huh!

GINA. It wasn't me that got Grandfather his copying to do. It was Berta, that time she was here.

HJALMAR. Your voice seems to be trembling.

GINA [*putting on the shade*]. Is it?

HJALMAR. And your hands are shaking. Aren't they?

GINA [*firmly*]. Tell me straight, Hjalmar. What's he gone and told you about me?

HJALMAR. Is it true . . . *can* it really be true . . . that there was something between you and Old Werle when you were in service there?

GINA. It's not true. Not then, there wasn't. Mr. Werle pestered me plenty, that I will say. And his wife thought there was something in it. What a fuss she kicked up! She just went for me, played merry hell, she did. So I left.

HJALMAR. But then afterwards?

GINA. Well, then I went home. And my mother . . . she wasn't quite what you thought she was, Hjalmar. She kept on at me, about one thing and another. . . . Because Werle was a widower by then.

HJALMAR. Well, what then?

GINA. Well, you might as well know it. He wouldn't be satisfied till he'd had his way.

HJALMAR [*clasping his hands together*]. Is this the mother of my child! How could you keep a thing like that hidden from me!

GINA. Yes, it was wrong of me. I should have told you long ago.

HJALMAR. You should have told me at the time—then I'd have known what sort of woman you were.

GINA. But would you have married me just the same?

HJALMAR. However can you think that?

GINA. There you are! That's why I didn't dare say anything at the time. Because I'd come to like you so very much, you know. I couldn't go and make my whole life a misery. . . .

HJALMAR [*walking about*]. Is this my Hedvig's mother! To think that everything I see around me here . . . [*Kicks a chair.*] My entire home, all of it I owe to your previous lover. Ah, that lecherous old Werle!

GINA. Do you regret the fourteen or fifteen years we have lived together?

HJALMAR [*standing in front of her*]. Tell me this. Haven't you—every day, every hour—regretted this web of deceit you've spun around me like a spider? Answer me that! Haven't you in fact been suffering agonies of worry and remorse?

GINA. Oh, my dear Hjalmar, really I've had far too many other things to think of, what with running the house and everything. . . .

HJALMAR. And this past of yours, do you never give it a thought now?

GINA. No. God knows, I'd pretty nearly forgotten all that old business.

HJALMAR. Oh, how can you stand there so calm and unconcerned! That's what I find so absolutely outrageous. Imagine—not the slightest sign of regret.

GINA. But tell me now, Hjalmar—where would you have been now if you hadn't had somebody like me for a wife?

HJALMAR. Like you!

GINA. Yes, because I've always been as you might say a bit more down-to-earth and business-like than you. Well, that's understandable— I'm a year or two older, after all.

HJALMAR. Where would I have been?

GINA. You were in a pretty bad way all round when you first met me. You can hardly deny that.

HJALMAR. You call that being in a bad way? Oh, you don't understand what it means when a man is weighed down with worry and despair—especially a man with my fiery temperament.

GINA. Well, well, have it as you will. I don't want to make too much of a song and dance about it, either, because you turned out to be a right good husband once you'd got your own house and home.— And we'd made things so nice and cosy, and Hedvig and me were just starting to manage a little bit extra for ourselves in the way of food and clothes.

HJALMAR. Yes, in this swamp of deceit.

GINA. Ugh! That horrible man! What did he have to go and shove his nose in here for!

HJALMAR. I too used to think our home was a good place. What a mistake that was. Now where am I going to find the stimulus I need to make my invention a reality? Perhaps it will die with me; and your past, Gina, will be what's killed it.

GINA [*close to tears*]. Oh Hjalmar, you mustn't say things like that. When all my days I've spent only doing what I thought was best for you.

HJALMAR. I ask you—what about the breadwinner's dream now? When I used to lie in there on the sofa turning the invention over in my mind, I vaguely knew it would drain the very last bit of my strength. I had the feeling that the day I held the patent in my hands, would mark my own . . . last hour. And it was my dream that you should be left comfortably settled, to take your place as the widow of the one-time inventor.

GINA [*drying her tears*]. No, Hjalmar you *mustn't* talk like that. God forbid I should ever live to see the day I'm left a widow!

HJALMAR. Oh, it's all the same either way. Everything's over and done with now. Everything!

[GREGERS WERLE *cautiously opens the hall door and looks in.*]

GREGERS. May I come in?

HJALMAR. Yes, come in.

GREGERS [*advances, his face beaming with joy and holds out his hands to them*]. Well now, my dear people. . . ! [*Looks from one to the other and whispers to* HJALMAR.] Haven't you done it yet, then?

HJALMAR [*aloud*]. I *have* done it.

GREGERS. You *have*?

HJALMAR. I have experienced the bitterest moment of my life.

GREGERS. But also the most sublime, I should think.

HJALMAR. Well, we've got it off our chests, anyway.

GINA. May God forgive you, Mr. Werle.

GREGERS [*greatly astonished*]. But I don't understand.

HJALMAR. What don't you understand?

GREGERS. Now that you have laid bare your souls—this exchange on which you can now build a completely new mode of life—a way of living together in truth, free of all deception. . . .

HJALMAR. Yes, I know; I know all that.

GREGERS. I was absolutely convinced when I came in through that door that I should be greeted by the light of radiant understanding on the faces of husband and wife alike. And all I see is this dull, gloomy, miserable . . .

GINA. Very well then. [*She takes the shade off the lamp.*]

GREGERS. You're not trying to understand me, Mrs. Ekdal. Well, well; in your case perhaps with time . . . But *you* now, Hjalmar? Surely this passage of arms has brought you to some higher resolve.

HJALMAR. Yes, of course it has. That is . . . in a sort of way.

GREGERS. For there is surely no joy in life comparable with that of forgiving one who has sinned, and of raising her up again in love.

HJALMAR. Do you think a man so easily gets over the bitter draught I have just drunk?

GREGERS. No! No *ordinary* man, I dare say. But a man like you. . . !

HJALMAR. Yes, I know, I know. But you mustn't rush me, Gregers. It takes time you know.

GREGERS. There's a *lot* of the wild duck about you, Hjalmar.

[RELLING *has come in by the entrance door.*]

RELLING. What's this now! Is the wild duck on the go again?

HJALMAR. The poor maimed victim of Mr. Werle's sport, yes.

RELLING. Mr. Werle? Is it *him* you're talking about?

HJALMAR. Him and . . . the rest of us.

RELLING [*to* GREGERS *under his breath*]. God damn you!

HJALMAR. What do you say?

RELLING. I was merely expressing the pious wish that this quack here would pack himself off where he belongs. If he stops here, he's just as likely to be the ruination of the pair of you.

GREGERS. Neither of them is being ruined, Mr. Relling. I needn't say anything about Hjalmar; him we know. But she too, deep down within her, surely has something trustworthy, something sincere. . . .

GINA [*near to tears*]. Then you should have just let me be as I was.

RELLING [*to* GREGERS]. Would it be impertinent if I asked what exactly it is you want in this house?

GREGERS. I want to lay the foundation of a true marriage.

RELLING. Don't you think the Ekdals' marriage is good enough as it is?

GREGERS. It's probably as good a marriage as most, I regret to say. But it has never been a *true* marriage.

HJALMAR. You've never given much attention to the claims of the ideal, Relling.

RELLING. Don't talk rubbish, my lad! Mr. Werle, just let me ask you how many—at a rough guess—how many true marriages you have seen in your life?

GREGERS. I hardly think I've seen a single one.

RELLING. Nor have I.

GREGERS. But I've seen innumerable marriages of the opposite kind. And I've had the chance of seeing at close quarters the havoc a marriage like that can wreak on both parties.

HJALMAR. The whole moral basis of a man's life can crumble beneath his feet—*that* is the terrible thing.

RELLING. Well, I've never actually been married myself, so I can't really judge these things. But one thing I do know: that the *child* is also part of the marriage. And you should leave the child in peace.

HJALMAR. Ah, Hedvig! My poor Hedvig!

RELLING. Yes, you'd better just see that you keep Hedvig out of all this. You are both grown people; God knows you can please

yourself how much you want to muck up your own personal
affairs. But I'm telling you this: just you be careful the way you
treat Hedvig, or else you'll perhaps end up by doing her serious
harm.

HJALMAR. Harm?

RELLING. Yes, or else she'll do herself some harm—and maybe others
with her.

GINA. But how can you tell a thing like that, Mr. Relling?

HJALMAR. There's no immediate danger for her eyes, is there?

RELLING. None of this has got anything to do with her eyes. But
Hedvig is at a difficult age. She might get hold of all sorts of funny
ideas.

GINA. Why, that's just what she does do! I don't like the way she's
started playing with the fire out in the kitchen. She calls it playing
houses on fire. Many a time I'm frightened she *will* set the house on
fire.

RELLING. There you are, you see. I knew it.

GREGERS [*to* RELLING]. But how do you explain a thing like that?

RELLING [*disdainfully*]. She's reached the age of puberty, my dear sir.

HJALMAR. As long as the child has *me* . . . ! As long as I can keep body
and soul together . . . !

[*There is a knock at the door.*]

GINA. Hush, Hjalmar! There's somebody in the hall. [*Calls.*] Come in.

[MRS. SÖRBY, *in outdoor clothes, comes in.*]

MRS. SÖRBY. Good evening!

GINA [*walks over to her*]. Why, Berta, it's you!

MRS. SÖRBY. Yes, it's me. But perhaps I've come at an awkward time?

HJALMAR. Not at all. A messenger from *that* house. . . !

MRS. SÖRBY [*to* GINA]. To be quite honest, I hoped I'd find the men-
folk out at this time of day; I just thought I'd pop in for a little
chat and say goodbye.

GINA. Oh? Are you leaving?

MRS. SÖRBY. Yes, first thing tomorrow morning . . . up to Höidal. Mr. Werle left this afternoon. [*Casually to* GREGERS.] He sends his regards.

GINA. Well fancy!

HJALMAR. Mr. Werle's gone, d'you say? And you are going to follow him?

MRS. SÖRBY. Yes. What have you got to say to *that*, Mr. Ekdal?

HJALMAR. Watch out, that's all I've got to say.

GREGERS. Let me explain. My father and Mrs. Sörby are going to be married.

HJALMAR. Going to be married!

GINA. Oh, Berta! At last!

RELLING [*with a tremor in his voice*]. Surely this is never true?

MRS. SÖRBY. Yes, my dear Mr. Relling, it's perfectly true.

RELLING. You want to marry again?

MRS. SÖRBY. Yes, that's what it amounts to. Mr. Werle got a special licence, and we'll just have a quiet wedding up at Höidal.

GREGERS. Then I must wish you every happiness, like a good stepson.

MRS. SÖRBY. Thank you, if you really mean it. I can only hope it's going to bring happiness both for me and Mr. Werle.

RELLING. You are safe in hoping that. Mr. Werle never gets drunk— as far as *I* know, at any rate. And I don't suppose he's in the habit of knocking his wives about either, like our late lamented horse doctor.

MRS. SÖRBY. Oh, let Sörby rest in peace, now. He had his good points too, like everybody else.

RELLING. Mr. Werle has some even better points, I dare say.

MRS. SÖRBY. At any rate he hasn't gone and squandered what was best in him. Any man who does *that* must take the consequences.

RELLING. Tonight I am going to go out with Molvik.

MRS. SÖRBY. You shouldn't, Mr. Relling; please don't—for my sake.

RELLING. There's nothing else for it. [*To* HJALMAR.] You can come too, if you want.

GINA. No thank you. Hjalmar's not going out with you to *them* kind of places.

HJALMAR [*angrily in an undertone*]. Oh, shut up!

RELLING. Goodbye, Mrs.—— Werle.

[*He goes out through the hall door.*]

GREGERS [*to* MRS. SÖRBY]. It seems as though you and Dr. Relling know each other pretty well.

MRS. SÖRBY. Yes, we've known each other for years. Once upon a time it looked as if we might have made something of it, the two of us.

GREGERS. Just as well for you that you didn't.

MRS. SÖRBY. Yes, you might well say that. But I've always taken care not to act on impulse. A woman can't just throw herself away, either.

GREGERS. And you're not the least bit afraid I might drop my father a hint about this old affair?

MRS. SÖRBY. You may take it I've already told him myself.

GREGERS. Indeed?

MRS. SÖRBY. Your father knows every conceivable thing that anybody could truthfully think of saying about me. I've told him everything. It was the very first thing I did, when he began to make his intentions plain.

GREGERS. Then I think you must be more than usually frank.

MRS. SÖRBY. Frank is something I've always been. It's the best policy for us women.

HJALMAR. What do you say to that, Gina?

GINA. Oh, we women are so different—some one way, and some another.

MRS. SÖRBY. Well, Gina, I think it's wisest to do things the way I've done them now. And for his part, Mr. Werle hasn't tried to hide anything either. And that's mainly what's brought us together. Now he can sit and talk to me quite openly, just like a child. The whole of his youth and the best years of his manhood, all he heard was a lot of sermonizing about his sins—a healthy and vigorous man like him. And many's the time, from what I've heard, those sermons were about entirely imaginary offences.

GINA. Yes, it's true enough what you say.

GREGERS. If you ladies are going to start on *that* topic, it would no doubt be best if I went.

MRS. SÖRBY. There's no need to go on that account. I won't say another word. But I wanted to make it quite clear to you that nothing's been hushed up and everything's been above board. It might seem as though this is a great piece of luck for me; and so it is, in one way. But at the same time I don't think I'm taking more than I'm giving. I'll never let him down. And I can look after him and take care of him, as nobody else can, now that he'll soon be helpless.

HJALMAR. Be helpless?

GREGERS [*to* MRS. SÖRBY]. Yes, yes. Don't talk about it here.

MRS. SÖRBY. There's no point in hiding it any longer, however much he would like to. He's going blind.

HJALMAR [*with a start*]. Going blind? That's very strange. He's going blind too?

GINA. Lots of people in the same position.

MRS. SÖRBY. And you can imagine what that means for a businessman. Well, I shall try to use my eyes for him as best I can. But now I mustn't stay any longer; I've got so many things to see to at the moment.—Oh yes, something I had to tell you, Mr. Ekdal: if there was anything Mr. Werle could do for you, would you please just approach Graaberg about it.

GREGERS. An offer Hjalmar Ekdal will certainly decline.

MRS. SÖRBY. Indeed? I don't seem to remember him in the past . . .

GINA. No, Berta! Hjalmar doesn't have to take anything from Mr. Werle now.

HJALMAR [*slowly and weightily*]. Give my regards to your future husband and tell him from me that in the near future I intend to call on Graaberg . . .

GREGERS. What! You mean that!

HJALMAR. . . . As I was saying, to call on Graaberg and ask for a statement of the amount I owe his employer. I will pay this debt of honour—ha! ha! debt of honour, that's good! But enough of that. I will repay everything, with five per cent interest.

GINA. But, Hjalmar dear, heaven knows we haven't any money to do that.

HJALMAR. Tell your *fiancé* I am working away steadily at my invention. Tell him the thing that sustains me in this exhausting task is the desire to be rid of a painful burden of debt. That is why I am working on the invention. All the proceeds from it will go towards discharging those obligations imposed on me by your future husband's pecuniary outlay.

MRS. SÖRBY. Something's happened in this house.

HJALMAR. Yes, it has.

MRS. SÖRBY. Very well, goodbye, then! I still had a few things I'd have liked to talk to you about, Gina, but they'd better wait now till another time. Goodbye!

[HJALMAR *and* GREGERS *bow silently*. GINA *accompanies* MRS. SÖRBY *to the door*.]

HJALMAR. Not across the threshold, Gina!

[MRS. SÖRBY *goes;* GINA *shuts the door after her*.]

HJALMAR. There now, Gregers. Now I've got that load of debt off my shoulders.

GREGERS. Soon you will, anyway.

HJALMAR. I think it must be said that my behaviour was most correct.

GREGERS. You are the man I always took you for.

HJALMAR. In certain cases it is impossible to disregard the claim of the ideal. As head of a family there's nothing I can do but grin and bear it. Believe me it's no joke for a man without private means to have to pay off a debt from many years ago, on which, as it were, the dust of oblivion had already settled. But that makes no difference— I have certain human rights, too, that crave satisfaction.

GREGERS [*placing a hand on his shoulder*]. My dear Hjalmar, wasn't it a good thing I came?

HJALMAR. Yes.

GREGERS. So you saw quite clearly how things were—wasn't that a good thing?

HJALMAR [*a little impatiently*]. Yes, of course it was a good thing. But there is one thing that offends my sense of justice.

GREGERS. And what is that?

HJALMAR. The fact that . . . Well, I don't really know if I ought to speak so freely about your father.

GREGERS. Don't mind me at all.

HJALMAR. Well then. . . . You see, what I think is so distressing is the fact that it's now not me who is founding a true marriage, but him.

GREGERS. How can you say that!

HJALMAR. But it's true. Your father and Mrs. Sörby are entering upon a marriage based on full confidence, based on complete and unqualified frankness on both sides; they are not keeping anything back; there's no deception underneath it all. If I might so put it, it's an agreement for the mutual forgiveness of sin.

GREGERS. What of it?

HJALMAR. Well, *there* it all is. But from what you said, you had to go through all this difficult business before you could found a true marriage.

GREGERS. But that's something quite different, Hjalmar. Surely you're not going to compare either yourself or her with those two. . . ? You see what I mean, don't you?

HJALMAR. But I can't get over the fact that there's something in all this that offends my sense of justice. It looks for all the world as though there were no justice at all in things.

GINA. Good gracious, Hjalmar! You mustn't say things like that.

GREGERS. Hm, let's not get ourselves involved in questions like that.

HJALMAR. Yet, on the other hand, I might almost claim to see the guiding finger of fate. He is going blind.

GINA. Oh, perhaps it's not so certain.

HJALMAR. There's no doubt about it. At least we *ought* not to doubt it, for that is precisely what makes it a just retribution. He at one time has blinded a trusting fellow creature. . . .

GREGERS. He has, I regret to say, blinded many.

HJALMAR. And now comes this mysterious implacable power and demands the man's own eyes.

GINA. Ugh, how can you say such awful things! You make me feel scared.

HJALMAR. It profits a man occasionally to immerse himself in the darker things of life.

[HEDVIG, *in her hat and coat, comes in through the hall door, happy and breathless.*]

GINA. You back again already?

HEDVIG. Yes, I didn't want to go any further. And it was just as well, because I met somebody at the door.

HJALMAR. That must have been Mrs. Sörby.

HEDVIG. Yes.

HJALMAR [*walking up and down*]. I'd like to think you'd seen her for the last time.

[*Silence.* HEDVIG *looks shyly from one to the other as though trying to estimate their mood.*]

HEDVIG [*going over to* HJALMAR, *coaxingly*]. Daddy!

HJALMAR. Well—what is it, Hedvig?

HEDVIG. Mrs. Sörby had something for me.

HJALMAR [*halts*]. For you?

HEDVIG. Yes. It's something for tomorrow.

GINA. Berta has always had some little thing for your birthday.

HJALMAR. What is it?

HEDVIG. Oh, you mustn't know what it is yet. Mother has to bring it to me in bed first thing in the morning.

HJALMAR. Oh, all this secrecy, and me being kept in the dark!

HEDVIG [*hastily*]. But you can see it if you like. A big letter.

[*She takes a letter out of her coat pocket.*]

HJALMAR. A letter, too?

HEDVIG. There's only the letter. I suppose the rest is to come later. But just imagine, a letter! I've never had a letter before. And it says 'Miss' on the front. [*Reads.*] 'Miss Hedvig Ekdal.' Fancy, that's me.

HJALMAR. Let me see the letter.

HEDVIG [*hands it to him*]. There, you see.

HJALMAR. That's old Mr. Werle's writing.

GINA. Are you sure, Hjalmar?

HJALMAR. Look yourself.

GINA. Oh, you don't think I would know, do you?

HJALMAR. Hedvig, may I open the letter . . . and read it?

HEDVIG. Yes, of course you may, if you want to.

GINA. Please, not tonight, Hjalmar. You know it's meant for tomorrow.

HEDVIG [*softly*]. Oh, please let him read it! It's sure to be something nice. And then Daddy will be pleased and we'll all be happy again.

HJALMAR. I may open it, then?

HEDVIG. Yes, Daddy, please do. It will be fun to find out what it is.

HJALMAR. Very well. [*He opens the letter, reads it, and seems a little taken aback.*] What's this. . . ?

GINA. What does it say?

HEDVIG. Yes, Daddy, do tell us.

HJALMAR. Be quiet. [*Reads it through again; he has turned pale, but controls himself.*] It is a deed of gift, Hedvig.

HEDVIG. Well, fancy that! What am I getting?

HJALMAR. Read it yourself.

[HEDVIG *walks over to the lamp and reads for a moment or two.*]

HJALMAR [*in an undertone, clenching his hands*]. The eyes, the eyes . . . and now this letter.

HEDVIG [*interrupts her reading*]. Yes, but it looks to me as though it's Grandfather who is getting it.

HJALMAR [*takes the letter from her*]. Gina—can you understand this?

GINA. I don't know the first thing about it. Tell me what it is.

HJALMAR. Mr. Werle writes to Hedvig to say that her old grandfather needn't bother about doing any more copying, and that in future he can draw one hundred crowns a month straight from the office. . . .

GREGERS. Aha!

HEDVIG. A hundred crowns, Mother. I read that bit.

GINA. That will be nice for Grandfather.

HJALMAR. . . . a hundred crowns, for as long as he needs it. That means, of course, until he's passed away.

GINA. Well, that's him provided for, poor old soul.

HJALMAR. That's not all. You didn't read far enough, Hedvig. After that, it's to come to you.

HEDVIG. To me? All that?

HJALMAR. You are assured a like amount for the rest of your life, he writes. Do you hear that, Gina?

GINA. Yes, I heard.

HEDVIG. Fancy—all that money I'm going to get! [*Shakes him.*] Daddy, Daddy, aren't you glad?

HJALMAR [*moving away from her*]. Glad! [*Walks up and down.*] Oh, this puts quite a new perspective on things! It opens my eyes to all sorts of possibilities. It's Hedvig. She's the one he's being so generous to!

GINA. Yes, because she's the one who's having the birthday. . . .

HEDVIG. You shall have it, all the same, Daddy. You know I'll give all the money to you and Mother.

HJALMAR. To your mother, yes. That's just it.

GREGERS. Hjalmar, this is a trap that's being set for you.

HJALMAR. Could it be another trap, do you think?

GREGERS. When he was here this morning, he said: 'Hjalmar Ekdal is not the man you take him to be.'

HJALMAR. Not the man . . . !

GREGERS. 'Just wait, you'll see,' he said.

HJALMAR. See that I'd let myself be bought off for a price. . . !

HEDVIG. Mother, what is all this about?

GINA. Go and take your things off.

[*Near to tears,* HEDVIG *goes out by the kitchen door.*]

GREGERS. Yes, Hjalmar. Now we'll see who's right, him or me.

HJALMAR [*slowly tears the document in two, and places the pieces on the table*]. There's my answer.

GREGERS. As I expected.

HJALMAR [*goes over to* GINA *who is standing by the stove and says in a low voice*]. Now let's have no more pretence. If this affair was over and done with when you . . . 'got fond' of me as you put it . . . why did he go and arrange things so that we could afford to get married?

GINA. I suppose he thought he'd be able to come and go here as he liked.

HJALMAR. Is that all? Wasn't he afraid of a certain possibility.

GINA. I don't know what you mean.

HJALMAR. I want to know if . . . your child has a right to live under my roof.

GINA [*drawing herself up, her eyes flashing*]. *You* ask me that!

HJALMAR. I want a straight answer. Is Hedvig mine . . . or . . . ? Well!

GINA [*looking at him coldly and defiantly*]. I don't know.

HJALMAR [*trembling slightly*]. You don't know!

GINA. How should *I* know? A person like *me*. . . .

HJALMAR [*quietly turning away from her*]. This house is no place for me any more.

GREGERS. Think well what you are doing, Hjalmar!

HJALMAR [*putting on his topcoat*]. There's no need to think here, not for a man like me.

GREGERS. Yes there is. There's a tremendous lot to think about. The three of you must remain together if you, Hjalmar, are to win through to that sublime mood of magnanimity and forgiveness.

HJALMAR. I don't *want* to. Never, never! My hat! [*Takes his hat.*] My home has collapsed in ruins about my ears! [*Bursts into tears.*] Gregers, I have no child!

HEDVIG [*who has opened the kitchen door*]. What are you saying? [*Crosses to him.*] Daddy! Daddy!

GINA. There, there.

HJALMAR. Don't come near me, Hedvig! Go away! I can't bear to look at you. Oh, those eyes. . . ! Goodbye.

[*He makes for the door.*]

HEDVIG [*clings tight to him and screams*]. No! No! Don't leave me.

GINA [*shouts*]. Look at the child, Hjalmar! Look at her!

HJALMAR. I will not! I cannot! Let me go. I must get away from all this.

[*He tears himself free of* HEDVIG *and goes out by the hall door.*]

HEDVIG [*with despair in her eyes*]. He's leaving us, Mother! He's leaving us. He's never coming back any more!

GINA. Don't cry, Hedvig. Your father's coming back all right.

HEDVIG [*throws herself sobbing on the sofa*]. No, no, he's never coming back to us again.

GREGERS. You do believe I meant it all for the best, Mrs. Ekdal?

GINA. Yes, I dare say you did. But may God forgive you, all the same.

HEDVIG [*lying on the sofa*]. Oh, I just feel as though I want to die! What have I done? Mother, you must get him to come home again!

GINA. Yes, yes. Be quiet now, and I'll just go out and see if I can see him. [*Puts on her outdoor things.*] He might have gone into Relling's. But you mustn't lie there crying, now. Promise?

HEDVIG [*sobbing convulsively*]. Yes, I'll stop crying. As long as Daddy comes back.

GREGERS [*to* GINA, *who is about to leave*]. Wouldn't it perhaps be better to let him fight his bitter fight to the end.

GINA. Oh, he can do that afterwards. The first thing is to get the child quietened down.

[*She goes out through the hall door.*]

HEDVIG [*sits up and dries her eyes*]. Now you must tell me what's the matter. Why doesn't Daddy want me any more?

GREGERS. You mustn't ask *that* until you've grown up into a big girl.

HEDVIG [*sobbing*]. But I can't go on feeling as awful and miserable as this all the time till I'm grown-up.—I know what it is.—Perhaps I'm not really Daddy's.

GREGERS [*uneasily*]. How could *that* be?

HEDVIG. Mother could have found me, maybe. And now perhaps Daddy's found out. I've read about things like that.

GREGERS. Well, but even so . . .

HEDVIG. Then I think he might have been just as fond of me. Even more. After all, we got the wild duck sent to us as a present, and I'm awfully fond of that.

GREGERS [*leading her off the subject*]. Yes, the wild duck, that's right. Let's talk a bit about the wild duck, Hedvig.

HEDVIG. Poor little wild duck! He can't bear the sight of it, either. D'you know he wanted to wring its neck.

GREGERS. Oh, I'm sure he wouldn't do that.

HEDVIG. No, but that's what he said. And I thought it was rather horrid of Daddy to say that. Because I say a prayer for the wild duck every night, and I ask for it to be delivered from death and all evil.

GREGERS [*looking at her*]. Do you always say your prayers?

HEDVIG. Yes.

GREGERS. Who taught you that?

HEDVIG. I taught myself. It was once when Daddy was very ill, and had to have leeches on his neck. And he said he was at death's door.

GREGERS. Well?

HEDVIG. So I said a prayer for him, after I'd gone to bed. And I've done it ever since.

GREGERS. And now you pray for the wild duck as well?

HEDVIG. I thought I'd better include the wild duck, too. She was so poorly to begin with.

GREGERS. Do you say your prayers in the morning, too?

HEDVIG. Oh no, I don't.

GREGERS. Why don't you say your prayers in the morning as well?

HEDVIG. Well, it's light in the mornings; there's nothing to be afraid of any more.

GREGERS. And the wild duck you are so terribly fond of—your father wants to wring its neck.

HEDVIG. No, he said if *he* had his way, he'd do it. But he said he'd spare it for my sake. That was sweet of him.

GREGERS [*coming closer*]. Supposing you offered to sacrifice the wild duck for *his* sake?

HEDVIG [*rising*]. The wild duck!

GREGERS. Suppose you were ready to sacrifice for him the most precious thing you had in the world?

HEDVIG. Do you think *that* would help?

GREGERS. Try it, Hedvig.

HEDVIG [*quietly, with shining eyes*]. Yes, I will try it.

GREGERS. Have you the proper strength of mind, do you think?

HEDVIG. I'll ask Grandfather to shoot the wild duck for me.

GREGERS. Yes, do that. But not a word to your mother about this!

HEDVIG. Why not?

GREGERS. She doesn't understand us.

HEDVIG. The wild duck. I'll try it first thing tomorrow morning.

[GINA *enters through the hall door.*]

HEDVIG [*goes to meet her*]. Did you find him, Mother?

GINA. No, but I heard he'd called and gone out with Relling.

GREGERS. Are you sure?

GINA. Yes, the caretaker's wife said so. Molvik was with them too, she said.

GREGERS. At a time like this, when his soul desperately needs solitude to win through. . . !

GINA [*takes her things off*]. Yes, men are funny, they are that. God alone knows where Relling has dragged him off to! I rushed over to Ma Eriksen's, but they weren't there.

HEDVIG[*fighting her tears*]. Oh! What if he never comes back home again!

GREGERS. He will come back. I shall take a message to him in the morning, and you'll see he'll come. Sleep well and rest assured about *that*, Hedvig. Good night. [*Goes out through the hall door.*]

HEDVIG [*throws her arms round* GINA'*s neck, sobbing*]. Mother! Mother!

GINA [*pats her on the back and sighs*]. Ah yes. Relling was right. This is what happens when you get these stupid idiots coming round with their fancy demands.

ACT FIVE

HJALMAR EKDAL's *studio, in the cold grey light of morning; wet snow is lying on the large panes of the skylight.* GINA, *wearing an overall, comes in from the kitchen carrying a brush and a duster and walks over towards the living-room door. At that moment,* HEDVIG *rushes in from the hall.*

GINA [*stops*]. Well?

HEDVIG. Yes, Mother, I think he's very likely in with Relling . . .

GINA. You see, now!

HEDVIG. . . . because the caretaker's wife said she heard two other people come in with Relling last night.

GINA. I fancied as much.

HEDVIG. But that doesn't help very much if he won't come back here.

GINA. At least I can pop down and talk to him.

[OLD EKDAL, *in dressing-gown and slippers and smoking a pipe, appears at the door of his room.*]

EKDAL. Hjalmar! Isn't Hjalmar at home?

GINA. No, he's gone out.

EKDAL. So early? When it's snowing as heavily as this? Oh well, all right, I can go this morning by myself.

[*He pulls the loft door aside;* HEDVIG *helps him; he goes in and she shuts the door behind him.*]

HEDVIG [*in an undertone*]. Oh, Mother, what will poor Grandfather say when he hears Daddy's going to leave us.

GINA. Oh, rubbish! Grandfather mustn't hear anything about it. What a godsend he wasn't around yesterday when all that business was going on.

HEDVIG. Yes, but . . .

[GREGERS *enters through the hall door.*]

GREGERS. Well? Found any trace of him?

GINA. As like as not, he's down there in with Relling, they say.

GREGERS. In with Relling! Has he really been out with those fellows?

GINA. He has that.

GREGERS. But how *could* he? When he desperately needed solitude and a chance to collect himself. . . .

GINA. Ah, you might well say that.

[RELLING *enters from the hall.*]

HEDVIG [*crosses to him*]. Is Daddy in with you?

GINA [*at the same time*]. Is he there?

RELLING. Indeed he is.

HEDVIG. And you never told us!

RELLING. Yes, I'm a bea . . . east. But I had to see to that other bea . . . east first, the demonic one, I mean, of course. And then I fell right off to sleep, so I . . .

GINA. What's Hjalmar got to say today?

RELLING. He doesn't say anything.

GINA. Hasn't he said anything at all?

RELLING. Not a blessed word.

GREGERS. Ah no, I understand that so well.

GINA. What's he doing with himself, then?

RELLING. He's lying on the sofa, snoring.

GINA. Is he? Yes, Hjalmar's pretty good at snoring.

HEDVIG. Is he asleep? Can he really sleep?

RELLING. It certainly looks like it.

GREGERS. Quite understandable! Torn as he was by the conflict in his soul. . . .

GINA. And him not used to late nights.

HEDVIG. Perhaps it's best for him to get some sleep, Mother.

GINA. That's what I'm thinking too. There's no point then in waking him up too soon. Thanks, Mr. Relling. Now I'd better get the house tidied up a bit first . . . then . . . come and help me, Hedvig.

[GINA *and* HEDVIG *go into the living-room.*]

GREGERS [*turns to* RELLING]. Have you any views on the spiritual turmoil going on in Hjalmar Ekdal?

RELLING. I'm damned if I can see any spiritual turmoil going on in him.

GREGERS. What! At a crisis like this, when his whole life has been put on a completely new basis. . . ? How do you suppose a personality like Hjalmar's . . . ?

RELLING. Personality? Him! If he ever showed any signs of anything as abnormal as a personality, it was all thoroughly cleared out of him, root and branch, when he was still a lad—that I can assure you.

GREGERS. That would seem very strange . . . after being brought up with such affectionate care, as he was.

RELLING. By those two crazy, hysterical maiden aunts of his, you mean?

GREGERS. Let me tell you they were women who never shut their eyes to the claim of the ideal.—Ah, I suppose you are just trying to be funny again.

RELLING. No, I'm in no mood for that. Besides, I know all about it. The amount of rhetoric he's brought up about these two 'soul-mothers' of his! But I don't think he has much to thank them for. Ekdal's misfortune is that in his own little circle he's always been considered a shining light. . . .

GREGERS. And don't you think he is? Deep down within, I mean.

RELLING. I've never seen any sign of it. Whether his father thought that—that might well be. The dear Lieutenant has always been a bit of a blockhead, all his life.

GREGERS. He's always been a man with the spirit of a child. *That's* what you don't understand.

RELLING. All right, all right! But when our dear, sweet little Hjalmar began as a student of sorts, he was immediately regarded by his fellow-students too as a man with a brilliant future. He was handsome, too, quite captivating—pink and white—the sort the girls all fall for. And because he was the sentimental sort, and there was something appealing in his voice, and because he learned the knack of reciting other people's poetry and other people's ideas . . .

GREGERS [*indignantly*]. Is this Hjalmar Ekdal you are talking about?

RELLING. It is, with your permission. For that's the inside view of this little demi-god you are grovelling to.

GREGERS. I wouldn't have said I was as completely blind as all that.

RELLING. Oh yes, you are. Pretty well, anyway. You see, *you* are a sick man, too.

GREGERS. You are right there.

RELLING. Well then. In your case there are complications. First there are these troublesome inflamed scruples. But then there's something much worse: you are subject to serious fits of hero-worship. You've always got to go round finding something to admire that's not really any of your business.

GREGERS. I must indeed look for something beyond my own self.

RELLING. But then you go and make such tremendous blunders about these wonderful beings you imagine you see and hear around you. Now you are at it again, coming to another labourer's cottage with that claim of the ideal. There just aren't any solvent people living here.

GREGERS. If you haven't any higher opinion of Hjalmar Ekdal than that, I wonder you find any pleasure at all in being everlastingly in his company.

RELLING. Good God, I'm supposed to be a doctor of sorts, aren't I, though I'm ashamed to say it? I have to do something in the way of looking after the sick who are living in the same house as me, poor things.

GREGERS. Really! Is Hjalmar Ekdal sick too?

RELLING. Pretty nearly everybody's sick, unfortunately.

GREGERS. And what treatment are you giving Hjalmar?

RELLING. The usual. I try to keep his life-lie going.

GREGERS. Life . . . lie? I don't think I quite caught . . . ?

RELLING. That's right. That's what I said: the life-lie. You see, the life-lie is the stimulating principle.

GREGERS. May I ask what sort of a life-lie Hjalmar has been inoculated with?

RELLING. I'm afraid not; I don't give secrets like that away to quacks. You would just be in a position to mess him up even worse for me. But it's a tried and tested method; I have used it on Molvik as well. I have made him a 'demonic'. That's the particular cure I had to apply to him.

GREGERS. Isn't he demonic?

RELLING. What the devil do you think being demonic means? It's just a bit of silly nonsense I thought up to keep him alive. If I hadn't done that, the poor devil would have succumbed to mortification and despair years ago. Same with the old Lieutenant there. But he's managed to find his own course of treatment.

GREGERS. Lieutenant Ekdal? What about him?

RELLING. Well, what do you think? Him, the great bear-hunter, shooting rabbits there in the loft? There isn't a happier sportsman in the world than that old man when he gets a chance of raking round in there among all the rubbish. He's collected up four or five withered old Christmas trees, and there's no difference for him between them and the whole tremendous living forest of Höidal. The cocks and the hens are the game birds in the tree tops; and the rabbits hopping about the floor, they are the bears that this intrepid he-man goes in pursuit of.

GREGERS. Poor old, unhappy Lieutenant Ekdal. He certainly has had to relinquish a lot of his youthful ideals.

RELLING. While I remember, Mr. Werle junior—don't use this fancy word 'ideals'; we've got a plain word that's good enough: 'lies'.

GREGERS. Are you trying to say the two things are related?

RELLING. Yes, not unlike typhus and putrid fever.

GREGERS. Dr. Relling, I shall not rest until I have rescued Hjalmar Ekdal from your clutches!

RELLING. So much the worse for *him*. Take the life-lie away from the average man and straight away you take away his happiness. [*To* HEDVIG, *who comes in from the living-room.*] Well, now my little wild duck mother, I'll pop down now and see whether that father of yours is still lying there thinking about his wonderful invention.

[*He goes out through the hall door.*]

GREGERS [*approaches* HEDVIG]. I can see from your face nothing's been done.

HEDVIG. What? Oh, the wild duck. No.

GREGERS. Your courage failed you, I imagine, when it came to the point.

HEDVIG. No it isn't that. But when I woke up early this morning and remembered what we'd talked about, it seemed so strange.

GREGERS. Strange?

HEDVIG. Yes, I don't know. . . . Last night when I first heard it, it seemed such a lovely idea; but when I thought about it again after I had slept on it, it didn't seem much of an idea.

GREGERS. Ah no. You could hardly be expected to grow up here without being the worse for it in some way.

HEDVIG. Oh, what do I care about that. If only Daddy would come. . . .

GREGERS. Ah, if only you'd had your eyes opened to what really makes life worth while! If you had the genuine, joyous, courageous spirit of self-sacrifice, then you would see how quickly he would come back to you. But I still have faith in you, Hedvig.

[*He goes out through the hall door.* HEDVIG *wanders about the room; she is about to go into the kitchen when there is a knocking from within the loft.* HEDVIG *goes over and opens the door slightly.* OLD EKDAL *comes out; he pushes the door to again.*]

EKDAL. Huh! It's not much fun having to go for your morning walk by yourself.

HEDVIG. Didn't you fancy going shooting, Grandfather?

EKDAL. It's not the weather for it today. So dark you can hardly see anything.

HEDVIG. Don't you ever feel like shooting anything else but rabbits?

EKDAL. Aren't the rabbits good enough, then, eh?

HEDVIG. I mean, what about the wild duck?

EKDAL. Ha! ha! Are you frightened I'll go and shoot your wild duck. Not for the world, my dear! I'd never do that!

HEDVIG. No, I dare say you couldn't. It's supposed to be very difficult to shoot wild duck.

EKDAL. Couldn't I? I should jolly well think I could.

HEDVIG. How would you set about it, Grandfather? I don't mean with *my* wild duck, but with others.

EKDAL. I'd try to make sure I shot them in the breast, you know. That's the best place. And then you have to shoot them *against* the lie of the feathers, you see—never with the feathers.

HEDVIG. Do they die then, Grandfather?

EKDAL. I'll say they do . . . if you shoot them properly. Well, I'd better go and tidy myself up. Hm . . . you see . . . hm!

[*He goes into his room.* HEDVIG *waits a moment, glances towards the living-room door, walks across to the bookcase and, standing on tiptoe, she takes the double-barrelled pistol down off the shelf and looks at it.* GINA *with her brush and duster, enters from the living-room.* HEDVIG *quickly replaces the pistol without being noticed.*]

GINA. Don't go upsetting your father's things, Hedvig.

HEDVIG [*moving away from the bookcase*]. I was just tidying up a bit.

GINA. Go into the kitchen instead and see if the coffee is still hot. I'll take a tray of something down with me when I go and see him.

[HEDVIG *goes out.* GINA *begins dusting up the studio. A moment later the passage door is hesitantly opened and* HJALMAR EKDAL *looks in. He has his topcoat on, but no hat; he is unwashed, his hair is ruffled and untidy; he looks heavy and dull about the eyes.*]

GINA [*stops what she is doing, her broom in her hand and looks at him*]. Oh, Hjalmar . . . so you've come back?

HJALMAR [*enters and answers in a dull voice*]. I've come . . . but I'm leaving again at once.

GINA. Yes, yes, I suppose that's all right. But good Lord, there's a sight you look!

HJALMAR. A sight?

GINA. Just look at your good winter coat! Not much use for any thing now.

HEDVIG [*at the kitchen door*]. Mother, shall I . . . ? [*Sees* HJALMAR, *screams with joy and runs across to him.*] Oh, Daddy! Daddy!

HJALMAR [*turns aside and waves her away*]. Go away, go away! [*To* GINA.] Take her away from me, I tell you!

GINA [*in a low voice*]. Go into the living-room, Hedvig.

[HEDVIG *goes in silently.*]

HJALMAR [*busying himself pulling out the table drawer*]. I must have my books with me. Where are my books?

GINA. What books?

HJALMAR. My scientific works, of course—the technical periodicals I use for my invention.

GINA [*looks in the bookcase*]. Are these them, without any backs on.

HJALMAR. Of course they are.

GINA [*putting a pile of unbound books on the table*]. Shouldn't I get Hedvig to cut the pages for you?

HJALMAR. I don't need any cutting doing.

[*Short silence.*]

GINA. So you haven't changed your mind about moving out and leaving us, Hjalmar.

HJALMAR [*rummaging among the books*]. I should have thought that was pretty evident.

GINA. Ah, well.

HJALMAR [*angrily*]. I can't stay on here having a knife twisted in my heart every hour of the day.

GINA. God forgive you for thinking I could be that bad.

HJALMAR. Prove to me that . . . !

GINA. Strikes me *you're* the one that should think about proving.

HJALMAR. With a past like yours? There are certain claims . . . I might almost be tempted to call them claims of the ideal. . . .

GINA. What about Grandfather? What's to be done with *him*, poor old fellow?

HJALMAR. I know my duty. The helpless old man will come along with me. I shall go to town and make the necessary arrangements. . . . Hm! [*Hesitates.*] Has anybody seen my hat on the stairs?

GINA. No, have you lost your hat?

HJALMAR. There's no doubt I had it on when I got back last night. But I couldn't find it again today.

GINA. Lord! Wherever did you land up with them two old soaks?

HJALMAR. Oh, don't ask questions about things that don't matter. Do you think I'm in a mood to remember details?

GINA. As long as you haven't caught cold, Hjalmar.

[*She goes out into the kitchen.*]

HJALMAR [*talking angrily to himself in an undertone as he empties the table drawer*]. You are a blackguard, Relling. Nothing but a scoundrel, a shameless rake. If only I could get somebody to do you in!

[*He puts some old letters to one side, finds the torn document of the day before, picks it up and looks at the pieces. As* GINA *comes in he quickly puts them down again.*]

GINA [*puts a breakfast tray on the table.*] Just a drop of something to warm you up, if you can fancy it. And some bread and butter and some cold meat.

HJALMAR [*glances at the tray*]. Meat? Never again under this roof! I don't care if I haven't had a bite for nearly twenty-four hours.— My notes! The start of my autobiography! Where's my diary and all my important papers? [*He opens the living-room door, but draws back.*] There she is again.

GINA. Heavens above, the child has to be somewhere!

HJALMAR. Come out.

[*He stands back; and* HEDVIG, *terrified, comes into the studio.*]

HJALMAR [*his hand on the door handle, speaks to* GINA]. As I spend these last moments in what was once my home, I wish to remain undisturbed by those who have no business to be here. . . .

HEDVIG [*runs across to her mother and asks in a low trembling voice*]. Does he mean me?

GINA. Stay in the kitchen, Hedvig. Or no—go into your own room instead. [*Speaking to* HJALMAR, *as she goes in to where he is.*] Just a minute, Hjalmar. Don't upset everything in that chest of drawers. *I* know where everything is.

[HEDVIG *stands motionless for a moment, frightened and confused; she bites her lip to stop herself from crying, and clenches and unclenches her hands.*]

HEDVIG [*softly*]. The wild duck!

[*She creeps across and takes the pistol from the shelf, opens the loft door a little way, slips in and pulls the door behind her.* HJALMAR *and* GINA *begin to argue in the living-room.*]

HJALMAR [*comes out carrying some exercise books and old sheets of paper, which he puts on the table*]. Oh, that old valise isn't much use. There are thousands of things I've got to hump away with me.

GINA [*follows with the valise*]. Well, leave the other things for the time being; just take a shirt and a pair of pants with you now.

HJALMAR. Phew! All these exhausting preparations!

[*He takes off his topcoat and throws it on the sofa.*]

GINA. Your coffee's getting cold.

HJALMAR. Hm!

[*He takes a mouthful without thinking, and then another.*]

GINA [*dusting the backs of the chairs*]. Your worst job now will be finding another loft big enough for the rabbits.

HJALMAR. What! Have I to drag all those rabbits along with me as well?

GINA. Yes, you know Grandfather couldn't live without his rabbits.

HJALMAR. He'll damn' well have to get used to the idea. There are more important matters in life than rabbits among the things *I'm* having to do without.

GINA [*dusting the bookcase*]. Shall I put your flute in your valise?

HJALMAR. No. I don't want any flute. But give me the pistol.

GINA. You want to take that pistol!

HJALMAR. Yes. My loaded pistol.

GINA [*looks for it*]. It's gone. He must have taken it in with him.

HJALMAR. Is he in the loft?

GINA. Oh, he's bound to be.

HJALMAR. Hm. Poor lonely old fellow.

[*He takes a piece of bread and butter, eats it, and drinks up the coffee.*]

GINA. If only we hadn't let that room, you could have moved in there.

HJALMAR. Me live under the same roof as . . . ! Never! Never!

GINA. But couldn't you shake down for a day or two in the living-room? You could be all on your own there.

HJALMAR. Never within these walls!

GINA. Well, what about going in with Relling and Molvik?

HJALMAR. I don't want to hear their names. Just thinking of them is enough to put me off my food, nearly. . . . Ah no! I must out into the storm and the snow . . . go from house to house seeking shelter for my father and myself.

GINA. But, Hjalmar, you haven't any hat. You've lost your hat, remember?

HJALMAR. Oh, the scum. Can't trust them with anything! I'll have to get myself a hat on the way. [*He takes another piece of bread.*] The necessary arrangements will have to be made. I've no desire to go risking my life as well.

[*He looks for something on the tray.*]

GINA. What are you looking for?

HJALMAR. Butter.

GINA. I'll get some straight away. [*Goes out into the kitchen.*]

HJALMAR [*calls after her*]. Oh, you needn't bother. I can just as well eat it dry.

GINA [*brings a butter dish*]. There you are, now. Supposed to be freshly churned.

[*She pours him a fresh cup of coffee; he sits down on the sofa, spreads more butter on the bread, eats and drinks in silence for a moment or two.*]

HJALMAR. Would I, without being disturbed by anybody—anybody at all—be able to move into the living-room for a day or two?

GINA. Yes, you could very nicely, and for as long as you wanted to.

HJALMAR. Because I can't see much likelihood of moving all Father's things out very fast.

GINA. There's something else as well. You'll have to tell him first about not wanting to live here with the rest of us any longer.

HJALMAR [*pushes his coffee cup away*]. Yes, that's another thing. All these complicated arrangements to be revised. I must consider things first, I must have a breathing space. I can't take all these burdens on in one single day.

GINA. No, and when it's such awful weather, too, on top of everything.

HJALMAR [*fingers Werle's letter*]. I see this paper's lying about here still.

GINA. Yes, *I* haven't touched it.

HJALMAR. Not that this bit of paper's got anything to do with me . . .

GINA. Well, I've got no use for it.

HJALMAR. . . . but there's not much point in letting it get destroyed, all the same. In all the upset when I move, it could so easily . . .

GINA. I'll take care of it, Hjalmar.

HJALMAR. After all, this letter belongs in the first place to Father; and it will have to be for him to decide whether he wants to make use of it or not.

GINA [*sighs*]. Yes, poor old Father.

HJALMAR. Might as well be on the safe side. . . . Where will I find the paste?

GINA [*goes to the bookcase*]. Here's the paste pot.

HJALMAR. And a brush?

GINA. Here's the brush as well.

[*She brings him the things.*]

HJALMAR [*taking the scissors*]. Just needs a strip of paper along the back. . . . [*He cuts and pastes.*] Far be it from me to lay hands on anybody else's property, least of all on a penniless old man's. And not on . . . the other person's, either, for that matter. . . . There we are. It can stay there for the present. And when it's dry, put it away. I don't want to see that document ever again. Never!

[GREGERS WERLE *comes in from the hall.*]

GREGERS [*a little surprised*]. What! You here, Hjalmar?

HJALMAR [*gets up quickly*]. I had sunk down from exhaustion.

GREGERS. I see you've had some breakfast.

HJALMAR. The body too makes known its claims on us at times.

GREGERS. What have you decided to do?

HJALMAR. For a man such as me there is but one way open. I am in the process of collecting together the more important of my possessions. But it takes time, you understand.

GINA [*a little impatiently*]. Shall I get the room ready for you, or shall I pack the valise?

HJALMAR [*with an irritated glance at* GREGERS]. Pack . . . and get the room ready.

GINA [*takes the valise*]. All right, I'll put the shirt and the other things in, then.

[*She goes into the living-room and shuts the door behind her.*]

GREGERS [*after a short silence*]. I would never have thought that it would end like this. Is it really essential that you should leave house and home?

HJALMAR [*walking about restlessly*]. What do you expect me to do, then?
—I am not made for unhappiness, Gregers. Everything around me
has got to be nice and secure and peaceful.

GREGERS. But can't that be done? Try. To my mind you've got a firm
foundation to build on . . . just begin at the beginning. Remember
you've got your invention to live for, too.

HJALMAR. Oh, shut up about the invention. That's probably pretty
far away.

GREGERS. Really?

HJALMAR. Good Lord, what in fact do you expect me to invent?
Practically everything's been invented by other people already.
It gets more and more difficult every day.

GREGERS. After you've put such a lot of work into it!

HJALMAR. It was that devil Relling who put me up to it.

GREGERS. Relling?

HJALMAR. Yes, he was the one who first suggested I was capable of
making some special invention in photography.

GREGERS. Aha! . . . It was Relling!

HJALMAR. It's a thing that's made me intensely happy. Not so much
because of the invention itself, as because Hedvig believed in it—
believed in it with all the passion of a child. . . . What I mean is that
I, like a fool, went and imagined that she believed in it.

GREGERS. Do you really suppose Hedvig went out of her way to
deceive you!

HJALMAR. I'm ready to think anything now. Hedvig's the stumbling
block now. She'll finish up by taking all the sunshine out of my
life.

GREGERS. Hedvig! D'you mean Hedvig! How could *she* ever do
anything like that?

HJALMAR [*without answering*]. I can't tell you how I loved that child.
I can't tell you how happy I felt every time I came home to my
modest room and she would come running across to me, with her
poor sweet, strained little eyes. Oh, gullible fool that I was! I was

so inexpressibly fond of her . . . and I deluded myself into imagining she was equally fond of me, too.

GREGERS. Can you say that *that* was merely a delusion?

HJALMAR. How should I know? I cannot get anything out of Gina. And anyway she has absolutely no understanding of the element of idealism in this situation. But I feel the need to unburden myself to you, Gregers. There's this terrible uncertainty—perhaps Hedvig never really loved me at all.

GREGERS. That is something you might very well get proof of. [*Listens.*] What's that? I thought I heard the wild duck cry.

HJALMAR. It's the wild duck quacking. Father is in the loft.

GREGERS. Is he! [*Joy lights up his face.*] What I was saying is that you might well have proof that poor misunderstood Hedvig does love you!

HJALMAR. Oh, what proof can she give me! I can hardly place any reliance on anything she says.

GREGERS. I'm sure there's nothing deceitful about Hedvig.

HJALMAR. Oh, Gregers, that's just what isn't so certain. Who knows what Gina and that Mrs. Sörby have sat here whispering and gossiping about? And Hedvig's got long ears. Perhaps that deed of gift wasn't so unexpected. I fancy I noticed something of the sort.

GREGERS. What's this that's got into you?

HJALMAR. I have had my eyes opened. You just watch—you'll see this deed of gift is only a beginning. Mrs. Sörby has always been specially fond of Hedvig, and now she has the power to do whatever she wants for the child. They can take her away from me any time they like.

GREGERS. Hedvig will never, never leave *you*.

HJALMAR. Don't you be so sure. What if they stand there with full hands beckoning to her. . . ? Oh, and I can't tell you how much I loved her! How it would have given me supreme happiness just to have taken her by the hand and led her along, as one leads a child that is afraid of the dark through a great empty room! I'm now convinced that the bitter truth is that the poor photographer up in his attic flat never really meant anything to her at all. All she did in her cunning was to take care that she kept on good terms with him until the right moment came.

GREGERS. You don't really believe that yourself, Hjalmar.

HJALMAR. That's the terrible thing, of course. I just don't know what to believe . . . and I'll never know. But surely you don't doubt it's as I say? Ha! ha! You rely too much on people's idealism, my dear Gregers! Suppose the others came along, their hands full, and they called to the child: 'Come away from him. With us, life is at your feet. . . .'

GREGERS [*quickly*]. Well, what then, d'you think?

HJALMAR. If I then asked her: 'Hedvig, are you willing to give up this life for my sake?' [*Laughs scornfully.*] Oh, yes! I must say. You would soon hear the sort of answer I would get!

[*A pistol shot is heard within the loft.*]

GREGERS [*shouts with joy*]. Hjalmar!

HJALMAR. Look at that, now. He has to go shooting!

GINA. Oh, Hjalmar, I think Grandfather's banging away there in the loft by himself.

HJALMAR. I'll look in.

GREGERS [*quickly, excitedly*]. Wait a minute! Do you know what that was?

HJALMAR. Of course I know what it was.

GREGERS. No, you don't. But *I* do. That was the proof!

HJALMAR. What proof?

GREGERS. That was the child's sacrifice. She's got your father to shoot the wild duck.

HJALMAR. Shoot the wild duck!

GINA. Well . . . !

HJALMAR. What's *that* for?

GREGERS. She wanted to sacrifice the most precious thing she had in the world, for your sake. Then, she thought, you couldn't help loving her again.

HJALMAR [*softly, with emotion*]. Oh, that child!

GINA. The things she thinks of!

GREGERS. All she wanted was for you to love her again, Hjalmar; she didn't think she could live without that.

GINA [*fighting back her tears*]. There you see, Hjalmar.

HJALMAR. Gina, where is she?

GINA [*sniffing*]. Poor little thing, she's sitting out in the kitchen, I expect.

HJALMAR [*crosses, and throws open the kitchen door*]. Hedvig, come out! Come to me! [*Looks round.*] No, she's not here.

GINA. Then she must be in her own room.

HJALMAR [*from outside*]. No, she isn't here either. [*Comes in.*] She must have gone out.

GINA. Well, you wouldn't have her anywhere in the house.

HJALMAR. Oh, if only she'd come back home again soon . . . so that I can tell her properly. . . . Everything's going to be all right, Gregers. Now I really believe we can begin life all over again.

GREGERS [*quietly*]. I knew it—knew that redemption would come through the child.

[*OLD EKDAL appears at the door of his room, dressed in full uniform and busy trying to buckle on his sword.*]

HJALMAR [*astonished*]. Father! Are you there!

GINA. Were you shooting in your room, Father?

EKDAL [*indignantly, coming into the room*]. What d'you mean by going shooting alone, Hjalmar?

HJALMAR [*tense, bewildered*]. Wasn't it you who fired that shot in the loft?

EKDAL. Me? A shot? Huh!

GREGERS [*calls to* HJALMAR]. She's shot the wild duck herself!

HJALMAR. What's all this! [*He rushes to the door of the loft, pulls it to one side, looks in and screams.*] Hedvig!

GINA [*running to the door*]. Dear God, what's the matter!

HJALMAR [*goes in*]. She's lying on the floor!

GREGERS. Hedvig! On the floor!

[*He goes in to* HJALMAR.]

GINA [*at the same time*]. Hedvig! [*She goes into the loft.*] Oh no! No!

EKDAL. Aha! *She's* gone off shooting too, eh?

[HJALMAR, GINA, *and* GREGERS *carry* HEDVIG *into the studio; her right hand hangs down, her fingers still gripping the pistol.*]

HJALMAR [*desperately*]. The pistol's gone off. She's been shot. Call for help! Help!

GINA [*runs into the hall and shouts down*]. Relling! Relling! Dr. Relling! Come up as fast as you can!

[HJALMAR *and* GREGERS *lay* HEDVIG *down on the sofa.*]

EKDAL [*quietly*]. The forest's revenge!

HJALMAR [*beside her on his knees*]. She'll come round soon. She'll come round. . . . Yes, yes.

GINA [*who has come in again*]. Where's she been shot? I can't see anything. . . .

[RELLING *hurries in, followed closely by* MOLVIK; *the latter has neither waistcoat nor collar, and his coat is flying open.*]

RELLING. What's going on here?

GINA. They say Hedvig has shot herself.

HJALMAR. Come here and help!

RELLING. Shot herself! [*He shifts the table to one side, and begins examining her.*]

HJALMAR [*looking anxiously up at him*]. It can't be anything serious, eh, Relling? She's hardly bleeding. Surely it can't be serious?

RELLING. How did this happen?

HJALMAR. Oh, how do I know. . . !

GINA. She wanted to shoot the wild duck.

RELLING. The wild duck?

HJALMAR. The pistol must have gone off.

RELLING. Hm! Indeed!

EKDAL. The forest's revenge. Still I'm not frightened.

[*He goes into the loft and shuts himself in.*]

HJALMAR. Well, Relling . . . why don't you say something?

RELLING. The bullet hit her in the breast.

HJALMAR. Yes, but she'll be coming round.

RELLING. Can't you see Hedvig is dead?

GINA [*bursts into tears*]. Oh my little one!

GREGERS [*huskily*]. In the briny deep . . .

HJALMAR [*springing up*]. No, no, she *must* live! Oh, for God's sake, Relling . . . just for a moment, just long enough for me to tell her how infinitely I loved her all the time!

RELLING. She was hit in the heart. Internal hæmorrhage. She died instantaneously.

HJALMAR. And I drove her away from me like some animal. And in terror she crept into the loft and died, for love of me. [*Sobbing.*] I can never make it up to her again! Never be able to tell her . . . ! [*He clenches his hands and cries to heaven.*] Oh, God on high . . . if Thou *art* there! Why hast Thou done this to me?

GINA. Hush, hush, you mustn't say such terrible things. We had no right to keep her, I dare say.

MOLVIK. The child is not dead; it sleeps.

RELLING. Rubbish!

HJALMAR [*more composed, goes over to the sofa and looks down on* HEDVIG *with folded arms*]. There she lies, stiff and still.

RELLING [*trying to free the pistol*]. It's so tight, so tight.

GINA. Please, Relling, don't force her little fingers. Leave the pistol there.

HJALMAR. She shall take it with her.

GINA. Yes, let her. But she mustn't lie out here for everybody to see. She shall go into her own little room, she shall. Help me with her, Hjalmar.

[HJALMAR *and* GINA *take* HEDVIG *between them.*]

HJALMAR [*as they carry her out*]. Oh, Gina, can you bear this?

GINA. We must help one another. For *now* she's as much yours as mine, isn't she?

MOLVIK [*stretches out his arms and mutters*]. Praised be the Lord. Earth to earth . . . earth to earth. . . .

RELLING [*whispers*]. Shut up, man! You are drunk!

[HJALMAR *and* GINA *carry the body out by the kitchen door.* RELLING *shuts it after them.* MOLVIK *sneaks out into the hall.*]

RELLING [*crosses to* GREGERS]. Nobody's ever going to persuade me this was an accident.

GREGERS [*who has stood horror-stricken, his face twitching*]. Nobody can say how this dreadful thing happened.

RELLING. There was a powderburn on her dress. She must have pressed the pistol right against her breast and fired.

GREGERS. Hedvig has not died in vain. Didn't you see how grief brought out what was noblest in him?

RELLING. Most people feel some nobility when they stand grieving in the presence of death. But how long do you suppose this glory will last in *his* case?

GREGERS. Surely it will continue and flourish for the rest of his life!

RELLING. Give him nine months and little Hedvig will be nothing more than the theme of a pretty little party piece.

GREGERS. You dare say that about Hjalmar Ekdal!

RELLING. We can discuss it again when the first grass starts showing on her grave. Then he'll bring it all up, all about 'the child so untimely torn from a loving father's heart'. Then you'll see him wallowing deeper and deeper in sentimentality and self-pity. Just you watch!

GREGERS. If *you* are right and *I* am wrong, life will no longer be worth living.

RELLING. Oh, life wouldn't be too bad if only these blessed people who come canvassing their ideals round everybody's door would leave us poor souls in peace.

GREGERS [*staring into space*]. In that case I am glad my destiny is what it is.

RELLING. If I may ask—what is your destiny?

GREGERS [*turning to leave*]. To be thirteenth at table.

RELLING. The devil it is!

ROSMERSHOLM

[Rosmersholm]

PLAY IN FOUR ACTS

(1886)

CHARACTERS

JOHANNES ROSMER, of Rosmersholm, a former clergyman

REBECCA WEST, resident at Rosmersholm

KROLL, Rosmer's brother-in-law, a headmaster

ULRIK BRENDEL

PETER MORTENSGAARD

MRS. HELSETH, housekeeper at Rosmersholm

The action takes place at Rosmersholm, an old family estate near a small coastal town in Western Norway

ACT ONE

The living-room at Rosmersholm, spacious, old-fashioned and comfortable. Against the wall, right front, is a stove decorated with fresh birch twigs and wild flowers. Further back is a door. On the back wall, folding doors open on to the entrance hall. On the wall, left, is a window in front of which is a stand with flowers and plants. Near the stove is a table with a sofa and easy chairs. The walls are hung with past and recent portraits of clergymen, officers and officials in their robes and uniforms. The window is open, so also is the hall door and the outer door. Outside can be seen an avenue of ancient trees leading to the estate. It is a summer evening; the sun has set.

REBECCA WEST is sitting in an easy-chair near the window, crocheting a large white woollen shawl which is nearly finished. From time to time she peeps out of the window from behind the flowers. Presently MRS. HELSETH enters from right.

MRS. HELSETH. Hadn't I better start laying the table for supper now, miss?

REBECCA. Yes, please. The pastor will probably be back soon.

MRS. HELSETH. Isn't there an awful draught where you are sitting, miss?

REBECCA. Yes, there is rather. Perhaps you would shut the window.

[MRS. HELSETH *goes over and shuts the door to the hall, then she crosses to the window.*]

MRS. HELSETH [*about to shut the window, looks out*]. But isn't that the pastor coming over there?

REBECCA [*quickly*]. Where? [*Rises.*] Yes, that's him. [*Behind the curtain.*] Come away from there. Don't let him see us.

MRS. HELSETH [*away from the window*]. Well, fancy that, miss! He is starting to use the path by the mill again.

REBECCA. He came by the mill-path a couple of days ago, too. [*Peeping from behind the curtain.*] But now we'll see whether . . .

MRS. HELSETH. Will he dare come across the footbridge?

REBECCA. That's just what I want to see. [*Pause.*] No, he's turning off. He's going round the top again today. [*Away from the window.*] It's a long way round.

MRS. HELSETH. Lord, so he is. I suppose it can't be easy for the pastor to face crossing *that* bridge again. Not after what happened there. . . .

REBECCA [*gathering up her crochet work*]. They cling long to their dead here at Rosmersholm.

MRS. HELSETH. It's my belief it's the dead that cling to Rosmersholm, miss.

REBECCA [*looking at her*]. The dead?

MRS. HELSETH. Yes, as though they couldn't tear themselves away from the ones they left behind, as you might say.

REBECCA. What makes you think that?

MRS. HELSETH. Well, otherwise that White Horse thing wouldn't keep coming around here, I'm sure.

REBECCA. Now, Mrs. Helseth, what *is* all this about the White Horse?

MRS. HELSETH. Oh, there's no point in talking about it. *You* wouldn't believe any of it anyway.

REBECCA. Do you believe in it then?

MRS. HELSETH [*goes and shuts the window*]. Oh, I'm not going to let you try to make me look a fool, miss. [*Looks out.*] Isn't that surely the pastor again, down on the path by the mill?

REBECCA [*looks up*]. Over there? [*Goes to the window.*] Of course not, it's the headmaster!

MRS. HELSETH. So it is of course, the headmaster.

REBECCA. Well, isn't that nice! He'll be on his way to visit us, you'll see.

MRS. HELSETH. Straight over the footbridge for him. Even though it *was* his own sister. Well, I'll go and lay the supper table now, miss.

[*She goes out to the right.* REBECCA *stands a moment at the window, then she waves, smiling and nodding. It is beginning to get dark.*]

REBECCA [*crosses to the door on the right and calls through it*]. Oh, Mrs. Helseth! You will try to find something special for supper please, won't you? You know what the headmaster likes best.

MRS. HELSETH [*outside*]. All right, miss. I'll see what can be done.

REBECCA [*opens the door to the entrance hall*]. Fancy, after all this time...! How delightful to see you again, Mr. Kroll. Do come in.

KROLL [*in the entrance hall, puts down his stick*]. Thank you. I hope I am not disturbing you?

REBECCA. You! For shame, Mr. Kroll, saying a thing like that!

KROLL [*comes in*]. You are always very kind. [*Looks about him.*] Is Rosmer up in his room by any chance?

REBECCA. No, he is out for a walk. He is rather later than usual. But he is bound to be back any minute now. [*Points to the sofa.*] Won't you sit down till he comes?

KROLL [*puts down his hat*]. Thank you very much. [*Sits down and looks round the room.*] How nice and gay you have got this old room looking. Flowers everywhere!

REBECCA. Mr. Rosmer is very fond of having fresh flowers about the place.

KROLL. And you are too, I imagine.

REBECCA. Yes, I find their fragrance so wonderfully soothing. That was a pleasure we had to deny ourselves earlier, of course.

KROLL [*nods sadly*]. Poor Beata couldn't bear the scent of flowers.

REBECCA. Nor the colours either. They used to upset her.

KROLL. Yes, I remember only too well. [*In a brisker tone.*] Well now, and how are things going out here?

REBECCA. Oh, it's all very quiet and uneventful. One day very much like another. And how are things with you? Is your wife...?

KROLL. Ah, my dear Miss West, don't let's talk about my affairs. In a family there's always something or other that's not quite as it should be. Especially in times like these.

REBECCA [*after a pause, sits in an easy-chair near the sofa*]. You haven't once been out to see us during the vacation. Why is that?

KROLL. Well, you can't always be knocking on people's doors . . .

REBECCA. If you only knew how we had missed you. . . .

KROLL. . . . and apart from that I have been away, you know.

REBECCA. Yes, but just for a week or two. You have been going round all the political meetings, I gather?

KROLL [*nods*]. And what do you say to that? Did you ever imagine I would turn political agitator in my old age? Eh?

REBECCA [*smiles*]. You have always been *something* of an agitator, now, Mr. Kroll.

KROLL. Well yes, but just for my own private amusement. From now on, however, it's going to be in real earnest, I can tell you. Do you ever read any of these Radical papers?

REBECCA. Well, Mr. Kroll, I won't deny that . . .

KROLL. My dear Miss West, there can be no objection to that. Not in *your* case.

REBECCA. That's what I think, too. I have to keep up with things, find out what's going on. . . .

KROLL. Well now, I should never expect you . . . as a woman, I mean . . . to get mixed up in this dispute—this civil war, I might almost call it—that is raging here. But doubtless you have read the abusive things these 'men of the people' have been pleased to say about me? The outrageous insults they thought they could get away with?

REBECCA. Yes, but I thought you bit back pretty sharply.

KROLL. Indeed I did, although I say it myself. And now I have tasted blood, I'll show them that I'm not the sort of man to take things lying down. [*Breaks off.*] But there—don't let us go into that unpleasant and distressing business this evening.

REBECCA. No indeed, my dear Mr. Kroll.

KROLL. Tell me instead, how are you getting along here at Rosmersholm, now that you are on your own? Now that our poor Beata . . . ?

REBECCA. Oh, I get on quite well here, thank you. Of course, in many ways the place seems very empty now that she's gone. She is greatly missed, and greatly mourned . . . naturally. But otherwise . . .

KROLL. Do you intend staying on here? More or less permanently, I mean?

REBECCA. My dear Mr. Kroll, I haven't really thought about it, one way or the other. I have become so used to the place now, I almost feel I belong here.

KROLL. And so you do, I should say.

REBECCA. And as long as Mr. Rosmer feels that I can be of any use or comfort to him—well then, I'll be only too happy to stay, I suppose.

KROLL [*looks at her with some emotion*]. You know . . . there's something rather splendid about that—a woman giving up the best years of her young life, sacrificing them for the sake of others.

REBECCA. Oh, what else would I have had to live for?

KROLL. First, there was the constant strain of looking after your crippled foster-father who was so difficult. . . .

REBECCA. You mustn't think Dr. West was so difficult when we lived up in Finmark. It was those terrible sea voyages that finally broke him. But after we had moved down here . . . well yes, it was hard going for a year or two before he finally went to rest.

KROLL. And those years that followed, weren't they even harder for you?

REBECCA. No indeed, how can you say such a thing! When I was so genuinely fond of Beata. . . . And she, poor thing, so desperately in need of care and friendly sympathy.

KROLL. Thank you for speaking so charitably of her; it does you much credit.

REBECCA [*moves a little closer*]. Dear Mr. Kroll, you said that so sweetly and sincerely that I am sure you don't hold anything against me after all.

KROLL. Hold anything against you? What do you mean?

REBECCA. Well, it wouldn't really be very surprising if it upset you to see a stranger like me running things here at Rosmersholm.

KROLL. What on earth . . . ?

REBECCA. But it seems you don't. [*Holds out her hand.*] Thank you, Mr. Kroll, thank you for that.

KROLL. But what on earth made you think a thing like that?

REBECCA. When you didn't come out as often as before, I began to get a bit worried.

KROLL. Then, believe me, Miss West, you have been on the wrong track entirely. And besides, there's been no real change in things here. Towards the end, and while poor Beata was still alive, you were already in charge of things here. You and you alone.

REBECCA. But I was only acting on her behalf, in the wife's name, as it were.

KROLL. Well, anyway . . . do you know, Miss West . . . I shouldn't at all object, speaking personally, if ever you . . . But perhaps it doesn't do to say things like that.

REBECCA. What things?

KROLL. If it should ever happen that you were to take over the vacant place. . . .

REBECCA. I have the place I want, Mr. Kroll.

KROLL. Yes, in one sense perhaps. . . .

REBECCA [*interrupts him earnestly*]. For shame, Mr. Kroll. How can you sit there and joke about such things?

KROLL. Ah well, I dare say our good Johannes Rosmer thinks that he has had more than enough of matrimony. But all the same . . .

REBECCA. You know, I can't help smiling at you.

KROLL. All the same . . . Tell me, Miss West, if you don't mind my asking: how old are you, in fact?

REBECCA. Twenty-nine, I'm ashamed to say, Mr. Kroll. Going on for thirty.

KROLL. Quite so. And Rosmer . . . let me see, how old is he? He is five years younger than me, so he must be about forty-three. I think it would be very suitable.

REBECCA [*rises*]. Yes, yes. Eminently suitable I'm sure. . . . Will you stay for a cup of tea with us this evening. . . ?

KROLL. Thank you. I *had* thought of staying on a while. There's something I must talk to our good friend about.—Well now, Miss West, just so that you won't start getting any more wrong ideas, I must look out here a bit more often—as I did in the old days.

REBECCA. Oh yes, you *must*. [*Takes both his hands.*] Thank you, thank you. You really are awfully kind after all.

KROLL [*gruffly*]. Am I? That's more than they tell me at home.

[JOHANNES ROSMER *comes in by the door on the right.*]

REBECCA. Mr. Rosmer! Do you see who's sitting here?

ROSMER. Mrs. Helseth told me.

[KROLL *has risen.*]

ROSMER [*in a low choking voice, taking his hands*]. Welcome to this house again, my dear Kroll. [*Places his hands on* KROLL'S *shoulders and looks into his eyes.*] My dear old friend! I felt sure things would come all right again between us.

KROLL. But my dear fellow! Don't say you also had this silly idea that something was wrong!

REBECCA [*to* ROSMER]. Isn't it marvellous! It was just our imagination.

ROSMER. Was it really, Kroll? But why were you so obviously keeping away from us?

KROLL [*earnestly and quietly*]. Because I didn't want to appear as a living reminder of those unhappy years . . . and of her who met her end in the millstream.

ROSMER. How good of you to think like that. You always were considerate. But it was quite unnecessary for you to stay away on that account. Come along now, let us sit down on the sofa. [*They sit.*] No, it really doesn't upset me to think about Beata. We talk about her every day. We feel as though she still belonged to the house.

KROLL. Do you really?

REBECCA [*lights the lamp*]. Yes, we really do.

ROSMER. It's rather what you might have expected. We were both so devoted to her. And both Reb . . . both Miss West and I, we know ourselves that we did everything in our power for the poor thing in her affliction. We have nothing to reproach ourselves with. That is why I find myself thinking quite calmly and tenderly about Beata now.

KROLL. You dear, good people! From now on I shall come out to see you every day.

REBECCA [*sits down in an easy-chair*]. Yes, and now all we've got to do is to see that you keep your word.

ROSMER [*rather hesitantly*]. Kroll, my dear fellow . . . I honestly wish there hadn't been this break between us. Ever since we first knew each other, it seemed the obvious thing that you should be the one I always turned to for advice. Ever since I was a student.

KROLL. I know, and it is something that I value very highly. Is there anything in particular now by any chance. . . ?

ROSMER. There are a great many things I would dearly like to talk over frankly with you. A sort of heart to heart talk.

REBECCA. Yes, there are, aren't there, Mr. Rosmer? I think it would be such a good thing . . . two old friends together. . . .

KROLL. And I have even more to talk to you about, believe me. Because I have now become an active politician, as you probably know.

ROSMER. Yes, I know you have. How did that happen?

KROLL. I had to, you know! Had to, whether I liked it or not. You just can't stand idly looking on any longer. Now that these wretched Radicals have got into power . . . it's high time . . . That's why I've persuaded our little circle of friends in town to get together. And not before time, I can tell you.

REBECCA [*with a faint smile*]. Yes, but isn't it a bit late, perhaps?

KROLL. I don't deny it would have been better to have stemmed the torrent a bit earlier. But who could have foreseen what was to come? Not me, anyway. [*Rises and walks up and down.*] Yes, now I've really had my eyes opened. For now these subversive ideas have found their way even into the school.

ROSMER. Into the school? But surely not into your school?

KROLL. Yes they have, I tell you. Into my own school! And what do you think? It has come to my knowledge that the sixth-form boys— or some of them, I should say—have been holding secret meetings for the past six months, and they have been taking Mortensgaard's paper!

REBECCA. Ah, the *Beacon*!

KROLL. Yes, there's a nice thing for future civil servants to feed their minds on, isn't it? But the saddest thing about the affair is that it's all the *clever* lads in the class who have banded together in this conspiracy against me. Only the duffers and the thickheads have kept out of it.

REBECCA. Do you feel very badly about it, Mr. Kroll?

KROLL. Very badly! When I see all my life's work thwarted and undermined like this! [*Lower.*] Yet I might almost have said I was ready to bear even *that*. But that's not the worst. [*Looks round.*] I suppose nobody is likely to be listening at the door?

REBECCA. No, of course not.

KROLL. Then you ought to know that this spirit of defiance and revolt has intruded even into my own home. Into the quiet of my own home! Destroying the peace and quiet of my family life!

ROSMER [*gets up*]. What's that you say? In your own home. . . ?

REBECCA [*goes over to* KROLL]. But my dear Mr. Kroll, what has happened?

KROLL. Would you believe that my own children . . . ? To put it in a nutshell, Lauritz is the ringleader of the group at school. And Hilda has embroidered a red cover to keep the *Beacon* in.

ROSMER. I would never have dreamt such a thing . . . to *you* . . . in your own house. . . .

KROLL. Quite! Who ever would have dreamt a thing like that was possible? In my own house, where obedience and order have always been the rule . . . where until now we've all thought and acted with one mind. . . .

REBECCA. How does your wife take all this?

KROLL. Now that is the most incredible thing of all. All her life she has shared my opinions and agreed with my views—in big things as well as small. Yet even she tends sometimes to take the children's side in some things. And then she puts the blame on *me* for what has happened. She says I domineer the children, bully them. . . . As though it weren't necessary to. . . . Well, that's the sort of upset going on at home. But naturally I talk about it as little as possible. Things like that are best hushed up. [*Wanders about the room.*] Yes, indeed.

[*He stops at the window, hands behind back, and looks out.*]

REBECCA [*goes over to* ROSMER *and speaks quickly in a low voice so that* KROLL *does not hear*]. Go on, do it!

ROSMER [*in the same tone*]. Not tonight.

REBECCA [*as before*]. Yes, do it now!

[*She moves away and busies herself with the lamp.*]

KROLL [*comes forward*]. Yes, my dear Rosmer, now you know how the spirit of the age has cast its shadow over both my domestic life and my professional activities. And these pernicious, demoralizing, disruptive ideas, don't you think I should fight them with all the weapons I can lay my hands on? Of course, my friend, that is what I mean to do. With the written as well as the spoken word.

ROSMER. And do you have any hopes of achieving anything that way?

KROLL. I can at least do my bit as a citizen, anyway. And I think it is incumbent on every patriotic and right-minded man to do the same. In fact, that is mainly why I have come to see you tonight.

ROSMER. But my dear friend, what do you mean? What do you want me to . . . ?

KROLL. You are going to stand by your old friends. Do as the rest of us are doing. Lend a hand as best you can.

REBECCA. But Mr. Kroll, you know how Mr. Rosmer dislikes that sort of thing.

KROLL. He must try and get over that dislike now. You don't keep properly abreast of things, Rosmer, sitting out here and burying yourself in this historical research of yours. Heavens above, man!

Family trees and things like that are all very well, but unfortunately this just isn't the time for pursuits of that kind. You simply can't imagine the state things are in up and down the country. Hardly a single idea but what it hasn't been turned upside down. And what an enormous job that's going to be, putting all these things right again.

ROSMER. That I can well believe. But that kind of job isn't in my line at all.

REBECCA. And besides I rather think that Mr. Rosmer has come to see things with a clearer vision than before.

KROLL [*with a start*]. Clearer vision!

REBECCA. Yes, or more independent then. Less prejudiced.

KROLL. What is the meaning of this? Rosmer, surely you are not going to let yourself be taken in so easily by this snap victory the mob politicians have won.

ROSMER. My dear fellow, you know very well how little understanding I have of politics. But I certainly feel that in recent years people have shown a rather greater measure of independence in their ways of thinking.

KROLL. Indeed! And I suppose you obviously regard that as a good thing! Anyway, you are vastly mistaken, my friend. Just you try making a few inquiries about the views that are current among the Radicals, both out here and in town. There's not a scrap of difference between them and the precious words of wisdom the *Beacon* keeps putting out.

REBECCA. Yes, Mortensgaard has a great deal of influence over people in these parts.

KROLL. Yes, think of him too. A man with his murky past. A person sacked from his teaching post for immoral conduct! A creature like that setting himself up as a leader of the people. And he carries it off! Actually carries it off! He's going to expand his paper, I hear. I know on good authority he is looking for a capable assistant.

REBECCA. I'm only surprised that you and your friends don't set up in opposition to him.

KROLL. That's precisely what we are now thinking of doing. We bought the *County Times* today. There was no difficulty about money. But . . . [*turns to* ROSMER] now I come to the real point of my visit to you. Our difficulty is going to be running it, you see . . . on the editorial side. Tell me, Rosmer, don't you feel in a way it's up to you to take it on, for the sake of the cause?

ROSMER [*in consternation*]. Me?

REBECCA. Whatever makes you think a thing like that!

KROLL. I can quite understand your horror of public meetings, not wanting to face all the heckling and things that go on there. But the more sequestered work of an editor, or is it more correct to say . . . ?

ROSMER. No, no, my dear friend. You must not ask me to do it.

KROLL. I would dearly love to have a shot at a thing like that myself, too. But it would be far too much for me. I have taken on such a mass of other things as it is. . . . But you, on the other hand, now that you are no longer burdened with any official duties . . . The rest of us will help you, of course, as best we can.

ROSMER. I can't, Kroll. I would be no good at it.

KROLL. No good at it! You said the same thing when your father got you your living. . . .

ROSMER. I was right. That was why I gave it up.

KROLL. Oh, if you are no worse an editor than you were a clergyman, we'll be content.

ROSMER. My dear Kroll . . . I must insist, once and for all, I cannot do it.

KROLL. All right. But anyway you will let us use your name.

ROSMER. My name?

KROLL. Yes, the name of Johannes Rosmer will in itself be an asset to the paper. The rest of us are looked on as distinct party men. I am told they are even trying to brand me personally as some desperate fanatic. So that if we use our own names for the paper, we cannot count on much of a circulation among the poor misguided masses. You, on the other hand, have always held yourself aloof from the fray. You are known as a tolerant and fair-minded man; your fine brain, your indisputable integrity are appreciated by everybody in the district. Then there's the esteem and respect that come from your once having been a clergyman. And on top of all there's the family name and all that that means.

ROSMER. Oh, the family name . . .

KROLL [*points to the portraits*]. The Rosmers of Rosmersholm . . . clergymen and soldiers . . . high officials . . . men of the highest principles, all of them . . . the foremost family in the district with its seat here now for nearly two hundred years. [*Lays his hand on* ROS-MER's *shoulder*.] Rosmer, you owe it to yourself and to the traditions of your family to join in the fight to defend those things that have hitherto been held sacred in our community. [*Turns round*.] What do you say, Miss West?

REBECCA [*with a faint laugh*]. Mr. Kroll . . . I can't tell you how ludicrous all this sounds.

KROLL. What's that! Ludicrous!

REBECCA. Yes. For now I'm going to tell you straight. . . .

ROSMER [*quickly*]. No, no, don't! Not now!

KROLL [*looks from one to the other*]. But, my dear friends, what on earth . . . ? [*Breaks off*.] Hm!

[MRS. HELSETH *comes in by the door on the right*.]

MRS. HELSETH. There's a man at the kitchen door. He says he wants to see you, sir.

ROSMER [*relieved*]. Oh, is there? Ask him to come in, then.

MRS. HELSETH. In *here*, sir?

ROSMER. Certainly.

MRS. HELSETH. But he hardly looks the sort of person you would want in the living-room.

REBECCA. What does he look like, then, Mrs. Helseth?

MRS. HELSETH. Well, he's not all that much to look at, miss.

ROSMER. Didn't he tell you his name?

MRS. HELSETH. Yes, I think he said he was called Hekman or something like that.

ROSMER. I don't know anybody by that name.

MRS. HELSETH. He also said his name was Uldrik.

ROSMER [*with a start*]. Ulrik Hetman! Was that it?

MRS. HELSETH. Yes, Hetman, that was it.

KROLL. I seem to have heard that name before. . . .

REBECCA. Surely that was the name he used to write under, wasn't it, that strange man. . . ?

ROSMER [*to* KROLL]. It is Ulrik Brendel's pen-name.

KROLL. That waster Ulrik Brendel. So it is.

REBECCA. So he is still alive.

ROSMER. I thought he was on tour with some theatrical company.

KROLL. The last I heard of him he was in the workhouse.

ROSMER. Ask him to come in, Mrs. Helseth.

MRS. HELSETH. Very good, sir. [*She goes out.*]

KROLL. You are not really going to let this man into your house?

ROSMER. He was once my tutor, you know.

KROLL. Yes, I know that he went and crammed your head full of revolutionary ideas, and that your father drove him out of the house with a horsewhip.

ROSMER [*rather bitterly*]. Even at home Father was very much the major.

KROLL. You should thank him for that in his grave, my dear Rosmer. Well!

[MRS. HELSETH *opens the door on the right for* ULRIK BRENDEL *and then goes out, shutting the door. He is an impressive figure, with grey hair and beard, rather gaunt, but alert and vigorous. He is dressed like a common tramp. Threadbare frock-coat, down at heel, no sign of a shirt. He is wearing old black gloves, and carries a dirty soft hat crumpled under his arm and a walking stick in his hand.*]

BRENDEL [*first hesitates, then walks quickly over to* KROLL *with his hand outstretched*]. Good evening, Johannes!

KROLL. I beg your pardon. . . .

BRENDEL. You never expected to see me again, did you? Not inside these hated walls?

KROLL. I beg your pardon, but . . . [*points*] . . . over there.

BRENDEL [*turns round*]. Quite right. There we have him. Johannes . . . my boy . . . my well-beloved. . . .

ROSMER [*shakes his hand*]. My dear old teacher!

BRENDEL. In spite of certain memories, I felt I could not pass Rosmersholm without paying you a fleeting visit.

ROSMER. You are heartily welcome here now. Of that you may be sure.

BRENDEL. And this charming lady? [*Bows.*] Your lady wife, of course.

ROSMER. Miss West.

BRENDEL. A close relative, presumably. And yonder gentleman whom I do not know? A colleague, I see.

ROSMER. Mr. Kroll, headmaster of the grammar school.

BRENDEL. Kroll? Kroll? Wait a moment. Did you do languages when you were a student?

KROLL. Certainly I did.

BRENDEL. *Donnerwetter*, then I know you!

KROLL. I beg your pardon. . . .

BRENDEL. Weren't you . . .

KROLL. I beg your pardon. . . .

BRENDEL. . . . one of those paragons of virtue that had me thrown out of the Debating Society?

KROLL. That may well be. But I disclaim any closer acquaintance with you.

BRENDEL. All right! *Nach Belieben, Herr Doktor.* It doesn't make the slightest difference to me. Ulrik Brendel will remain the man he is, just the same.

REBECCA. I take it you are on your way to town, Mr. Brendel?

BRENDEL. Exactly, my good lady. At certain recurrent intervals I am compelled to exert myself in the battle for life. That is not something I enjoy doing; but ... *enfin* ... compelling necessity. ...

ROSMER. But my dear Mr. Brendel, won't you please let me give you something to help you out? Help you in some way or other, I mean. ...

BRENDEL. Ha! The very idea! Do you want to defile the bond that links us? Never, Johannes, never!

ROSMER. But what were you thinking of doing in town? Believe me, you won't find it easy. ...

BRENDEL. Leave that to me, my boy. The die is cast. What you see standing before you is one who has embarked on a great campaign, greater by far than all my previous enterprises put together. [*To* KROLL.] May I be allowed to inquire of the Herr Professor—*unter uns*—is there any reasonably decent and respectable and capacious meeting hall in your esteemed town?

KROLL. The biggest is in the Working Men's Institute.

BRENDEL. And has my learned friend any inside influence in this no doubt admirable institution?

KROLL. I have nothing whatever to do with it.

REBECCA [*to* BRENDEL]. You'll have to apply to Peter Mortensgaard.

BRENDEL. *Pardon, madame* ... and what sort of idiot is he?

ROSMER. What makes you think he is an idiot?

BRENDEL. Can't I tell straight away from his name that he is nothing but a plebeian.

KROLL. That's an answer I hadn't expected.

BRENDEL. But I shall control my feelings. There's nothing else for it. When one comes—as I have come—to a turning point in one's career. . . . That's settled. I shall make contact with this individual . . . initiate direct negotiations. . . .

ROSMER. Are you in earnest about having reached a turning point?

BRENDEL. Does my young friend not know that no matter where Ulrik Brendel is, he is always in earnest? Yes, Johannes, I am going to put on a new man . . . throw off this modesty and reserve I have hitherto observed.

ROSMER. How. . . ?

BRENDEL. I shall lay hold on life with eager hands . . . I shall step forth . . . mount up. It is the air of a tempestuous, cataclysmic age we breathe. . . . I intend now to place my mite on the altar of liberty.

KROLL. You too?

BRENDEL [*to them all*]. Is the general public here in any way acquainted with my occasional writings?

KROLL. No, quite frankly I must admit that . . .

REBECCA. I have read quite a number of them. My foster-father had them.

BRENDEL. Then, my dear lady, you have been wasting your time. They are just so much trash, I tell you.

REBECCA. Really?

BRENDEL. Those you have read, yes. My really important works are known to nobody, man or woman. Not a soul . . . except myself.

REBECCA. How is that?

BRENDEL. Because they are unwritten.

ROSMER. But my dear Mr. Brendel . . .

BRENDEL. You know, my dear Johannes, that I am a bit of a sybarite, a gourmet. Have been all my days. I like to take my pleasures in solitude. For then I enjoy them twice as much. So you see, whenever golden dreams came over me . . . enveloping me . . . whenever new ideas were born within me, dazzling, audacious . . . when I felt the rush of their beating wings . . . these things I formed into poems and visions and images. In rough outline, as it were, you understand.

ROSMER. Yes, of course.

BRENDEL. Oh, what passions, what rapture have I known in my time, Johannes! The mysterious bliss of creation . . . in rough outline, as I said . . . the applause, the gratitude, the eulogies, the laurel crowns . . . all this I have abundantly gathered in with glad and trembling hands. Indulged myself in secret fantasies that my mind reeled with ecstasy. . . .

KROLL. Hm!

ROSMER. But you never wrote it down?

BRENDEL. Not a word! I have always felt quite nauseated at the thought of solemnly writing it all out. And anyway, why should I profane my own ideals when I could enjoy them in all their purity, and keep them to myself? But now they shall be sacrificed. In truth, I feel like a mother who gives her young daughters into the arms of their husbands. But sacrifice them I shall—sacrifice them on the altar of liberty. A series of well-conceived lectures . . . over the whole country. . . !

REBECCA [*animatedly*]. How splendid of you, Mr. Brendel! You are giving the most precious thing you have.

ROSMER. The only thing.

REBECCA [*looks significantly at* ROSMER]. How many are there who do that? *Dare* do that?

ROSMER [*returns the look*]. Who knows?

BRENDEL. My audience is touched. That comforts my heart . . . and strengthens my will. And with that I thereby proceed to action. Yet there is *one* thing. . . . [*To* KROLL.] Can you tell me, my dear sir, whether there is such a thing as a Temperance Society in town? For total abstainers? Yes, of course, there must be.

KROLL. Yes, there is. I am its president, at your service.

BRENDEL. As if I couldn't tell by looking at you! Well, it is not impossible that I may look in on you and enrol myself for a week.

KROLL. You must forgive me—but we don't accept members by the week.

BRENDEL. *A la bonne heure*, my good sir! Ulrik Brendel never comes knocking round the door of societies of that kind. [*Turns.*] But I must not outstay my welcome in this house, so rich in memories. I must go to town and select a suitable lodging. There is, I presume, a decent hotel?

REBECCA. Won't you have a drink to warm you up before you go?

BRENDEL. How do you mean, gracious lady—to warm me up?

REBECCA. A cup of tea, or . . .

BRENDEL. To my generous hostess, my thanks. But I cannot impose any longer on private hospitality. [*Waves his hand.*] Farewell, good people. [*Goes towards the door but turns.*] Oh, by the way . . . Johannes . . . Pastor Rosmer, could you for old time's sake do your former tutor a favour?

ROSMER. With the greatest of pleasure.

BRENDEL. Good. Could you . . . for a day or two . . . lend me a clean dress shirt?

ROSMER. Is that all!

BRENDEL. You see I am travelling on foot . . . this time. My trunk is being sent on.

ROSMER. Of course. But is there nothing else, then?

BRENDEL. Well, as a matter of fact, there is. . . . Perhaps you could spare an old overcoat you have done with?

ROSMER. Yes, yes, certainly I can.

BRENDEL. And if there happened to be a decent pair of boots to go with the overcoat. . . .

ROSMER. We'll manage that too. We'll send them on as soon as we know your address.

BRENDEL. I wouldn't dream of it! All that inconvenience on my account. I can easily take these few odd things along with me.

ROSMER. Very well. Just come upstairs with me.

REBECCA. Let me go. Mrs. Helseth and I will see to it.

BRENDEL. I could never think of allowing this distinguished lady to . . .

REBECCA. Oh nonsense. Come along, Mr. Brendel.

[*She goes out to the right.*]

ROSMER [*holds* BRENDEL *back*]. Tell me . . . isn't there anything else I can do for you?

BRENDEL. I can't imagine what else there *could* be. Ah, yes, damn it all, there is . . . now that I think about it. . . ! Johannes . . . you haven't by any chance got eight crowns on you?

ROSMER. Let me see. [*Opens his purse.*] I have a couple of ten crown notes.

BRENDEL. Well, well, never mind. I'll just take those. I can always get them changed in town. Meanwhile, thanks very much. Don't forget, it was two ten crowns I got. Good night, Johannes, my own dear boy! And a respectful good night to you, sir!

[*He goes out to the right, where* ROSMER *takes leave of him and shuts the door behind him.*]

KROLL. Good God. . . . So that is the Ulrik Brendel people once believed would make something of himself in the world.

ROSMER [*quietly*]. At least he has had the courage to live his life in his own way. I don't think *that's* such a small thing after all.

KROLL. What! A life like his! I almost believe he's the sort who could turn your ideas upside down all over again.

ROSMER. Oh, no. Now I have got all my ideas straightened out.

KROLL. If only I could believe that, my dear Rosmer. You are so terribly impressionable in many ways.

ROSMER. Let us sit down. I want to talk to you.

KROLL. By all means.

[*They sit down on the sofa.*]

ROSMER [*after a pause*]. Don't you think it is nice and comfortable out here?

KROLL. Yes, it certainly is nice and comfortable—and peaceful. Yes, you have got yourself a home, Rosmer. And I have lost mine.

ROSMER. My dear friend, don't say that. The wound will always heal again.

KROLL. Never, never, the sting will always rankle. Things can never be as they were before.

ROSMER. I want you to listen to me, Kroll. We two have been close friends for many, many years now. Can you ever imagine our friendship finishing up on the rocks?

KROLL. I can't imagine anything in the world ever coming between us. Whatever has put this into your mind?

ROSMER. Because obviously it's immensely important to you to have your friends holding the same views and opinions as you.

KROLL. Well, yes. But we two are pretty well agreed. On the big questions, at any rate.

ROSMER [*quietly*]. No, not any longer.

KROLL [*makes to jump up*]. What is that!

ROSMER [*restraining him*]. You must sit still. I beg you, Kroll.

KROLL. What is all this? I don't understand you. Tell me straight.

ROSMER. In my mind, it is high summer once more. I see with a new youthful vision. And therefore I have taken my stand. . . .

KROLL. Where? Where do you stand?

ROSMER. Where your children stand.

KROLL. You? You! Surely it is impossible! Where, do you say?

ROSMER. I take my stand on the same side as Lauritz and Hilda.

KROLL [*bows his head*]. A renegade! Johannes Rosmer a renegade!

ROSMER. I ought to have been so glad, so sublimely happy, being what you call a renegade. But I suffered greatly, all the same, because I knew well enough it would come as a bitter disappointment to you.

KROLL. Rosmer . . . Rosmer! I shall never get over this. [*Looks sadly at him.*] Oh, to think that even you should want to lend yourself to the work of corrupting and perverting this unhappy country.

ROSMER. It is the work of liberation I want to take part in.

KROLL. Oh yes. That's what it's called both by those at the top and their poor dupes. But do you really think any sort of liberation can be expected from the doctrines now busy poisoning our whole social life?

ROSMER. I am no supporter of any prevailing doctrine, nor indeed of either side in the dispute. I want to try to bring men together from all sides. As many and as sincerely, as I can. I will devote my life and all my strength to this one thing: to create a true democracy in this land.

KROLL. Don't you think we have enough democracy already? For my part I think the whole lot of us are well on the way to being dragged down into the mud where the only ones to thrive are the common people.

ROSMER. That is precisely what makes me define the true aim of democracy.

KROLL. What is that?

ROSMER. To make all my countrymen noblemen.

KROLL. All. . . .

ROSMER. As many as possible, anyway.

KROLL. By what means?

ROSMER. By liberating their minds and purifying their wills, I should say.

KROLL. Rosmer, you are a dreamer. Are *you* going to liberate them? Are *you* going to purify them?

ROSMER. No, my dear friend. I only want to try and rouse them to it. As for *doing* it, that is their own affair.

KROLL. And you think they can?

ROSMER. Yes.

KROLL. And by their own power?

ROSMER. Exactly! By their own power! There is no other.

KROLL [*rises*]. Are these words that befit a clergyman?

ROSMER. I am no longer a clergyman.

KROLL. Yes, but . . . the religion you were brought up to. . . ?

ROSMER. Is no longer mine.

KROLL. No longer . . . !

ROSMER [*rises*]. I have given it up. I *had* to give it up, Kroll.

KROLL [*controlling his agitation*]. Indeed. Yes, yes. The two things doubtless go together. . . . Was that the reason you left the service of the church?

ROSMER. Yes. As soon as I had straightened out my ideas . . . when I was absolutely certain that it wasn't just some temporary aberration but instead something that I could not and would not escape from—then I left.

KROLL. And it has been working up inside you all this time. And we, your friends, were given no hint of it. Rosmer, Rosmer, how could you hide the sorrowful truth from us!

ROSMER. Because I thought it was something that concerned nobody but myself. And I didn't want to cause you or any of my other friends any unnecessary sorrow. I thought I could go on living here as before, quietly and happily. I wanted to read and to bury myself in all those works that had previously been closed books to me. To make myself thoroughly familiar with that great world of truth and freedom that has now been revealed to me.

KROLL. Apostasy! Every word proves it. But what makes you want to confess this secret apostasy at all? And why *now* exactly?

ROSMER. You yourself made me do it, Kroll.

KROLL. *I* made you. . . !

ROSMER. When I heard how violently you had been carrying on at the public meetings . . . when I read about all the uncharitable speeches you made there . . . all the hateful things you said about the people on the other side . . . the sneers, the contempt of your opponents . . . Oh, Kroll . . . how could you turn like that! There was no escaping my duty. In the present struggle men are growing evil. Their minds must be given a sense of peace and happiness and conciliation. That is why I now stand forth and openly confess to being what I am. I too want to try out my powers. Couldn't you . . . from your side . . . stand by me, Kroll?

KROLL. Never as long as I live will I compromise with these subversive forces in society.

ROSMER. Then let us at least fight with honourable weapons—since fight we must.

KROLL. Any man who is not with me in these critical matters, I want nothing whatever to do with. Nor do I owe him any consideration.

ROSMER. Does that also mean me?

KROLL. It is you who have broken with me, Rosmer.

ROSMER. *Is* this a breach then?

KROLL. This! It is a breach with all those who have previously stood by you. Now you must take the consequences.

[REBECCA WEST *comes in from the right and opens the door wide.*]

REBECCA. There we are. He is on his way now to his great sacrificial feast. Now we can have our supper. Won't you come in, Mr. Kroll?

KROLL [*takes his hat*]. Good night, Miss West. There is nothing more to keep me here.

REBECCA [*eagerly*]. What is this? [*Shuts the door and goes nearer.*] Have you told him. . . ?

ROSMER. Now he knows.

KROLL. We will not let you get away, Rosmer. We will force you back on our side again.

ROSMER. I shall never come back.

KROLL. We shall see. You are not the man to hold out alone.

ROSMER. I shall not be entirely alone, after all. There are two of us to bear the loneliness.

KROLL. Ah. . . ! [*A suspicion seems to cross his mind.*] Even that too! Beata's very words!

ROSMER. Beata. . . ?

KROLL [*dismissing the thought*]. No, no . . . that wasn't nice. . . . Forgive me.

ROSMER. What? What wasn't nice?

KROLL. No, let us not talk about it. Ugh! Forgive me. Goodbye!

[*He goes towards the hall door.*]

ROSMER [*follows him*]. Kroll! Things must not end like this between us. I'll look in on you tomorrow.

KROLL [*in the entrance hall, turns*]. You shall not set foot in my house.

[*He takes his stick and goes.* ROSMER *stands for a moment in the open door, then he shuts it and goes over to the table.*]

ROSMER. Never mind, Rebecca. We'll manage all right, we two firm friends. You and I.

REBECCA. What do you think he meant, Johannes, when he said 'That wasn't nice'?

ROSMER. Don't worry about that, my dear. He himself didn't really believe what he thought. But I'll look in and see him tomorrow. Good night!

REBECCA. You are not going up early again tonight? After this?

ROSMER. Tonight, as every night. I feel so relieved now that it is all over. You see, I am quite calm. And you, my dear Rebecca, you mustn't get upset either. Good night!

REBECCA. Good night, my dear. Sleep well.

[ROSMER *goes out by the hall door, and is then heard climbing the stairs.* REBECCA *walks over and pulls a bell-pull beside the stove. Shortly after* MRS. HELSETH *comes in from the right.*]

REBECCA. You might as well clear the table again, Mrs. Helseth. The pastor doesn't want anything . . . and the headmaster has gone home.

MRS. HELSETH. The headmaster gone! What was the matter with him, then?

REBECCA [*takes her crochet work*]. He thought it was blowing up for a storm. . . .

MRS. HELSETH. That's funny. There isn't a cloud in the sky tonight.

REBECCA. As long as he doesn't meet the White Horse, that's all. Because I am afraid it won't be long before we hear again from some of these spooks of yours.

MRS. HELSETH. God forgive you, miss! Don't say such dreadful things.

REBECCA. Well, well. . . .

MRS. HELSETH [*in a lower voice*]. Do you really think that somebody here is meant to go soon?

REBECCA. Of course not! I don't think anything of the sort. But there are so many kinds of White Horses in the world, Mrs. Helseth. Well, good night, I'm going to my room now.

MRS. HELSETH. Good night, miss.

[REBECCA *takes her crochet work and goes out right.*]

MRS. HELSETH [*turns down the lamp, shakes her head and mutters to herself*]. Lord! . . . Lord! . . . That Miss West. The things she says sometimes.

ACT TWO

JOHANNES ROSMER's *study. The way into it is through a door, left. At the back is a doorway with a curtain drawn back, leading to his bedroom. Right, a window, and in front of it a writing-table covered with books and papers. Bookshelves and cupboards line the walls. Simply furnished. Left, an old-fashioned sofa, with a table in front of it.* ROSMER, *in a smoking-jacket, is sitting on a high-backed chair at the writing-table. He is cutting the pages of a periodical, pausing now and again to read it. There is a knock on the door on the left.*

ROSMER [*without turning round*]. Come in.

[REBECCA WEST *enters, in a dressing-gown.*]

REBECCA. Good morning.

ROSMER [*thumbing through his book*]. Good morning, my dear. Was there something you wanted?

REBECCA. I just wanted to ask if you had slept well.

ROSMER. Oh, I had such a lovely deep sleep. No dreams. . . . [*Turns.*] And you?

REBECCA. Yes, thanks . . . eventually, in the early hours of the morning. . . .

ROSMER. I can't remember feeling as light-hearted as this for a long time. Oh, what a good thing I got it off my chest.

REBECCA. Yes, you shouldn't have kept it to yourself so long, Johannes.

ROSMER. I can't understand how I could be such a coward.

REBECCA. Well, it wasn't exactly cowardice. . . .

ROSMER. Oh yes, it was. When I look closely at things, I can see it was partly cowardice.

REBECCA. All the more courageous of you then to make a clean break. [*Sits down on a chair beside him at the writing-table.*] But now I want to tell you something I've done . . . but you mustn't be angry with me about it.

ROSMER. Angry? My dear, whatever makes you think . . . ?

REBECCA. Yes, because I did perhaps rather take it upon myself.

ROSMER. Well, let me hear it then.

REBECCA. Last night, when this man Ulrik Brendel was leaving . . . I wrote him two or three lines to give to Mortensgaard.

ROSMER [*rather doubtfully*]. But, my dear Rebecca. . . . Well, what did you say then?

REBECCA. I said that if he could do anything for this unfortunate man, and help him in any way, he would be doing you a service.

ROSMER. My dear, you shouldn't have done that. You won't have done Brendel any good by it. And Mortensgaard is a man I would much rather keep away from. You remember the business I had with him once before.

REBECCA. But don't you think it might be as well to be on good terms with him again?

ROSMER. Me? With Mortensgaard? Whatever makes you think that?

REBECCA. Well, because things might be a bit uncertain now, you know . . . now this business has arisen between you and your friends.

ROSMER [*looks at her and shakes his head*]. You don't really imagine that Kroll or the others would feel in any way vindictive. . . ?

REBECCA. In their first flush of anger, my dear . . . nobody can be sure. After the way Mr. Kroll took it . . .

ROSMER. Oh, you know him better than that, surely. Kroll is every inch a gentleman. I am going to town this afternoon to have a talk with him. I want to talk to them all. Oh, it will all be all right, you'll see. . . .

[MRS. HELSETH *appears at the door, left.*]

REBECCA [*gets up*]. What is it, Mrs. Helseth?

MRS. HELSETH. Mr. Kroll is downstairs in the hall.

ROSMER [*gets up quickly*]. Kroll!

REBECCA. Mr. Kroll! Well!

MRS. HELSETH. He asked if he could come up and have a word with the pastor.

ROSMER [*to* REBECCA]. What did I tell you! Of course he can. [*Goes to the door and shouts down the stairs.*] Do come up, my dear fellow. I am delighted to see you.

[ROSMER *stands holding the door open.* MRS. HELSETH *goes.* REBECCA *draws the curtain over the doorway, then tidies up the room a little.* KROLL *enters, carrying his hat.*]

ROSMER [*quietly, with emotion*]. I knew it . . . knew it couldn't be the last time. . . .

KROLL. Today I see things in an altogether different light from yesterday.

ROSMER. Yes, of course you do, Kroll, don't you? Now that you have had time to give it more thought. . . .

KROLL. You completely misunderstand me. [*Puts his hat on the table near the sofa.*] It is important I talk to you alone.

ROSMER. Why can't Miss West . . . ?

REBECCA. No, no, Mr. Rosmer. I'll go.

KROLL [*looks her up and down.*] You must excuse me, Miss West, for calling so early in the morning . . . for catching you unawares before you had time to . . .

REBECCA [*surprised*]. What do you mean? Do you think it's not right I should wear a dressing-gown about the house?

KROLL. Heaven forbid! I have, of course, no idea what the done thing is now at Rosmersholm.

ROSMER. But, Kroll . . . you are like a different person today.

REBECCA. Good morning to you, Mr. Kroll.

[*She goes out left.*]

KROLL. If you will allow me. . . . [*He sits down on the sofa.*]

ROSMER. Yes, my dear fellow, let's sit down together comfortably and talk things over. [*He sits down in a chair facing* KROLL.]

KROLL. I didn't sleep a wink last night. I lay awake the whole night, thinking and thinking.

ROSMER. And what do you say today?

KROLL. It's a long story, Rosmer. Let me begin with a sort of introduction. I can give you a short report about Ulrik Brendel.

ROSMER. Has he been to see you?

KROLL. No. He settled himself in a low public house, in the lowest of company, of course, drinking and standing drinks as long as his money lasted. Then he began abusing the whole company as a lot of riff-raff—in which incidentally he was quite right—whereupon they set on him and threw him out into the gutter.

ROSMER. It seems he is quite incorrigible.

KROLL. He had also pawned your coat, but they say that has been redeemed for him. Can you guess by whom?

ROSMER. By you yourself, perhaps?

KROLL. No. By our worthy Mr. Mortensgaard.

ROSMER. Indeed.

KROLL. I have been given to understand that Mr. Brendel's first call was upon this 'idiot' and 'plebeian'.

ROSMER. Well, it was very lucky for him. . . .

KROLL. Indeed it was. [*Leans over the table towards* ROSMER.] But that brings us to something which—for the sake of our old . . . our former friendship—it is my duty to warn you about.

ROSMER. My dear fellow, whatever can *that* be?

KROLL. I'll tell you: some game or other is going on in this house behind your back.

ROSMER. What makes you think that? Is it Reb . . . is it Miss West you are referring to?

KROLL. Exactly. I can well understand her point of view. She's been used to having her way so long now in this place. But all the same . . .

ROSMER. My dear Kroll, you are completely mistaken about this. She and I—we have no secrets from each other about anything in the world.

KROLL. Has she confessed, then, that she has been in correspondence with the editor of the *Beacon*?

ROSMER. Oh, you are referring to the few lines she wrote for Ulrik Brendel to take.

KROLL. So you are on to that. And do you approve of her thus forming an association with that scandalmonger who week after week sets out to make a laughing stock of me, both as a schoolmaster and as a public figure?

ROSMER. My dear Kroll, I am sure that side of things never once occurred to her. And in any case, she is a completely free agent, of course, just as I am.

KROLL. Indeed? I take it that's another of these new ideas you have gone in for. I suppose Miss West takes the same view of things as you?

ROSMER. She does. We two have advanced together, trusting in each other.

KROLL [*looks at him and slowly shakes his head*]. Oh, you poor, blind, dupe!

ROSMER. Me? What makes you say a thing like that?

KROLL. Because I dare not . . . *will* not think the worst. No, no, let me finish. You really do value my friendship, don't you, Rosmer? And my respect, too? Don't you?

ROSMER. Surely I don't have to answer that question.

KROLL. All right. But there are other things that do demand an answer . . . a full explanation from you. Would you be willing to submit to a sort of interrogation. . . ?

ROSMER. Interrogation?

KROLL. Yes . . . to let me ask some questions about one or two things that you might find it painful to be reminded of? For instance, this business of your apostasy . . . well, your emancipation, as you like to call it. . . . It's all bound up with so many other things that you must, for your own sake, try to explain.

ROSMER. My dear Kroll, ask about whatever you like. I have nothing to hide.

KROLL. Tell me then . . . what do you think in fact was the *real* reason why Beata went and put an end to her life?

ROSMER. Can you be in any doubt about that? Or rather is it possible to inquire into the reasons why a sick unhappy woman of unsound mind does what she does?

KROLL. Are you certain that Beata really was of unsound mind? The doctors at any rate thought perhaps it wasn't certain.

ROSMER. If the doctors had ever seen her as I so often saw her, day and night, they would never have had any doubt.

KROLL. Nor had I, then.

ROSMER. Oh, no! There wasn't a shadow of doubt, I regret to say. I told you, didn't I, about her wild fits of sensual passion . . . which she expected me to respond to. Oh! how she appalled me. And then there was the way she used to reproach herself quite unnecessarily about certain things towards the end.

KROLL. Yes, when she had been told that she would never have any children.

ROSMER. Well, I put it to you. . . . All this dreadful agony of mind about something that wasn't her fault at all. . . ! And is she really supposed to have been in her right mind?

KROLL. Hm! Can you remember if you had any books in the house at the time dealing with the institution of marriage, giving the modern, advanced view.

ROSMER. I remember Miss West did lend me a book of that sort. She inherited Dr. West's library. But my dear Kroll, you could never imagine we were so thoughtless as to let the poor ailing creature get hold of ideas like that? I give you my solemn assurance we are not to blame. It was her own disordered mind that drove her to those wild aberrations.

KROLL. One thing, however, I can now tell you. And that is that poor Beata, tormented and over-wrought, put an end to her own life so that you might be happy . . . and free to live your own life as you wanted.

ROSMER [*half rising from his chair*]. What do you mean by that?

KROLL. Listen to me quietly, Rosmer. Now I can speak about it. Twice in the last twelve months before her death she came to see me, and she poured out all her feelings of agony and despair.

ROSMER. About what you just said?

KROLL. No, the first time she came, she declared you were well on the way to apostasy. That you were going to abandon the faith of your fathers.

ROSMER [*eagerly*]. What you are saying is impossible, Kroll. Quite impossible! You must be mistaken.

KROLL. Why is that?

ROSMER. Because while Beata was alive I was still wrestling with my own doubts. It was a fight I fought alone and in utter secrecy. I don't even believe that Rebecca . . .

KROLL. Rebecca?

ROSMER. Well, then . . . Miss West. I call her Rebecca for convenience.

KROLL. So I have noticed.

ROSMER. That's why I find it quite incomprehensible that anything of the kind should ever have occurred to Beata. And why didn't she talk to me about it? She never did, never a single word.

KROLL. Poor soul. She begged and implored me to speak to you.

ROSMER. And why didn't you?

KROLL. Do you think at that time I doubted for one moment that she might not have been out of her mind. An accusation of that kind against a man like you! And then . . . it must have been about a month after . . . she came again. This time she looked a bit calmer.

But as she was leaving she said: 'They can expect to see the White Horse at Rosmersholm again soon.'

ROSMER. Yes, yes. The White Horse—she was always talking about that.

KROLL. And when I tried to distract her from these morbid ideas, she just answered: 'I haven't much time left. Because now Johannes must marry Rebecca at once.'

ROSMER [*almost speechless*]. What did you say? I marry . . . !

KROLL. That was the Thursday afternoon. On the Saturday evening she threw herself off the bridge into the millstream.

ROSMER. And you never warned us!

KROLL. You knew yourself how often she used to make remarks about not having long to live.

ROSMER. I know. But all the same, you *should* have warned us!

KROLL. I did think of it. But by then it was too late.

ROSMER. And all this time you didn't . . . ? Why have you kept quiet about all this?

KROLL. What was the good of coming here and worrying you and upsetting you still more. Naturally I took it all as a mere figment of her disordered brain. Until yesterday evening.

ROSMER. And now you think differently?

KROLL. Didn't Beata see things clearly enough when she said you were going to abandon the faith you were brought up to?

ROSMER. Yes, that I don't understand. I find that absolutely incomprehensible.

KROLL. Incomprehensible or not, there it is. And now I ask you, Rosmer, how much truth is there in that other accusation of hers? In the last one, I mean?

ROSMER. Accusation? Was that an accusation?

KROLL. Perhaps you didn't notice how it was phrased. She wanted to go, she said. . . . Why? Well?

ROSMER. So that I might marry Rebecca. . . .

KROLL. That wasn't quite the way it was put. Beata expressed herself rather differently. She said, 'I haven't much time left. Because now Johannes must marry Rebecca at once.'

ROSMER [*looks at him for a moment, then rises*]. Now I understand you, Kroll.

KROLL. Well, then? What is your answer?

ROSMER [*quietly and controlled*]. To anything so absolutely unheard-of. . . ! The only proper answer would be to point to the door.

KROLL [*rises*]. Very well.

ROSMER [*stands facing him*]. Listen to me. For over a year now—in fact ever since Beata died—Rebecca West and I have lived on here at Rosmersholm alone. All that time you have known of Beata's charge against us. But never at any time have I observed the slightest sign that you disapproved of Rebecca and me living here together.

KROLL. I didn't know until last night that it was a question of an apostate and . . . an emancipated woman living under one roof.

ROSMER. Ah. . . ! So you don't think there is any sense of virtue to be found among free-thinkers? Doesn't it strike you they might have a natural instinct for morality?

KROLL. I don't place much reliance on any kind of morality that is not rooted in the faith of the Church.

ROSMER. And you include Rebecca and me in that too? My relations with Rebecca. . . !

KROLL. I cannot bring myself, merely on your account, to abandon my view that there is no tremendous gulf between free-thinking and . . . hm!

ROSMER. And what?

KROLL. . . . and free-love, if you must have it.

ROSMER [*gently*]. And you have no shame in saying that to me? You who have known me since I was a boy.

KROLL. That's exactly why. I know how easily you are influenced by those you associate with. And this Rebecca of yours . . . well, Miss West, then . . . we don't really know very much about her. I tell

you straight, Rosmer, I'm not letting you go. And you yourself . . .
you must try and save yourself while there's time.

ROSMER. Save myself? What . . . ?

[MRS. HELSETH *looks in through the door on the left.*]

ROSMER. What do you want?

MRS. HELSETH. I wanted to ask Miss West if she would come downstairs.

ROSMER. Miss West is not up here.

MRS. HELSETH. Isn't she? [*Looks about her.*] That's funny. [*She goes.*]

ROSMER. You were saying . . . ?

KROLL. Listen. Whatever went on here in secret while Beata was still
alive . . . and whatever is still going on here . . . I don't want to
inquire into any further. Your marriage was admittedly a very
unhappy one. And in one way that might well be taken as an
excuse. . . .

ROSMER. Oh, how little you really know me. . . !

KROLL. Don't interrupt me. What I want to say is this: if you *must* go
on living here with Miss West, then it's absolutely essential that
this change of heart of yours—this tragic defection she has led you
into—is kept hushed up. Let me speak! Let me speak! What I say
is this: if this madness must go on, then in Heaven's name go ahead
and *think* whatever you like . . . about anything under the sun. But
see that you keep your opinions to yourself. After all it's a purely
personal affair. There's no necessity to go shouting a thing like that
all over the countryside.

ROSMER. But there *is* a necessity for me to extricate myself from a
false and ambiguous position.

KROLL. But you have a duty towards the traditions of your family,
Rosmer. Remember that. Since time immemorial Rosmersholm has
been like a stronghold of order and high thinking . . . of respect and
esteem for all those things which are accepted and acknowledged by
the best people in our society. If ever the rumour got about that
you yourself had abandoned what I might call the Rosmer tradition,
it would lead to disastrous and irreparable confusion.

ROSMER. My dear Kroll, I cannot bring myself to see the matter in that light. To me it seems I have a bounden duty to bring a little light and happiness into those places where the Rosmers have spread gloom and oppression all these long years.

KROLL [*looks sternly at him*]. Yes, that would indeed be an undertaking worthy of the man who is the last of his line. Leave such things alone, Rosmer. You are not cut out for that sort of work. You were made for the academic life.

ROSMER. Yes, that may be so. But now I also want to take part in the battle of life.

KROLL. The battle of life . . . do you know what that will mean for you? It means a fight to the death against every one of your friends.

ROSMER [*quietly*]. I don't suppose they are all such fanatics as you.

KROLL. You are a gullible creature, Rosmer. Inexperienced, that's what you are. You have no idea of the fury of the storm that will break over your head.

[MRS. HELSETH *puts her head through the door, left.*]

MRS. HELSETH. Miss West would like to know . . .

ROSMER. What is it?

MRS. HELSETH. There's a man downstairs who would like a word with the pastor.

ROSMER. Is it the man who was here last night?

MRS. HELSETH. No, it's Mortensgaard.

ROSMER. Mortensgaard!

KROLL. Aha! So it's come to that, has it? Already!

ROSMER. What does he want with me? Why didn't you send him away?

MRS. HELSETH. Miss West told me to ask if he was to come up.

ROSMER. Tell him there's somebody here. . . .

KROLL [*to* MRS. HELSETH]. Let him come up.

[MRS. HELSETH *goes.*]

KROLL [*takes his hat*]. I quit the field—for the time being. But the main action is still to be fought.

ROSMER. As true as I stand here, Kroll . . . I have nothing to do with Mortensgaard.

KROLL. I don't believe you any more. Not in anything. Not on any matter at all can I believe you after this. Now it is war to the knife. We must see if we cannot render you harmless.

ROSMER. Oh, Kroll . . . how low you have sunk!

KROLL. I? You can talk! Remember Beata!

ROSMER. Are you going to bring that up all over again?

KROLL. No. The mystery of the millstream you must try to solve in the light of your own conscience . . . if you still have one.

[PETER MORTENSGAARD *enters softly and quietly through the door on the left. He is a small, slightly-built man with reddish hair and beard.*]

KROLL [*with a look of hate*]. So! The *Beacon*, eh! Burning at Rosmersholm. [*Buttons his coat.*] Well, now I can have no doubt about what course to steer.

MORTENSGAARD [*quietly*]. The *Beacon* will always be burning to guide Mr. Kroll home.

KROLL. Yes, you have given plenty of evidence of your good will. Actually, one of the Commandments does tell us that we shouldn't bear false witness against our neighbour. . . .

MORTENSGAARD. You don't have to teach me about the Commandments, Mr. Kroll.

KROLL. Not even the Seventh?

ROSMER. Kroll!

MORTENSGAARD. If anybody had to do it, then the obvious person would be the pastor here.

KROLL [*with suppressed scorn*]. The pastor? Yes, Pastor Rosmer is without doubt the obvious person for *that*. I wish you a profitable discussion, gentlemen.

[*He goes out, slamming the door after him.*]

ROSMER [*stares fixedly at the door, and speaks to himself*]. Well, well. . . . So be it then. [*Turns.*] Now will you tell me, Mr. Mortensgaard, what brings you out here to see me?

MORTENSGAARD. Actually, it was Miss West I was looking for. I felt I had to thank her for the kind letter I got from her yesterday.

ROSMER. I know she wrote to you. Have you had a word with her?

MORTENSGAARD. Yes, for a minute. [*With a slight smile.*] I hear that certain ideas have changed out here at Rosmersholm.

ROSMER. My ideas have changed about quite a lot of things. I might almost say . . . about everything.

MORTENSGAARD. That's what Miss West said. And that's why she thought I had better come up and have a little talk with you about certain things.

ROSMER. About what things, Mr. Mortensgaard?

MORTENSGAARD. Can I put it in the *Beacon* about you changing your ideas . . . that you support the radical progressive policy?

ROSMER. Certainly you may. Indeed I'd even go so far as to *ask* you to put it in.

MORTENSGAARD. It will be in first thing in the morning. It's news of considerable importance when Pastor Rosmer of Rosmersholm takes the view that he can seek the light in the other sense as well.

ROSMER. I don't altogether understand you.

MORTENSGAARD. What I mean is that it contributes to the moral backing of our party every time we get a supporter with serious Christian principles.

ROSMER [*in some surprise*]. Then you don't know . . . ? Didn't Miss West tell you *that* as well?

MORTENSGAARD. Tell me what, Pastor Rosmer? Miss West was in rather a hurry. She told me to come upstairs and hear the rest from you.

ROSMER. Then I must tell you that my emancipation is total. In all things. I have severed all connection with the teachings of the Church. From now on, such things are of absolutely no concern to me.

MORTENSGAARD [*looks at him in amazement*]. Never! If the moon fell out of the sky, I couldn't be more . . . ! Even the pastor himself renouncing . . .

ROSMER. Yes, I have reached the same stage that you reached long ago. So you can announce *that* in the *Beacon*, too.

MORTENSGAARD. That too? No, my dear pastor. Forgive me, but there's no point in mentioning that aspect of the thing.

ROSMER. Not mention it?

MORTENSGAARD. Not to begin with, I mean.

ROSMER. But I don't understand. . . .

MORTENSGAARD. Look, Pastor Rosmer. . . . I dare say you are not so familiar with the ins and outs of things as I am. But now that you have come over to the radical cause, and if—as Miss West says— you are thinking of taking an active part in the movement, then I suppose you'll want to do all you possibly can to help.

ROSMER. Yes, I most certainly do.

MORTENSGAARD. Well, I'd better just make clear, Pastor Rosmer, that if you come out with all this about throwing up the Church, it will be like tying your own hands right from the very start.

ROSMER. Do you think so?

MORTENSGAARD. Yes, you can be quite sure there'll not be very much you can do then in these parts. And besides, we've got plenty of free-thinkers already, Pastor Rosmer. I might almost say too many. What the party really needs is Christian elements—something that everybody has to respect. That's what we are badly short of. So the wisest thing for you to do is to keep quiet about any of the things that don't really concern the public. There, that's what I think.

ROSMER. I see. So you wouldn't dare have anything to do with me if I openly confessed my apostasy?

MORTENSGAARD [*shakes his head*]. I wouldn't like to risk it, Pastor Rosmer. Lately I have made it a rule never to support anybody or anything opposed to the Church.

ROSMER. And have you returned to the Church yourself then, of late?

MORTENSGAARD. We needn't go into that.

ROSMER. So that's how it is, then. Yes, now I understand you.

MORTENSGAARD. Pastor Rosmer, you ought to remember that I of all people am not wholly free to act as I wish.

ROSMER. What's stopping you then?

MORTENSGAARD. The thing that stops me is that I am a marked man.

ROSMER. Ah . . . of course.

MORTENSGAARD. A marked man, Pastor Rosmer. You in particular ought to remember that. For you more than anybody else were the person who had me branded.

ROSMER. If I had thought then as I now think, I would have dealt with your transgression much more considerately.

MORTENSGAARD. That I can well imagine. But now it is too late. You have branded me once and for all, branded me for life. I don't suppose you really understand what a thing like that means. But now, perhaps, you will soon see for yourself how painful it feels, Pastor Rosmer.

ROSMER. I?

MORTENSGAARD. Yes, surely you never believe that Kroll and his crowd will show any mercy for the way you have deserted them. And the *County Times* is out for blood, they say. You yourself could quite easily become a marked man, too.

ROSMER. I feel secure against any attack on personal grounds, Mr. Mortensgaard. My conduct cannot be impugned.

MORTENSGAARD [*with a faint smile*]. That's a bold thing to say, Pastor Rosmer.

ROSMER. Perhaps it is. But it is one I feel justified in being so bold about.

MORTENSGAARD. Even if you were to scrutinize your own conduct as thoroughly as you once scrutinized mine?

ROSMER. You say that so strangely. What are you getting at? Is there something specific?

MORTENSGAARD. Yes, there is *one* thing. Just one. But *that* could be bad enough if any of those malicious people on the other side got wind of it.

ROSMER. Be good enough to tell me what this thing is supposed to be.

MORTENSGAARD. Can't you guess, Pastor Rosmer?

ROSMER. No, I can't. I haven't the faintest idea.

MORTENSGAARD. In that case then, I might as well tell you. I have in my possession a strange letter that was written here at Rosmersholm.

ROSMER. Miss West's letter, you mean. Is it so strange?

MORTENSGAARD. No, there's nothing strange about that letter. But I got another letter from this place once.

ROSMER. Also from Miss West?

MORTENSGAARD. No, Pastor Rosmer.

ROSMER. Well, from whom, then? From whom?

MORTENSGAARD. From the late Mrs. Rosmer.

ROSMER. From my wife! *You* got a letter from my wife?

MORTENSGAARD. Yes, I did.

ROSMER. When?

MORTENSGAARD. Not long before she died. It must be about eighteen months ago, now. And that letter is the one that is strange.

ROSMER. You know of course that my wife had had a mental breakdown at that time.

MORTENSGAARD. Yes, I know there were many people who thought that. I doubt if you would think so from the letter. When I say the letter is strange, I mean in a different sense.

ROSMER. And what on earth did my poor wife want to write to you about?

MORTENSGAARD. I have the letter at home. She begins by saying more or less that she is living in fear and trembling; there are so many wicked people in the district, she says; and all these people think about is what harm they can do you.

ROSMER. Me?

MORTENSGAARD. So she said. And then came the strangest bit of all. Shall I go on, Pastor Rosmer?

ROSMER. Of course! Tell me all. Don't keep anything back.

MORTENSGAARD. Your wife begged and implored me to be magnanimous. She was aware, she said, that it was the pastor who had had me dismissed from the school. And she implored me earnestly not to revenge myself.

ROSMER. How did she imagine you might revenge yourself?

MORTENSGAARD. It says in the letter that if I heard any rumours about certain shameful things supposed to be going on at Rosmersholm, I hadn't to pay any attention to them; it would only be things put about by those wicked people in order to distress you.

ROSMER. Does it say that in the letter?

MORTENSGAARD. You can read it yourself, Pastor Rosmer, at any time.

ROSMER. But I don't understand. . . ! What did she imagine these wicked rumours would be about?

MORTENSGAARD. In the first place, that you were supposed to have renounced your religious beliefs. This your wife firmly denied—at that time. And then . . . hm. . . .

ROSMER. Then?

MORTENSGAARD. Yes, then she says . . . it's a bit confused, this . . . that she is quite unaware of any immoral relations at Rosmersholm. That she has never been wronged in any way. And if there ever should be any rumours to that effect, she implores me not to refer to them in the *Beacon*.

ROSMER. No mention of any names?

MORTENSGAARD. No.

ROSMER. Who brought you the letter?

MORTENSGAARD. I promised not to tell. It was brought to me one evening after dark.

ROSMER. If you had taken the trouble to inquire at the time, you would have learned that my poor unfortunate wife was not quite in her right mind.

MORTENSGAARD. I did inquire, Mr. Rosmer. But I must say, I didn't exactly get *that* impression.

ROSMER. You didn't? But why have you chosen this moment to tell me about this old and confused letter?

MORTENSGAARD. As a warning to be extremely careful, Pastor Rosmer.

ROSMER. In my personal affairs, you mean?

MORTENSGAARD. Yes, remember you have now lost any immunity you might have had in the past.

ROSMER. You seem convinced there's something here to hide.

MORTENSGAARD. I don't see any reason why an emancipated man shouldn't live as full a life as possible. But, as I said, just be careful from now on. If any rumours get around that offend against the proprieties, you can be sure the reputation of the whole radical movement will suffer. Goodbye, Pastor Rosmer.

ROSMER. Goodbye.

MORTENSGAARD. I am going straight to my office to put the great news in the *Beacon*.

ROSMER. Put it all in.

MORTENSGAARD. I'll put in everything that the dear public needs to know.

[*Bows and goes out.* ROSMER *remains standing in the doorway whilst* MORTENSGAARD *goes downstairs. The sound of the outer door being shut is heard.*]

ROSMER [*calls softly from the doorway*]. Rebecca! Reb . . . hm. [*Loudly.*] Mrs. Helseth, isn't Miss West down there?

MRS. HELSETH [*is heard downstairs in the hall*]. No, sir, she's not here.

[*The curtain at the back of the room is drawn back.* REBECCA *appears in the doorway.*]

REBECCA. Johannes!

ROSMER [*turns*]. Were you in my bedroom! My dear, what were you doing there?

REBECCA [*goes up to him*]. I was listening.

ROSMER. Oh, Rebecca, but how could you!

REBECCA. Certainly, why not? He was so nasty, the way he spoke about my dressing-gown. . . .

ROSMER. Ah, so you were also in there when Kroll . . . ?

REBECCA. Yes, I wanted to know what he was after.

ROSMER. I would have told you.

REBECCA. You would hardly have told me everything. And certainly not in his own words.

ROSMER. Did you hear everything?

REBECCA. Most of it I think. I had to go downstairs for a moment when Mortensgaard came.

ROSMER. And then you came up again. . . .

REBECCA. Don't take it so badly, my dear.

ROSMER. You must always do what you think is right and proper. You are a free agent. . . . But what do you make of all this, Rebecca. . . ? Oh, never before have I needed you as much as I do now.

REBECCA. But surely we've been prepared for something or other like this happening.

ROSMER. No, no! Not for this.

REBECCA. Not for this?

ROSMER. I did think that perhaps sooner or later our pure and beautiful friendship might be misinterpreted and sneered at. Not by Kroll. I never imagined anything like that of him. But all those others with their coarse minds and their shifty eyes. Oh yes, Rebecca, I had good grounds for keeping the relations between us so jealously concealed. It was a dangerous secret.

REBECCA. Oh, why must we worry about what others think? We know, you and I, that we have no reason to feel guilty.

ROSMER. I? Not feel guilty? Yes, so I thought . . . until today. But now . . . now, Rebecca. . . .

REBECCA. Well, what about now?

ROSMER. How am I to explain Beata's terrible accusation?

REBECCA [*vehemently*]. Oh, stop talking about Beata! Stop thinking about Beata any more! Just when you had begun to put her right out of your mind, now that she's dead.

ROSMER. Since I heard about all this, she seems in some uncanny way to be back among the living again.

REBECCA. Oh no, not that, Johannes, not that!

ROSMER. Yes, I tell you. We must try to get to the bottom of this. Whatever can have led Beata into this ghastly mistake?

REBECCA. Surely *you* are not beginning to doubt she was very nearly insane?

ROSMER. Yes, I am. That's just what I cannot be absolutely certain about any more. And besides . . . even if she were . . .

REBECCA. If she were! Well, what then?

ROSMER. What I mean is . . . where are we to look for the immediate cause that tipped her sick mind over into madness?

REBECCA. Oh, what's the use of going on brooding about it like this!

ROSMER. I can't help it, Rebecca. I can't get rid of this nagging doubt, however much I would like to.

REBECCA. Oh, but that's a dangerous thing to do . . . turning this morbid affair over and over in your mind.

ROSMER [*walks about restlessly, pondering*]. I must have let something slip, one way or another. She must have noticed how happy I began to feel after *you* had come to live here.

REBECCA. Yes, my dear, but even if you did . . . !

ROSMER. I tell you . . . it didn't escape her notice that we read the same books. That we liked to get together and talk about all the recent developments. Yet I don't understand! Because I was so careful to spare her any unpleasantness. When I look back, I think I did my utmost to keep her away from anything we were interested in. Or perhaps that wasn't so, Rebecca?

REBECCA. Yes, yes! You certainly did.

ROSMER. And you too. And yet . . . ! Oh, it's terrible to contemplate! She must have been going about here . . . sick with passion . . . never saying a word . . . watching us . . . noticing everything . . . and misinterpreting everything.

REBECCA [*wringing her hands*]. Oh, I should never have come to Rosmersholm.

ROSMER. To think what she must have suffered in silence! All the horrible things her sick brain must have been capable of believing about us. Did she never say anything to you that might have given you a hint?

REBECCA [*apparently startled*]. To me! Do you think I'd have stayed on here a day longer?

ROSMER. No, no, of course not. Oh, what a battle she must have fought. And fought alone, Rebecca. In despair, and quite alone. And then, in the end, her triumph . . . that agonizing indictment . . . in the millstream. . . .

[*He throws himself down on the chair near the writing-table, rests his elbows on the table and hides his face in his hands.*]

REBECCA [*approaches him cautiously from behind*]. Listen to me, Johannes. If it were in your power to call Beata back . . . to you . . . to Rosmersholm . . . would you do it?

ROSMER. Oh, how do I know what I would or wouldn't do? I can think of nothing but this one thing . . . this one irrevocable thing.

REBECCA. Now you were going to live, Johannes. You had already begun. You had made yourself completely free . . . in all things. You felt so happy and carefree. . . .

ROSMER. I know . . . I really did. And now this crushing weight.

REBECCA [*behind him, with her arms on the back of the chair*]. How lovely it was when we used to sit in the dusk downstairs in the living-room. Helping each other to plan our lives anew. You wanted to lay hold of life—the throbbing life of the day, as you used to say. You wanted to go from house to house like a messenger of deliverance, winning the minds and the wills of men. Creating all about you a nobility . . . in ever wider circles. Noble men.

ROSMER. Happy, noble men.

REBECCA. Yes, happy.

ROSMER. For it is happiness that brings nobility of mind, Rebecca.

REBECCA. Don't you think . . . perhaps suffering too? Great suffering.

ROSMER. Yes . . . so long as you come through . . . get over it . . . rise above it.

REBECCA. That's what *you* must do.

ROSMER [*shakes his head sadly*]. I shall never succeed in rising above this, never completely. There will always be some doubt remaining, some question. I shall never again know the joy of the one thing that makes life so wonderful to live.

REBECCA [*over the back of the chair, softly*]. And what do you think that is, Johannes?

ROSMER [*looks up at her*]. Quiet, happy innocence.

REBECCA [*takes a step back*]. Yes, innocence.

[*Short pause.*]

ROSMER [*with elbows on the table, his head in his hands and looking straight ahead*]. And how she must have worked things out, how systematically she must have pieced things together. Beginning first with suspicions about my faith. . . . However did she come by that idea at that time? Yet she did. And then it grew into certainty. And then . . . yes, it wasn't difficult for her then to suppose all the other things possible. [*Sits up in his chair and runs his hands through his hair.*] Oh, all these wild speculations. I'll never be rid of them. I'm sure of it. I know it. They'll always be there, ready to charge in and remind me of the dead.

REBECCA. Like the White Horse of Rosmersholm.

ROSMER. Exactly. Rushing out of the darkness. Out of the stillness.

REBECCA. So you are going to let life go by just when you had begun to lay hold of it, and all because of these morbid fantasies.

ROSMER. You are right, it's hard. Hard, Rebecca. But the choice isn't mine. How do you suppose I could ever put all this behind me?

REBECCA [*behind the chair*]. By forming new associations.

ROSMER [*starts and looks up*]. New associations!

REBECCA. Yes, new associations with the world outside. Living, working, doing things. Not sitting here brooding and stewing over insoluble problems.

ROSMER [*gets up*]. New associations? [*Walks across the room, stops near the door and comes back again.*] One question occurs to me. Haven't you asked yourself the same thing, Rebecca?

REBECCA [*breathing hard*]. Tell me . . . what . . . you mean.

ROSMER. How do you think our association will be after today?

REBECCA. I still think our friendship can endure . . . whatever happens.

ROSMER. Yes, but that wasn't exactly what I meant. I was meaning the thing that first brought us together . . . the thing that unites us so closely . . . the belief we share that a man and a woman can live together simply on terms of friendship.

REBECCA. Yes, yes . . . what of it?

ROSMER. I mean that *that* kind of relationship . . . like ours, in fact . . . doesn't it best go with the sort of life that's lived quietly, serenely, happily. . . .

REBECCA. Well?

ROSMER. But the sort of life I see opening up in front of me is one of strife and unrest and strong passion. For I do mean to live my life, Rebecca! I'm not going to be beaten down by any grim thoughts of what might be. Nobody is going to decide my life for me, neither the living nor . . . anybody else.

REBECCA. No, no, don't let them! Be a free man in all things, Rosmer!

ROSMER. Then do you know what I think? Don't you? Don't you see how I can best rid myself of all those nagging memories . . . from all the misery of the past?

REBECCA. Well?

ROSMER. By confronting it all with a new and living reality.

REBECCA [*feels for the back of a chair*]. A living . . . ? What do you mean?

ROSMER [*comes closer*]. Rebecca . . . if I were to ask you . . . will you be my wife?

REBECCA [*for a moment speechless, then gives a cry of joy*]. Your wife! Your . . . ! Me!

ROSMER. Good. Let us try. We two will be one. The space left here by the dead must remain empty no longer.

REBECCA. Me . . . in Beata's place. . . !

ROSMER. Then that puts her out of the picture. Right out. For good.

REBECCA [*in a soft, trembling voice*]. Do you think so, Johannes?

ROSMER. It must do! It *must*. I will not go through life with a corpse on my back. Help me to throw it off, Rebecca. And let us stifle all memory in freedom, in joy, in passion. You shall be to me the only wife I ever had.

REBECCA [*masters herself*]. Let us have no more talk of this. I will never be your wife.

ROSMER. What! Never! Oh, don't you think you might come to love me? Isn't there already a hint of love in our friendship?

REBECCA [*puts her hands over her ears as if in terror*]. You mustn't talk like that, Johannes! Mustn't say such things!

ROSMER [*seizes her arm*]. It's true! There *is* some tender promise in our feelings for each other. Oh, when I look at you, I see you feel the same. Don't you, Rebecca?

REBECCA [*once again firm and composed*]. Listen to me. I tell you this: if you persist in this, I shall leave Rosmersholm.

ROSMER. Leave! You! You can't. It's impossible.

REBECCA. It's even more impossible for me to become your wife. Never in this world can I be that.

ROSMER [*looks at her in surprise*]. You say 'can'. And you say it so strangely. Why can't you?

REBECCA [*takes both his hands in hers*]. Dear friend . . . for your sake as well as mine . . . don't ask me why. [*Lets go his hands.*] There it is, Johannes.

[*She goes towards the door on the left.*]

ROSMER. After today there can be for me only one question: Why?

REBECCA [*turns and looks at him*]. Then that will be the end.

ROSMER. Between you and me?

REBECCA. Yes.

ROSMER. Never can there be an end to things between us. You will never leave Rosmersholm.

REBECCA [*with her hand on the door latch*]. No, I don't suppose I shall. But if you ever ask me again . . . that's the end of things, all the same.

ROSMER. The end. . . ? What . . . ?

REBECCA. Yes, for then I go the way Beata went. Now you know, Johannes.

ROSMER. Rebecca. . . !

REBECCA [*in the doorway, nods slowly*]. Now you know. [*She goes.*]

ROSMER [*stares in bewilderment at the closed door, and says to himself*]. What . . . is . . . this?

ACT THREE

The living-room at Rosmersholm. The window and the hall door are open. The morning sun is shining outside. REBECCA WEST, *dressed as in Act I, is standing at the window, watering and arranging the flowers. Her crochet-work is lying on the armchair.* MRS. HELSETH *is going round dusting the furniture with a feather mop.*

REBECCA [*after a moment or two of silence*]. Strange that the pastor is staying so long upstairs today.

MRS. HELSETH. Oh, he often does that. He'll be down soon, I should think.

REBECCA. Have you seen anything of him?

MRS. HELSETH. Just for a minute. He was in his bedroom getting dressed when I went up with his coffee.

REBECCA. The reason I ask is because he wasn't feeling quite himself yesterday.

MRS. HELSETH. Yes, he did look a bit off-colour. I was wondering if there wasn't maybe a bit of trouble between him and his brother-in-law.

REBECCA. What sort of trouble do you think?

MRS. HELSETH. That I couldn't say. Perhaps it's this Mortensgaard that's made them fall out.

REBECCA. That's always possible. Do you know anything about Peter Mortensgaard?

MRS. HELSETH. Not me! Whatever gives you that idea, miss? A person like that!

REBECCA. You mean because he's the editor of that awful paper?

MRS. HELSETH. Oh, it's not just *that*. Surely, miss, you must have heard about him having a child by that married woman whose husband had gone away and left her?

REBECCA. Yes, I heard. But that must have been long before I came here.

MRS. HELSETH. Bless me, yes! He was quite young at the time. She at least might have had a bit more sense than him. He wanted to go ahead and marry her, but that just couldn't be done. So he had to suffer pretty heavily for it. But, my goodness, Mortensgaard has got on since those days. There are plenty of people ready to run after *him* now.

REBECCA. Many of the poor turn to him first when there's any trouble.

MRS. HELSETH. It needn't always be just the poor. . . .

REBECCA [*glances at her furtively*]. Really?

MRS. HELSETH [*vigorously dusting the sofa*]. People you would least expect, miss.

REBECCA [*arranging the flowers*]. Now, this is just some idea you have got hold of, Mrs. Helseth. You can hardly be expected to know anything like that for certain.

MRS. HELSETH. So you think I don't know, miss, do you? But I'm telling you I do. If you must know, I once took a letter to Mortensgaard myself.

REBECCA [*turns*]. Never! Did you?

MRS. HELSETH. Yes, that I did. And, what's more, the letter was written here at Rosmersholm.

REBECCA. Really, Mrs. Helseth?

MRS. HELSETH. Yes, that it was. And written on fine paper it was. And sealed with fine red sealing-wax, too.

REBECCA. And you were the one entrusted with taking it? Well then, my dear Mrs. Helseth, it's not difficult to guess who it was from.

MRS. HELSETH. Well?

REBECCA. Naturally it must have been something that poor Mrs. Rosmer, stricken as she was . . .

MRS. HELSETH. It's you who said it, Miss West, not me.

REBECCA. But what was in the letter? No, of course . . . how could you possibly know that?

MRS. HELSETH. Hm, maybe I do know, all the same.

REBECCA. Did she tell you what the letter was about?

MRS. HELSETH. No, she didn't exactly do that. But when Mortensgaard had finished reading it, he started asking me all sorts of questions, going on and on about it, so I had a pretty good idea what it was all about.

REBECCA. What do you think was in it then? Oh, dear, kind Mrs. Helseth, do tell me!

MRS. HELSETH. Certainly not, miss. Not for anything in the world.

REBECCA. Oh, surely you can tell *me*. You and I are such good friends, aren't we?

MRS. HELSETH. Heaven forbid I should tell you anything about *that*, miss. All I can say is it was something not very nice that they had gone and got the poor, sick lady to believe.

REBECCA. Who had got her to believe it?

MRS. HELSETH. Wicked people, Miss West. Wicked people.

REBECCA. Wicked . . . ?

MRS. HELSETH. Yes, I say it again. Downright wicked people it must have been.

REBECCA. And who do you think it could have been?

MRS. HELSETH. Oh, I know all right what I think. But God forbid that I should ever say anything. Not but what there isn't a certain lady in town . . . hm!

REBECCA. I can see you mean Mrs. Kroll.

MRS. HELSETH. Yes, she's a fine one, she is. She's always been so stuck up with me. And she's never been very fond of you, either.

REBECCA. Do you think Mrs. Rosmer was in her right mind when she wrote that letter to Mortensgaard?

MRS. HELSETH. The mind's a funny thing, miss. But I don't think she was completely gone.

REBECCA. But she went a bit queer when she was told she could never have any children. It was *then* the insanity first started.

MRS. HELSETH. Yes, she took that very badly, poor thing.

REBECCA [*takes her crochet-work and sits in a chair near the window*]. All the same, Mrs. Helseth, don't you think *that* was really a good thing for the pastor?

MRS. HELSETH. What was, miss?

REBECCA. That there were no children. Well?

MRS. HELSETH. Hm, I don't really know what to say to that.

REBECCA. Yes, it was, believe me. It was best for him. Pastor Rosmer is not the kind of man who can put up with a lot of crying children.

MRS. HELSETH. Children never cry at Rosmersholm, miss.

REBECCA [*looks at her*]. Never cry?

MRS. HELSETH. No. Children have never been known to cry in this house, not as long as anybody can remember.

REBECCA. That's strange.

MRS. HELSETH. Yes, isn't it strange? But it runs in the family. And there's another strange thing. When they grow up, they never laugh. Never laugh as long as they live.

REBECCA. But that's extraordinary. . . .

MRS. HELSETH. Have you ever seen or heard the pastor laugh, miss?

REBECCA. No, now I come to think about it, I almost believe you are right. But then I don't think people in this part of the world laugh very much at all.

MRS. HELSETH. They don't. People say it began at Rosmersholm. And then I suppose it spread, like a sort of infection.

REBECCA. You are a deep one, you are, Mrs. Helseth.

MRS. HELSETH. Oh, you mustn't sit there making fun of me, miss. . . . [*Listens.*] Hush, hush . . . the pastor is coming down now. He doesn't like seeing mops in here.

[*She goes out through the door, right.* JOHANNES ROSMER, *stick and hat in hand, comes in from the hall.*]

ROSMER. Good morning, Rebecca.

REBECCA. Good morning, my dear. [*After a while, crocheting.*] Are you going out?

ROSMER. Yes.

REBECCA. It's a lovely day.

ROSMER. You didn't come in to see me this morning.

REBECCA. No, I didn't. Not today.

ROSMER. Aren't you going to do it in future, either?

REBECCA. Oh, I don't know yet.

ROSMER. Has anything come for me?

REBECCA. The *County Times* has come.

ROSMER. The *County Times*. . . !

REBECCA. It's lying on the table there.

ROSMER [*puts down his hat and stick*]. Is there anything in about . . . ?

REBECCA. Yes.

ROSMER. Yet you didn't send it up. . . .

REBECCA. You would read it soon enough.

ROSMER. Well. [*Takes the paper and reads it standing at the table.*] What! . . . 'Cannot emphasize too strongly this warning against unprincipled deserters.' [*Looks across at her.*] They call me a deserter, Rebecca.

REBECCA. They mention no names.

ROSMER. That makes no difference. [*Reads on.*] 'Secret traitors to the good cause . . .' 'Judas-like creatures who have the impudence to confess their apostasy as soon as they believe the most opportune and . . . the most profitable moment has arrived.' 'A reckless outrage on the fair name of an honoured family . . .' '. . . in the expectation that those at present in power will not neglect to make some suitable reward.' [*Puts the paper on the table.*] How can they write such things about me! Men who have known me so well and so long. Things they don't even believe themselves. Things they know there isn't a single word of truth in—yet they write them all the same.

REBECCA. There's more yet.

ROSMER [*takes the paper again*]. 'Inexperience and lack of judgement . . .'
'. . . pernicious influence, perhaps even extending to matters which
for the present we are unwilling to make subjects for public discussion or censure . . .' [*Looks at her.*] What is this?

REBECCA. It's obviously aimed at me.

ROSMER [*puts down the paper*]. Rebecca . . . these are the doings of unscrupulous men.

REBECCA. Yes, I don't think they need talk about Mortensgaard.

ROSMER [*walks about the room*]. There is work for redemption here.
Everything that is good in man will be destroyed if this kind of thing
is allowed to go on. But it shall not. Oh, how happy I should feel
if I could bring a little light into all this murky nastiness.

REBECCA [*gets up*]. Oh, how right you are! That would be something
great and glorious for you to live for.

ROSMER. Just think if I could make them see themselves for what they
really are. Bring them to a sense of shame and repentance, get them
to approach one another in a spirit of tolerance . . . of love, Rebecca.

REBECCA. Yes, if you concentrate everything on this, you'll win—
you'll see.

ROSMER. I think it might be done. Oh, what joy then to be alive. No
more bitter strife, only friendly rivalry. All eyes fixed on the same
goal. Every mind, every will striving on and on . . . up and up . . .
each by the path best suited to its nature. Happiness for all . . . created
by all. [*Happens to look out through the window, starts and says sadly.*]
Ah! Not by me.

REBECCA. Not . . . not by you?

ROSMER. And not *for* me either.

REBECCA. Oh, Johannes, you mustn't let such misgivings get the better
of you.

ROSMER. Happiness . . . dear Rebecca . . . happiness is more than
anything that serene, secure, happy freedom from guilt.

REBECCA [*stares straight ahead*]. Ah, this question of guilt. . . .

ROSMER. Oh, that's nothing you are likely to know very much about. Whereas I . . .

REBECCA. You least of all!

ROSMER [*points out of window*]. The millstream.

REBECCA. Oh, Johannes. . . !

[MRS. HELSETH *looks in through the door, right.*]

MRS. HELSETH. Miss West!

REBECCA. Later, later. Not now.

MRS. HELSETH. Just one word, miss.

[REBECCA *walks over to the door.* MRS. HELSETH *tells her something. They whisper together for a moment.* MRS. HELSETH *nods and goes.*]

ROSMER [*uneasily*]. Was it anything for me?

REBECCA. No, only household matters. . . . Now you ought to go out for a walk in the fresh air, my dear Johannes. A good long walk, you should make it.

ROSMER [*takes his hat*]. Yes, come on. We'll go together.

REBECCA. No, my dear, I can't just now. You go on your own. But shake off all these gloomy thoughts. Promise me.

ROSMER. I'll never be able to shake them off, I am very much afraid.

REBECCA. Oh, why do you let these empty fears have such power over you. . . !

ROSMER. I am sorry, but they are not so empty as you think, Rebecca. I lay awake all night turning them over in my mind. Perhaps Beata saw straight after all.

REBECCA. What do you mean?

ROSMER. Saw straight when she believed I was in love with you, Rebecca.

REBECCA. You think *that*?

ROSMER [*places his hat on the table*]. One question has been tossing about in my mind. . . . Weren't we all the time simply deceiving ourselves about the way things were between us when we called it 'friendship'?

REBECCA. You mean it might just as well have been called . . . ?

ROSMER. . . . Love. Yes, Rebecca, that is what I mean. Even while Beata was still alive, my thoughts were all for you. It was you alone I longed for. It was with you that I found calm, happy, serene contentment. If we really think about it, Rebecca . . . we began our life together like two children falling sweetly and secretly in love. Making no demands, dreaming no dreams. Didn't you also feel that way about it? Tell me?

REBECCA [*struggling with herself*]. Oh . . . I don't know what to answer.

ROSMER. And it was this life of intimacy, *with* each other and *for* each other, we took for friendship. No, Rebecca, our life together has been a spiritual marriage . . . perhaps from the very first day. That is why the guilt is mine. I had no right to it . . . no right for Beata's sake.

REBECCA. No right to a happy life? Do you believe that, Johannes?

ROSMER. She looked on our relationship through the eyes of *her* love. Judged our relationship by the nature of *her* love. That was only natural. Beata could not have judged otherwise than she did.

REBECCA. But why should you reproach yourself for Beata's wild ideas?

ROSMER. It was for love of me . . . *her* kind of love . . . that she threw herself into the millstream. The fact is inescapable, Rebecca. I can never get away from it.

REBECCA. Oh, you must put everything out of your mind but the great and splendid task you have dedicated your life to.

ROSMER [*shakes his head*]. I fear that is something that can never be done, my dear. Not by me. Not after what I know now.

REBECCA. Why not by you?

ROSMER. There can be no victory for any cause that springs from guilt.

REBECCA [*vehemently*]. Oh, all these doubts, these fears, these scruples— they are just part of the family tradition. The people here talk about the dead coming back in the form of charging white horses. I think this is the same sort of thing.

ROSMER. Maybe it is, but what's the use if I can't escape them now? And believe me, Rebecca, it is just as I said. Any cause that is to win a lasting victory must have at its head a happy and guiltless man.

REBECCA. Is happiness something *you* can't exist without either, then, Johannes?

ROSMER. Happiness? Yes, my dear, it is.

REBECCA. Even though you can never laugh?

ROSMER. That makes no difference. Believe me, I have a great capacity for happiness.

REBECCA. Now you really must have your walk, my dear. A nice long one, really long, do you hear? Here is your hat and here is your stick.

ROSMER [*takes both*]. Thank you. You are not coming with me?

REBECCA. No, no. I can't just now.

ROSMER. Very well. But you'll be with me all the same.

[*He goes out through the hall. After a moment* REBECCA *peeps out after him from behind the open door. Then she goes over to the door on the right.*]

REBECCA [*opens the door and speaks in a low voice*]. All right, Mrs. Helseth. You can let him in now.

[*She goes over to the window. Shortly after,* KROLL *comes in from the right. He bows silently and formally and keeps his hat in his hand.*]

KROLL. Has he gone, then?

REBECCA. Yes.

KROLL. Does he generally stay out long?

REBECCA. Oh, yes. But he is a bit unpredictable today. So if you don't want to meet him . . .

KROLL. No, no. It's you I want to talk to. And quite alone.

REBECCA. Then we had best make the most of our time. Do sit down, Mr. Kroll.

[*She sits down in the easy-chair near the window.* KROLL *sits on a chair beside her.*]

KROLL. Miss West . . . you can hardly imagine how profoundly and how painfully this has affected me . . . this change in Johannes Rosmer.

REBECCA. We expected something of the sort . . . to begin with.

KROLL. Only to begin with?

REBECCA. Mr. Rosmer was quite confident that sooner or later you would join him.

KROLL. *I* should?

REBECCA. You and all his other friends as well.

KROLL. Ah, there you see! That shows you how uncertain he is in his judgement when it concerns his fellow men and their practical affairs.

REBECCA. Furthermore . . . now that he feels he has a duty to himself to carry on what he has begun . . .

KROLL. Yes, but look . . . that's exactly what I do not believe.

REBECCA. And what *do* you believe then?

KROLL. I believe that *you* are the one behind it all.

REBECCA. You got that idea from your wife, Mr. Kroll.

KROLL. It doesn't matter very much where I got it from. What is certain is the strong suspicion I feel . . . the extremely strong suspicion, I might say . . . when I start thinking of the way you have behaved ever since you got here.

REBECCA [*looks at him*]. I seem to remember there was a time when you felt an extremely strong *faith* in me, my dear Mr. Kroll. A warm faith, I might almost say.

KROLL [*in a subdued voice*]. Who is there you couldn't bewitch . . . if you tried?

REBECCA. Are you saying I tried to . . .

KROLL. Yes, you did. I'm no longer such a fool as to imagine you cared anything for me the way you carried on. All you wanted was to get your foot in at Rosmersholm. Get yourself established here. That's what I was supposed to help you with. I can see it all now.

REBECCA. Then you have completely forgotten that it was Beata who begged and prayed me to move out here.

KROLL. Yes, after you had managed to bewitch her as well. Or do you want to call that friendship, the way she came to feel about you? She idolized you, worshipped you. The outcome of it was . . . how shall I put it? . . . a kind of desperate infatuation. Yes, that's the only way to describe it.

REBECCA. You will please remember the state your sister was in. As far as I'm concerned, I don't think I can be said to be particularly highly-strung.

KROLL. No, you are not. But that's what makes you even more dangerous for those you want in your power. You find it easy to calculate all things and act with complete deliberation . . . precisely because you have a cold heart.

REBECCA. Cold? Are you so sure of that?

KROLL. I am absolutely certain of it now. Otherwise you could never have kept it up here year after year, never swerving in the pursuit of what you were after. Well, well . . . you have got what you wanted. You have got him and everything else in your power. But to get your way, you have had no scruples about making him unhappy.

REBECCA. That's not true. It wasn't me. It was *you* who made him unhappy.

KROLL. Me indeed!

REBECCA. Yes, when you allowed him to think he was to blame for Beata's terrible end.

KROLL. So that struck home deep, did it?

REBECCA. Surely you must realize that. A mind as sensitive as his . . .

KROLL. I thought these so-called emancipated men knew how to suppress all such scruples. . . . But there it is! Oh yes, I suppose deep down I knew it well enough. The descendant of these men here looking down at us . . . he'll not escape so easily from what has been handed down unbroken from generation to generation.

REBECCA [*looks down thoughtfully*]. Johannes Rosmer has roots that go deep into his ancestry. That is certainly very true.

KROLL. Yes, and you would have thought of that if you had had any pity for him. But I don't suppose you are capable of consideration of that kind. Your background and his are of course poles apart.

REBECCA. What do you mean . . . my background?

KROLL. I was thinking of your family background. Of your antecedents . . . Miss West.

REBECCA. I see. Yes, that's quite true, I do come from quite humble beginnings. But at the same time . . .

KROLL. It is not class or position I am referring to. I am thinking of the moral side of your background.

REBECCA. Of the . . . ? In what way?

KROLL. The very circumstances of your birth.

REBECCA. What's that you say?

KROLL. I mention it of course only because it explains your whole conduct.

REBECCA. I don't understand a word of all this. Tell me exactly what you mean!

KROLL. I thought surely you must know. Otherwise it wouldn't make sense . . . letting yourself be adopted by Dr. West. . . .

REBECCA [*gets up*]. Ah! Now I understand!

KROLL. . . . Taking his name. Your mother's name was Gamvik.

REBECCA [*walks across the room*]. My father's name was Gamvik, Mr. Kroll.

KROLL. Your mother's occupation must have brought her into pretty regular contact with the local doctor.

REBECCA. Yes, it did.

KROLL. And no sooner has your mother died than he takes you into his house. . . . He treats you harshly. Yet you stay with him. You know he won't leave you a penny. All you got was a case full of books. And yet you stick it out, put up with him, look after him right to the very end.

REBECCA [*by the table, looks scornfully at him*]. And what I did you put down to something immoral, something criminal, about the circumstances of my birth!

KROLL. What you did for him I attribute to some intuitive daughterly instinct. Indeed I consider your whole conduct derives from the circumstances of your birth.

REBECCA [*hotly*]. But there's not a word of truth in anything you say. And I can prove it! Dr. West didn't come to Finmark until after I was born.

KROLL. You will forgive me, Miss West, but he was already there the year before. I have gone into that.

REBECCA. You are wrong I tell you. You are completely wrong.

KROLL. You said yourself a couple of days ago that you were twenty-nine. Going on for thirty.

REBECCA. Really? Did I say that?

KROLL. Yes, you did. And from that I can work it out that . . .

REBECCA. Stop! There's no point in working it out. I might as well tell you at once. I am a year older than I pretend to be.

KROLL [*smiles incredulously*]. Really? This is something new. How does that happen?

REBECCA. When I was twenty-five, and still not married, I thought I was getting a bit too old. So I began subtracting a year.

KROLL. You? An emancipated woman. Have you still got old-fashioned ideas about the proper age for marriage?

REBECCA. Yes, it is silly . . . and ridiculous, too. But there's always some little thing or other that sticks and you just can't shake yourself free of it. It's just the way we are made.

KROLL. Just as you say. But my calculations can still be correct, just the same. For Dr. West was up there on a flying visit the year before he was appointed.

REBECCA [*vehemently*]. It's not true!

KROLL. Isn't it?

REBECCA. No. My mother never mentioned it.

KROLL. Didn't she now?

REBECCA. No, never. Nor Dr. West either. Never a word.

KROLL. Might it not be because they both had good reason to skip a year? Just as you did, Miss West. Perhaps it's a family peculiarity.

REBECCA [*walks about wringing her hands*]. It's impossible. It's just something you want to get me to believe. Never in the world is this true. It cannot be true! Never in the world. . . !

KROLL [*gets up*]. But my dear Miss West . . . why in Heaven's name are you taking it like this? You make me feel quite alarmed! What am I to think. . . ?

REBECCA. Nothing. You are not to think anything.

KROLL. Then you really must tell me why you are taking this little matter . . . this possibility . . . so much to heart.

REBECCA [*composes herself*]. It's quite simple, of course, Mr. Kroll. I have no desire to be looked on here as illegitimate.

KROLL. Indeed! Well, well, let's be content with that explanation . . . for the time being. But it seems you also have a certain . . . prejudice on this point, too.

REBECCA. Yes, I suppose I have.

KROLL. Well, I imagine it's pretty much the same with most of what you call your emancipation. You have read up a lot of new ideas and opinions. You have acquired a smattering of various ideas and theories—that somehow seem to upset a good many things that up to now we took for incontrovertible and inviolate. But in your case, Miss West, it never got beyond being anything but an abstraction. Book knowledge. It never got into your blood.

REBECCA [*thoughtfully*]. Perhaps you are right.

KROLL. Yes, just take a good look at yourself and you will see. And if it is like that in your case, it's easy enough to guess how it is with Johannes Rosmer. The very idea of *him* getting up and announcing his apostasy . . . why, it's sheer and utter madness . . . like hurling himself headlong to destruction. Think . . . a man of his retiring disposition. Imagine *him* rebuffed . . . hunted by the very circle he previously belonged to. Exposed to ruthless attack from the best people in the community. He's never the man to stand up to that.

REBECCA. He *must* stand up to it! It's too late now for him to draw back.

KROLL. It's not in the least too late. Not by any means. What has happened can be kept dark . . . or at least it can be interpreted as a purely temporary, though regrettable, aberration. But . . . there is in fact *one* measure that is absolutely imperative.

REBECCA. And what is that?

KROLL. You must get him to legalize the relationship, Miss West.

REBECCA. The relationship between us?

KROLL. Yes. You *must* see he does that.

REBECCA. You can't get away from the idea that our relationship needs . . . legalizing, as you put it?

KROLL. I have no wish to go personally into the matter any further. But I have been struck before by the fact that the easiest conventions to break with seem to be those that concern . . . hm!

REBECCA. Concern the relations between a man and a woman, I suppose you mean?

KROLL. Yes . . . speaking candidly . . . that's what I think.

REBECCA [*walks across the room and looks through the window*]. I could almost say . . . I wish you were right, Mr. Kroll.

KROLL. What do you mean by that? You said it so strangely.

REBECCA. Oh, I don't know. Don't let's talk any more about it. . . . Ah! There he comes.

KROLL. Already. Then I'll go.

REBECCA [*turns to him*]. No . . . please stay. There's something I want you to hear.

KROLL. Not now. I don't think I could bear to see him.

REBECCA. Don't go . . . I beg you! Or you will regret it later. It is the last time I shall ask anything of you.

KROLL [*looks at her in surprise and puts down his hat*]. Very well, Miss West. As you wish.

[*There is a moment's silence. Then* ROSMER *comes in from the hall.*]

ROSMER [*sees* KROLL, *stops in the doorway*]. What! Are *you* here!

REBECCA. He would have preferred not to meet you, Johannes, my dear.

KROLL [*involuntarily*]. 'My dear'?

REBECCA. Yes, Mr. Kroll. Johannes and I call each other 'dear'. That's one result of the 'relations' between us.

KROLL. Was it *that* you promised I should hear?

REBECCA. That . . . and a little more.

ROSMER [*comes closer*]. What is the purpose of your visit here today?

KROLL. I wanted to make one last attempt to stop you, to win you back.

ROSMER [*points at the newspaper*]. After what's in there?

KROLL. I didn't write it.

ROSMER. Did you do anything to try and stop it?

KROLL. That would have been unjustifiable interference with the cause I serve. Nor was it in my power.

REBECCA [*tears up the paper, crumples the pieces and throws them behind the stove*]. There. Now it's out of sight. And let it be out of mind as well. For there'll be no more of that sort of stuff, Johannes.

KROLL. Oh yes, if only you could make such things unnecessary.

REBECCA. Come, let's sit down, my dear. All three of us. Then I'll tell you everything.

ROSMER [*sits down involuntarily*]. What's come over you, Rebecca? So unnaturally calm. . . . What is it?

REBECCA. The calmness of resolution. [*Sits.*] You sit down too, Mr. Kroll.

[KROLL *sits on the sofa.*]

ROSMER. Of resolution, you say. What resolution?

REBECCA. I want to give you back again what you need to live your life. You shall have your happy innocence back again, my dear.

ROSMER. But what is all this!

REBECCA. I just want to tell you something. That's all that's necessary.

ROSMER. Well?

REBECCA. When I came down here from Finmark . . . together with Dr. West . . . I felt as though a great, new wide world were opening before me. The doctor taught me most things . . . indeed practically all the odds and ends of knowledge I possessed about life were from him. [*With a struggle, and scarcely audible.*] And then . . .

KROLL. And then?

ROSMER. But Rebecca . . . I know all this.

REBECCA [*collecting herself*]. Yes, yes . . . I suppose in one way you are right. You knew as much as was necessary.

KROLL [*looks hard at her*]. Perhaps I had better go.

REBECCA. No, stay where you are, my dear Mr. Kroll. [*To* ROSMER.] Yes, that was it, you see . . . I wanted to be in at the dawning of the new age, wanted to be in on everything, all the new ideas. One day Mr. Kroll told me about the great influence Ulrik Brendel had once had over you, while you were still a boy. I thought I might manage to pick up again where he left off.

ROSMER. You came here with this ulterior motive. . . !

REBECCA. I wanted us to go forward together in freedom. On and on, ever further. But between you and full and complete freedom was this grim, insurmountable barrier.

ROSMER. What do you mean . . . barrier?

REBECCA. I mean, Johannes, that you could only grow to freedom in the clear light of the sun. But there you were, wilting and sickly in the gloom of a marriage like yours.

ROSMER. Never until today have you spoken to me like that about my marriage.

REBECCA. No, I didn't dare, in case I frightened you off.

KROLL [*nods to* ROSMER]. Do you hear *that*?

REBECCA [*continues*]. But I knew very well where your salvation lay. Your only salvation. So I took action.

ROSMER. What do you mean . . . you took action?

KROLL. Do you mean to say . . . ?

REBECCA. Yes, Johannes. . . . [*Gets up.*] Don't get up. Nor you either, Mr. Kroll. Now it must be told. It wasn't you, Johannes. You are innocent. It was *I* who lured . . . who ended by luring Beata out on the twisted path. . . .

ROSMER [*jumping up*]. Rebecca!

KROLL [*getting up from the sofa*]. . . . The twisted path!

REBECCA. The path . . . that led to the millstream. Now you know, both of you.

ROSMER [*as if stunned*]. But I don't understand. . . . What is she saying . . . I don't understand a single word. . . !

KROLL. Oh yes, Rosmer. I am beginning to understand.

ROSMER. But what did you do? What could you possibly have told her? There was nothing. Not a thing!

REBECCA. She was informed that you were ridding yourself of all your old-fashioned prejudices.

ROSMER. Yes, but I wasn't . . . not then.

REBECCA. I knew you soon would.

KROLL [*nods to* ROSMER]. Aha!

ROSMER. Well, and what else? Now I must know everything.

REBECCA. Shortly after that . . . I begged and implored her to let me leave Rosmersholm.

ROSMER. Why did you want to leave . . . just then?

REBECCA. I didn't want to leave. I wanted to stay here where I was. But I told her it would be best for us all . . . if I left before it was too late. I gave her to understand that if I stayed on . . . certain things . . . might happen.

ROSMER. You actually said that? You did that?

REBECCA. Yes, Johannes.

ROSMER. So that's what you meant when you said you 'took action'.

REBECCA [*in a broken voice*]. That's what I meant.

ROSMER [*after a pause*]. Have you confessed everything now, Rebecca?

REBECCA. Yes.

KROLL. Not everything.

REBECCA [*looks at him in terror*]. What else do you think there is?

KROLL. Didn't you finally give Beata to understand that it was imperative—not just that it would be best, but that it was imperative—for your sake as well as Rosmer's, that you should leave and go somewhere else . . . as quickly as possible. . . ? Well?

REBECCA [*in a low, indistinct voice*]. Perhaps I did say something like that.

ROSMER [*sinks into the armchair near the window*]. And the poor sick creature went and believed it, all this web of lies and deceit. Believed every word of it . . . implicitly. [*Looks up at* REBECCA.] And she never turned to me. Never once said a word to me about it. Oh, Rebecca . . . I can see from your face . . . that was because *you* dissuaded her.

REBECCA. She had got it into her head that a childless wife had no right to stay on. So she persuaded herself it was her duty to you to make way for another.

ROSMER. And you . . . you did nothing to remove this idea?

REBECCA. No.

KROLL. Perhaps you even encouraged it? Answer me. Did you or did you not?

REBECCA. That might well have been the impression she got from me, I suppose.

ROSMER. Yes, yes . . . she always gave in when faced with your strength of will. And then she did make way. [*Jumps up.*] How could you . . . how could you play such a horrible game!

REBECCA. I thought it was a choice between two lives, Johannes.

KROLL [*sternly and peremptorily*]. That choice was not for *you* to make.

REBECCA [*vehemently*]. But do you think I set about these things deliberately in cold blood! I was different then from what I am now, standing here talking about it. And besides, it seems to me a person can want things both ways. I wanted to get rid of Beata, one way or another. But I never really imagined it would ever happen. Every little step I risked, every faltering advance, I seemed to hear something call out within me: 'No further. Not a step further!' . . . And yet I could not stop. I *had* to venture a little bit further. Just one little bit further. And then a little bit more . . . always just a little bit more. And then it happened. That's the way things like that do happen.

[*A short silence.*]

ROSMER [*to* REBECCA]. And how do you think things will be for *you* now? After this?

REBECCA. I shall take things as they are. It's not important now.

KROLL. Not the slightest hint of remorse. Perhaps you don't even feel any.

REBECCA [*coldly aloof*]. Forgive me, Mr. Kroll . . . but that's something that concerns nobody but me. That's something I shall settle with myself.

KROLL [*to* ROSMER]. And this is the woman you are living under the same roof with . . . in the closest intimacy. [*Looks round at the portraits.*] Oh, if only they could see you now, these men of the past.

ROSMER. Are you going into town?

KROLL [*takes his hat*]. Yes. And the quicker the better.

ROSMER [*also taking his hat*]. I'm coming with you.

KROLL. You are! Yes, I was sure we hadn't lost you for good.

ROSMER. Come on, Kroll! Come on!

[*They both go out through the hall without looking at* REBECCA. *After a moment,* REBECCA *walks cautiously over to the window and looks out from behind the flowers.*]

REBECCA [*speaks softly to herself*]. Not across the bridge today either. Round by the top. Never across the millstream. Never. [*Moves away from the window.*] Well, well.

> [*She crosses the room and pulls the bell-rope. A moment later* MRS. HELSETH *comes in from the right.*]

MRS. HELSETH. What is it, miss?

REBECCA. Mrs. Helseth, would you be so kind as to have my trunk brought down from the loft.

MRS. HELSETH. Your trunk?

REBECCA. Yes, you know, the brown sealskin trunk.

MRS. HELSETH. Certainly. Goodness, but are you going away?

REBECCA. Yes, I'm going away, Mrs. Helseth.

MRS. HELSETH. What! Now?

REBECCA. As soon as I have packed.

MRS. HELSETH. I've never heard the likes of it! But you'll be back again soon, won't you, miss?

REBECCA. I'm never coming back.

MRS. HELSETH. Never! But good heavens! What's it going to be like at Rosmersholm without Miss West here any longer. Just when poor Pastor Rosmer was nice and settled.

REBECCA. Yes, but today I have become afraid, Mrs. Helseth.

MRS. HELSETH. Afraid! Heavens . . . what of?

REBECCA. I thought I caught a glimpse of white horses.

MRS. HELSETH. White horses! In broad daylight!

REBECCA. Oh, they are out at all hours . . . the White Horses of Rosmersholm [*Breaks off.*] Well now, what about that trunk, Mrs. Helseth.

MRS. HELSETH. Yes, of course. The trunk.

> [*They both go out to the right.*]

ACT FOUR

The living-room at Rosmersholm. It is late afternoon. A shaded lamp is burning on the table.

REBECCA WEST is standing at the table, packing some things into a hold-all. Her cloak and hat and the white crocheted shawl are hanging over the back of the sofa.

MRS. HELSETH comes in from the right.

MRS. HELSETH [*seems ill at ease and speaks in a low voice*]. All your things have been brought down now, miss. They are in the kitchen passage.

REBECCA. Good. Is the coach ordered?

MRS. HELSETH. Yes. He wants to know what time he has to be here.

REBECCA. I think about eleven o'clock. The boat leaves at midnight.

MRS. HELSETH [*hesitates a little*]. But what about the pastor? Suppose he isn't back by then.

REBECCA. I'll just have to go. If I don't see him, you can tell him I shall write. A long letter. Tell him that.

MRS. HELSETH. Yes, I suppose that's all right . . . writing to him, but . . . poor Miss West . . . I think you ought to try and talk to him just once more.

REBECCA. Perhaps you're right. And yet, perhaps not.

MRS. HELSETH. Oh . . . that I should live to see a thing like this . . . I'd never have thought it!

REBECCA. What *did* you think then, Mrs. Helseth?

MRS. HELSETH. Well, really I thought Pastor Rosmer was more of a man than that.

REBECCA. More of a man?

MRS. HELSETH. Yes, really I did.

REBECCA. But, my dear Mrs. Helseth, what do you mean?

MRS. HELSETH. I mean what's right and proper, miss. He shouldn't be getting out of it like this, he shouldn't.

REBECCA [*looks at her*]. Listen to me, Mrs. Helseth. Tell me the plain, honest truth—why do you think I am going away?

MRS. HELSETH. Good heavens, I suppose because you have to, miss. Well, I mean to say! But really I don't think it's very nice of the pastor. Mortensgaard did have some excuse because *her* husband was still alive. So *they* couldn't get married however much they wanted to. But the pastor . . . well. . . !

REBECCA [*with a faint smile*]. Could you really think a thing like that about me and Pastor Rosmer?

MRS. HELSETH. Never in the world. What I mean is . . . not until today.

REBECCA. But today . . . ?

MRS. HELSETH. Well . . . after all the nasty things there's supposed to be about him in the papers. . . .

REBECCA. Aha!

MRS. HELSETH. What I mean is, you can believe anything of a man who's ready to go over to Mortensgaard's religion.

REBECCA. Oh yes, I suppose so. But what about me? What have you got to say about me?

MRS. HELSETH. Bless me, miss, I can hardly see it's any great fault of yours. When a woman's all on her own, it can't be easy for her to resist, I dare say. We're only human, Miss West, all of us.

REBECCA. That's very true, Mrs. Helseth. We are all only human. . . . What can you hear?

MRS. HELSETH [*in a low voice*]. Oh Lord! I think he's coming.

REBECCA [*starts*]. After all . . . ! [*Firmly.*] Well then, so be it.

[JOHANNES ROSMER *comes in from the hall.*]

ROSMER [*sees the luggage, turns to* REBECCA *and asks*]. What does this mean?

REBECCA. I'm leaving.

ROSMER. Now?

REBECCA. Yes. [*To* MRS. HELSETH.] Eleven o'clock then.

MRS. HELSETH. Very good, miss.

[*She goes out to the right.*]

ROSMER [*after a short pause*]. Where are you going, Rebecca?

REBECCA. North . . . with the boat.

ROSMER. North? What do you want up there?

REBECCA. That's where I came from, wasn't it?

ROSMER. But there's nothing for you up there now.

REBECCA. There's nothing down here either.

ROSMER. What did you think of doing?

REBECCA. I don't know. I just want to have done with everything.

ROSMER. Have done with everything?

REBECCA. Rosmersholm has broken me.

ROSMER [*suddenly attentive*]. What's that you say?

REBECCA. Completely and utterly broken me. When I first came here, I had some spirit; I wasn't afraid to do things. Now I feel crushed by a tradition quite foreign to me. I feel after this as though I hadn't any courage left for anything.

ROSMER. Why not? What do you mean by this tradition you say you . . . ?

REBECCA. My dear Johannes, let's not talk about that now. How did you get on with Mr. Kroll?

ROSMER. We have come to terms.

REBECCA. So! So it came to that in the end.

ROSMER. He invited all our old friends to join us at his house. They made it quite clear that the task of ennobling the minds of men . . . is not really the thing for me. And you know, it's a pretty hopeless kind of thing, anyway. I'm giving it up.

REBECCA. Yes . . . perhaps it's best that way.

ROSMER. So *that's* what you say now, is it? That's your view *now*?

REBECCA. I've come round to that. In the last few days.

ROSMER. You are lying, Rebecca.

REBECCA. Lying. . . ?

ROSMER. Yes, lying. You have never believed in me. You have never believed I had it in me to carry this thing through successfully.

REBECCA. I believed we two could manage it together.

ROSMER. That's not true! You thought that *you* yourself might be able to do something with your life; and that maybe you could utilize me for your own ends; you thought I might serve you somehow in your schemes. *That's* what you thought.

REBECCA. Listen to me, Johannes. . . .

ROSMER [*sits down wearily on the sofa*]. Oh, what's the use! I see through it all now. I have been like wax in your hands.

REBECCA. Listen to me, Johannes. We must get things straight. It will be our last chance. [*Sits on a chair near the sofa.*] I had thought of writing to you to tell you all about it . . . when I was back up North again. But perhaps it's better if you hear it now.

ROSMER. Is there still more to tell?

REBECCA. You still haven't heard the main thing.

ROSMER. The main thing?

REBECCA. Something you've never even suspected. Something that puts everything else in its true light.

ROSMER [*shakes his head*]. I don't understand you at all.

REBECCA. It's perfectly true I angled for admission here to Rosmersholm. Because I had the feeling I would succeed in doing rather well for myself here. In one way or another, if you see what I mean.

ROSMER. Well, you managed to achieve what you set out to do.

REBECCA. I think I could have achieved any mortal thing—then. For I still had the courage of a free mind. I felt no scruples; I wasn't prepared to give way for anything. But then came the start of something that finally broke my will . . . and turned me from then on into a poor frightened thing.

ROSMER. The start of what? Tell me plainly.

REBECCA. Something that came over me . . . a wild and uncontrollable passion . . . oh, Johannes!

ROSMER. Passion? You. . . ! For what?

REBECCA. For you.

ROSMER [*tries to spring up*]. What's that you say?

REBECCA [*restrains him*]. Stay where you are, my dear. There's more to tell.

ROSMER. Are you trying to tell me . . . you were in love with me . . . in that way?

REBECCA. I felt you couldn't call it anything else but being 'in love'— at that time. I really did think it was love. But it wasn't. It was what I said . . . wild, uncontrollable passion.

ROSMER [*with difficulty*]. Rebecca . . . is this really you . . . you . . . sitting here telling me all this?

REBECCA. Of course, what do you think, Johannes!

ROSMER. And it was as a result of this . . . under the influence of this . . . that you 'took action' as you put it.

REBECCA. It swept over me like a storm at sea. Like one of those storms we sometimes get in the winter up North. It takes hold of you . . . and carries you away with it . . . for as long as it lasts. It never occurs to you to resist.

ROSMER. Then it swept poor Beata into the millstream.

REBECCA. Yes, it was like a fight to the death between Beata and me at that time.

ROSMER. You were certainly the strongest of us at Rosmersholm. Stronger even than Beata and me together.

REBECCA. I knew you well enough to realize there was no way I could reach you until you had been set free . . . in mind and in deed.

ROSMER. But I don't understand you, Rebecca. You yourself . . . and the way you have behaved . . . it's all a complete mystery to me. Now I *am* free . . . in both respects. You are standing right within reach of the goal you set yourself from the very first. And yet . . . !

REBECCA. I have never been further from my goal than I am now.

ROSMER. . . . And yet yesterday, you know, when I asked you . . . begged you . . . to be my wife, you cried out as though in terror, saying it could never be.

REBECCA. I cried out in despair, Johannes.

ROSMER. Why?

REBECCA. Because Rosmersholm has paralysed me. My will-power has been sapped, my spirit crippled. Once I dared tackle anything that came my way; now that time is gone. I have lost the power to act, Johannes.

ROSMER. Tell me how this has happened.

REBECCA. Through living with you.

ROSMER. But how? How?

REBECCA. When I found myself living alone with you here . . . after you had found your real self . . .

ROSMER. Yes, yes?

REBECCA. . . . Because you were never wholly yourself as long as Beata was alive. . . .

ROSMER. I'm afraid you are right.

REBECCA. But when I began living here with you . . . in peace . . . in solitude . . . when without any kind of reserve you shared all your thoughts with me . . . all your feelings just as they came, so delicate and fine . . . *then* I felt the great transformation taking place. Gradually, you understand. Almost imperceptibly . . . but overwhelmingly in the end, and reaching right to the very depths of my soul.

ROSMER. Oh, what is all this you are saying, Rebecca!

REBECCA. All the rest . . . that horrible, sensual passion . . . faded far, far away. My restless agitation subsided in peace and quiet. A feeling of tranquillity came over me . . . a stillness like that which comes over a colony of sea-birds on the Northern coast under the midnight sun.

ROSMER. Tell me more of this. Everything you know.

REBECCA. There isn't very much more to tell, Johannes. Just that then I felt that this was the beginning of love . . . a great and selfless love that was content with being together as we *have* been together.

ROSMER. Oh, if I had had even the slightest inkling of all this!

REBECCA. It is best as it is. Yesterday . . . when you asked me if I would be your wife . . . I cried out with joy. . . .

ROSMER. Yes, you did, didn't you, Rebecca! I thought that was how it was.

REBECCA. For a moment, yes. I forgot myself. It was my old urgent spirit struggling to free itself again. But now it has no strength left . . . no stamina.

ROSMER. How do you explain what has happened to you?

REBECCA. It is the Rosmer philosophy of life . . . or in any case *your* philosophy . . . that has infected my will.

ROSMER. Infected?

REBECCA. And made it sick. Made it a slave to laws that had meant nothing to me before. You . . . being together with you . . . has given me some nobility of mind. . . .

ROSMER. Oh, if only I could believe that!

REBECCA. You need have no doubts about that. The Rosmer philosophy of life ennobles all right. But . . . [*shakes her head*] . . . but . . . but . . .

ROSMER. But what?

REBECCA. . . . But it kills happiness, Johannes.

ROSMER. Is that what you think, Rebecca?

REBECCA. For me, at least.

ROSMER. Yes, but are you quite certain? If I were to ask you again . . . ? Implore you . . .

REBECCA. Oh, my dear . . . please don't let us ever talk about that again. It's impossible. . . ! I think you ought to know, Johannes, I have . . . a past.

ROSMER. More than what you have already told me?

REBECCA. Yes. Something more, something different.

ROSMER [*with a faint smile*]. Isn't that strange, Rebecca. Do you know, I've occasionally suspected something of the sort.

REBECCA. Have you? And yet . . . in spite of that . . . ?

ROSMER. I never really believed it. I just toyed with the idea, you know.

REBECCA. If you want me to, I'll tell you that now as well.

ROSMER [*remonstrating*]. No! No! I don't want to hear a thing. Whatever it is, I want to forget it.

REBECCA. But I can't.

ROSMER. Oh, Rebecca. . . !

REBECCA. Yes, Johannes . . . that is the terrible thing . . . the very moment when I am being offered all the happiness in life I could wish for . . . it's now I see my own past confronting me like a barrier.

ROSMER. Your past is dead, Rebecca. It hasn't any hold on you any more . . . hasn't any connection with you . . . as you are *now*.

REBECCA. Oh, my dear, these are just empty phrases, you know. What about innocence? Where do I get *that*?

ROSMER [*sadly*]. Ah, yes . . . innocence.

REBECCA. Yes, innocence. Where happiness and contentment are found. Wasn't that after all the idea you wanted to foster in your new generation of happy and noble men. . . ?

ROSMER. Oh, don't remind me of *that*. That is nothing but a broken dream, Rebecca. An impetuous idea I don't believe in any more. . . . You know, people can't be ennobled from the outside.

REBECCA [*quietly*]. Not even by gentle love and affection, you think?

ROSMER [*thoughtfully*]. Yes . . . that could be a tremendous thing, of course. One of the most glorious things in life, I should think . . . if only it were so. [*Restlessly.*] But how can I be sure about a question like that? How can I know for certain?

REBECCA. Don't you believe me, Johannes?

ROSMER. Oh, Rebecca, how *can* I believe you . . . after the furtive way you have gone on here! And now you come along with this new idea. If there's anything behind it, please tell me straight out. If there's anything you want, I'll be only too glad to do all I can.

REBECCA [*wringing her hands*]. Oh, this killing doubt. . . ! Johannes . . . Johannes. . . !

ROSMER. Yes, it is terrible, Rebecca. But there's nothing I can do about it. I shall never be able to free myself from this doubt. Never know for certain that your love is whole-hearted and true.

REBECCA. But doesn't something deep within you tell you of the change that has taken place in me! And that this change is your doing . . . and yours alone!

ROSMER. Oh, Rebecca . . . I have no faith any longer in my power to change people. I have no faith in myself any more. No faith either in myself or in you.

REBECCA [*looks darkly at him*]. Then how are you going to live?

ROSMER. Yes, that I don't know. I simply can't imagine. I don't think I *can* live. . . . Nor can I think of anything in the world it might be worth living for.

REBECCA. Oh, life . . . life brings its own regeneration. Let us hold fast to it, Johannes. . . . We leave it soon enough.

ROSMER [*jumps up restlessly*]. Then give me back my faith again! My faith in *you*, Rebecca! Faith in your love. Proof! I must have proof!

REBECCA. Proof? How can I give you proof. . . ?

ROSMER. You *must*! [*Walks across the room.*] I can't stand this desolation . . . this terrible emptiness . . . this . . . this . . .

[*There is a loud knock on the hall door.*]

REBECCA [*starts up from her chair*]. Ah . . . do you hear that?

[*The door opens, and* ULRIK BRENDEL *comes in. He is wearing a dress shirt, a black coat and a good pair of boots with his trousers tucked in; otherwise he is dressed as on his previous appearance. He looks confused.*]

ROSMER. Oh, it's you, Mr. Brendel!

BRENDEL. Johannes, my boy! Greetings . . . and farewell!

ROSMER. Where are you going so late?

BRENDEL. Downhill.

ROSMER. What. . . ?

BRENDEL. I am going home, my dear pupil. I am homesick for the great void.

ROSMER. Something has happened to you, Mr. Brendel! What is it?

BRENDEL. So you observe the transformation? Yes . . . and well you may. When I last set foot in this room, I stood before you as a man of substance, patting my breast pocket.

ROSMER. Indeed! But I don't quite understand. . . .

BRENDEL. But what you see tonight is a deposed king standing amid the ashes of his burnt-out palace.

ROSMER. If there's anything I can do to help . . .

BRENDEL. You still have the heart of a little child, Johannes. Can you let me have a small loan?

ROSMER. Yes, of course. I'd be glad to.

BRENDEL. Could you manage me an ideal or two?

ROSMER. What did you say you wanted?

BRENDEL. One or two cast-off ideals. That would be doing a good deed. Because I'm cleaned out, my dear boy . . . absolutely flat.

REBECCA. Didn't you give your lecture?

BRENDEL. No, gracious lady. What do you think! Just as I was standing ready to shower out the contents of the cornucopia, I made the painful discovery that I was bankrupt.

REBECCA. But what about all those still unwritten works of yours?

BRENDEL. For twenty-five years I have been like a miser sitting on his padlocked chest. And then yesterday . . . when I opened it up to get at the treasure . . . there was none. . . . The mills of time had ground it all to dust. Not a blessed thing left, *nichts*.

ROSMER. Are you absolutely certain?

BRENDEL. There's no room for doubt, my dear boy. The President convinced me of that.

ROSMER. The President?

BRENDEL. Well . . . His Excellency, then. *Ganz nach Belieben*.

ROSMER. Whom do you mean?

BRENDEL. Peter Mortensgaard, of course.

ROSMER. What?

BRENDEL [*mysteriously*]. Hush, hush! Peter Mortensgaard is lord and master of the future. Never have I been in a more august presence. Peter Mortensgaard possesses the secret of omnipotence. He can do whatever he wants.

ROSMER. Oh, you can't believe that!

BRENDEL. Oh yes, I can, my boy! Because Peter Mortensgaard never wants to do more than he *can*. Peter Mortensgaard is quite capable of living his life without ideals. And it is precisely *that*, don't you see, that is the great secret of practical success. It is the sum of all the world's wisdom. *Basta!*

ROSMER [*in a low voice*]. Now I understand . . . why you are leaving here poorer than you came.

BRENDEL. *Bien!* Then be warned by the example of your old teacher. Cross out everything he ever tried to impress on you. Build not thy house on shifting sand. And watch yourself . . . and look carefully . . . before you build on this charming creature now sweetening life for you here.

REBECCA. Do you mean me?

BRENDEL. I do, my enchanting little mermaid.

REBECCA. And why shouldn't anybody build on me?

BRENDEL [*comes a step nearer*]. I gather that my one-time pupil has a mission to fulfil.

REBECCA. What if he has. . . ?

BRENDEL. His success is assured. But . . . I would have you know . . . on one inescapable condition.

REBECCA. What is that?

BRENDEL [*takes her gently by the wrist*]. That the woman who loves him goes out into the kitchen and gladly chops off her dainty, pink and white little-finger . . . *here*, just here near the middle joint. Furthermore, that the aforesaid woman in love . . . equally gladly . . . cuts off her incomparably formed left ear. [*Lets her go and turns to* ROSMER.] Farewell, my conquering Johannes.

ROSMER. Are you going now? On this dark night?

BRENDEL. The dark night is best. Peace be with you.

[*He goes. There is a moment of silence in the room.*]

REBECCA [*breathes heavily*]. Oh, how close and sultry it is in here!

[*She goes over to the window, opens it and remains standing there.*]

ROSMER [*sits down in the armchair over by the stove*]. There seems nothing else for it, Rebecca. I see that you must leave.

REBECCA. Yes, I can't see that there's any other choice.

ROSMER. Let us make the most of these last few minutes. Come over here and sit beside me.

REBECCA [*goes and sits down on the sofa*]. What is it, Johannes?

ROSMER. First I want to tell you this: you need have no worry about your future.

REBECCA [*smiles*]. Hm! *My* future!

ROSMER. I have prepared for all contingencies, long ago. Whatever happens, you are taken care of.

REBECCA. You even thought of that too, my dear!

ROSMER. That you might have known.

REBECCA. I have never given any thought to that kind of thing for many a long day.

ROSMER. Yes, yes. . . . You probably never imagined things could ever be any different between us from what they were.

REBECCA. Yes, that's what I thought.

ROSMER. I was the same. But if anything were to happen to me now . . .

REBECCA. Oh Johannes . . . you will live longer than me.

ROSMER. It is within my power to do with this miserable life of mine whatever I think best, you know.

REBECCA. What are you saying! Surely you are not thinking of . . . ?

ROSMER. Do you think that would be so strange? After the dismal, pitiful defeat I have suffered! I was going to carry a great cause on to victory . . . and now look! And now I've quit the whole thing . . . before the battle had even started!

REBECCA. Take up the fight again, Johannes! If only you would try . . . you'll see you'll win. Bringing nobility to the minds of hundreds . . . thousands. If only you would try!

ROSMER. Oh, Rebecca . . . when I don't believe any longer in my own cause.

REBECCA. But your cause has already stood the test. *One* person at least you have certainly ennobled . . . me, as long as I live.

ROSMER. Yes . . . if only I could believe you.

REBECCA [*wringing her hands*]. Oh, but Johannes . . . can't you think of anything . . . anything at all that would make you believe it?

ROSMER [*starts, as if in fear*]. Don't! You mustn't ask me about that! Please don't go on! Don't say another word!

REBECCA. I must. . . . This is just what we must talk about. Can't you think of anything that would wipe out this suspicion? *I* can't think of anything at all.

ROSMER. It's best that you can't . . . best for us both.

REBECCA. No, no, no . . . I'm not going to be put off like that. If you can think of any single thing that would acquit me in your eyes, then I demand as my right that you name it.

ROSMER [*as if impelled against his will*]. Let us see, then. Yours is a great love, you say. That through me you have won nobility of soul. Is it true? Are you sure you have reckoned things out right? Shall we prove it? Eh?

REBECCA. I am ready.

ROSMER. Any time?

REBECCA. Whenever you like. The sooner the better.

ROSMER. Then let me see, Rebecca . . . if you . . . for my sake . . . this very night . . . [*Breaks off.*] Oh no, no, no!

REBECCA. Yes, Johannes. Yes, yes! Tell me and you shall see.

ROSMER. . . . If you have the courage . . . gladly, as Ulrik Brendel said . . . for my sake, tonight . . . gladly . . . to go the same way . . . Beata went?

REBECCA [*rises slowly from the sofa and says almost inaudibly*]. Johannes. . . !

ROSMER. Yes, Rebecca . . . that is the question that will haunt me . . . after you have left. Every hour of the day my thoughts will keep returning to it. I seem to see you clearly in my mind's eye . . . standing right out in the middle of the bridge. Then you lean out over the railing! . . . You sway as the rush of the water draws you down. No . . . you draw back. You dare not do what *she* dared.

REBECCA. But supposing I did have the courage? If I did dare, and gladly. What then?

ROSMER. Then I should have to believe you. Then surely I would get back my faith again in the cause . . . faith in my power to bring nobility into the minds of men . . . faith in man's power to achieve that nobility of mind.

REBECCA [*slowly takes up her shawl, throws it over her head, and says with composure*]. You shall have your faith back again.

ROSMER. Have you the courage and the will . . . for that, Rebecca?

REBECCA. That is something you can judge in the morning . . . or later . . . when they drag me up.

ROSMER [*with his head in his hands*]. There is a horrible fascination in this. . . !

REBECCA. Because I don't want to lie there . . . not any longer than necessary. Make sure they find me.

ROSMER [*jumps up*]. But all this . . . it's sheer madness. Go . . . or else stay! I'll take you at your word . . . once more.

REBECCA. Empty phrases, Johannes. No easy way out now, my dear, no running away. How can you ever take my word for things after today?

ROSMER. But I do not want to see you defeated, Rebecca!

REBECCA. There will be no defeat.

ROSMER. There will. You'll never bring yourself to go the way Beata went.

REBECCA. Don't you think so?

ROSMER. Never. You are not like Beata. You are not in the power of some twisted view of life.

REBECCA. But I am in the power of the Rosmersholm view of life . . . *now*. Where I have sinned . . . it is right that I should atone.

ROSMER [*looks fixedly at her*]. Is *that* how you see it?

REBECCA. Yes.

ROSMER [*resolutely*]. Well then, I give *my* loyalty to our emancipated view of life. There is no judge over us. Therefore we must see to it that we judge ourselves.

REBECCA [*misunderstanding him*]. That's right . . . that too. My going will save what is best in you.

ROSMER. Oh, there's nothing left in me to save.

REBECCA. Oh, yes there is. But as for me . . . from now on I'd only be a drag on you, like some sea-troll slumped over the ship that is to carry you forward. I must go overboard. Do you expect me to go through life dragging behind me a crippled existence? . . . For ever brooding over the happiness I forfeited by my past? I must quit the game, Johannes.

ROSMER. If you go . . . I go with you.

REBECCA [*smiles almost imperceptibly, looks at him and says gently*]. Yes, come with me . . . and be my witness. . . .

ROSMER. I go with you, I said.

REBECCA. As far as the bridge, yes. You know you never dare go out on it.

ROSMER. Have you noticed that?

REBECCA [*sadly and brokenly*]. Yes. That was what made my love hopeless.

ROSMER. Rebecca . . . now I lay my hand on your head . . . [*does so*] and take you to be my truly wedded wife.

REBECCA [*takes both his hands and puts her head on his breast*]. Thank you, Johannes. [*Lets go.*] And now I go gladly.

ROSMER. Man and wife should go together.

REBECCA. Only as far as the bridge, Johannes.

ROSMER. Out on it, too. As far as *you* go . . . I too go with you. For now I dare.

REBECCA. Are you absolutely convinced . . . that this way is the best for you?

ROSMER. I know it's the only way.

REBECCA. Suppose you were only deceiving yourself. . . . Suppose it were all a delusion . . . one of those White Horses of Rosmersholm.

ROSMER. It could well be. We can never escape them, we of this house.

REBECCA. Then stay, Johannes!

ROSMER. The husband shall go with his wife, as the wife with her husband.

REBECCA. Yes, but first tell me this: is it you who goes with me, or I with you.

ROSMER. That is something we shall never fathom.

REBECCA. Yet I should so much like to know.

ROSMER. We go together, Rebecca. I go with you, you with me.

REBECCA. I rather think that too.

ROSMER. For now we two are one.

REBECCA. Yes, now we are one. Come! Let us go gladly.

[*They go out hand in hand through the hall and can be seen turning to the left. The door remains standing open after them. The room stands empty for a few moments. Then* MRS. HELSETH *opens the door on the right.*]

MRS. HELSETH. Miss West . . . the coach is . . . [*Looks about her.*] Not in? Gone out together at this time of night? Well . . . I must say that's . . . hm! [*Goes out into the hall, looks around and comes back in again.*] Not on the seat. Well . . . well . . . [*Goes to the window and looks out.*] Good God! That white thing there. . . ! Bless my soul . . . yes, they are both on the bridge. God forgive the sinful creatures! Putting their arms round each other! [*Screams.*] Oh . . . over the side . . . both of them! Into the millstream! Help! Help! [*Her knees tremble; shaking, she holds on to the back of a chair; she can scarcely utter the words.*] No, no help there . . . the dead woman has taken them.

SELECT BIBLIOGRAPHY

(i) general studies, in English, arranged chronologically

Edmund Gosse, *Studies in the Literature of Northern Europe* (London, 1879), pp. 35-69.

Georg Brandes, *Eminent authors of the Nineteenth Century*, tr. Rasmus B. Anderson (New York, 1886), pp. 405-60.

Havelock Ellis, *The New Spirit* (London, 1890), pp. 133-73.

George Bernard Shaw, *The Quintessence of Ibsenism* (London, 1891)—second edition 'completed to the death of Ibsen', London, 1913.

Philip H. Wicksteed, *Four lectures on Henrik Ibsen dealing chiefly with his metrical works* (London, 1892).

F. Anstey [i.e. Thomas Anstey Guthrie], *Mr. Punch's Pocket Ibsen*. A collection of some of the master's best-known dramas. Condensed, revised, and slightly rearranged for the benefit of the earnest student (London, 1893).

'Zanoni' [pseud.], *Ibsen and the Drama* (London, [? 1894]).

H. H. Boyesen, *A Commentary on the Works of Henrik Ibsen* (London, 1894).

Edward Russell, *Ibsen*. A lecture delivered at University College, Liverpool, 26 Jan. 1894 (Liverpool, 1894).

George Bernard Shaw, *Our Theatres in the Nineties*. 3 vols. (London, 1932)—being dramatic criticisms contributed week by week to *The Saturday Review* from Jan. 1895 to May 1898.

Henry James, *The Scenic Art*, ed. Allan Wade (London, 1949), pp. 243-60, 286-94—including: 'On the occasion of Hedda Gabler', *New Review*, June 1891; 'The Master Builder', *Pall Mall Gazette*, 17 Feb. 1893; 'Little Eyolf', 'John Gabriel Borkman', *Harper's Weekly*, 23 Jan., 6 Feb., 1897.

Edward Russell and Percy Cross Standing, *Ibsen on his merits* (London, 1897).

Georg Brandes, *Henrik Ibsen, Bjørnstjerne Bjørnson*. Critical studies (London, 1899).

Max Beerbohm, *Around Theatres* (London, 1953)—being dramatic criticisms May 1898—April 1910, including: 'An hypocrisy in play-going' [on *Hedda Gabler* played in Italian, Oct. 1903], pp. 277-81; 'Ibsen' [an obituary, May 1906], pp. 432-6; 'A memorable performance' [on *Rosmersholm*, Feb. 1908], pp. 497-501.

James Joyce, 'Ibsen's new drama', *Fortnightly Review*, 73, 1900, pp. 575-90.

James Huneker, *Iconoclasts: a book of dramatists* (London, 1905), pp. 1-138.

Arthur Symons, *Figures of Several Centuries* (London, 1916), pp. 222-67: 'Henrik Ibsen', written 1906.

Jeanette Lee, *The Ibsen Secret*. A key to the prose dramas of Henrik Ibsen (London, 1907).

Haldane Macfall, *Ibsen: the man, his art and his significance* (London, 1907).

Montrose J. Moses, *Henrik Ibsen: the man and his plays* (New York, 1908).

James Huneker, *Egoists: a book of supermen* (London, 1909), pp. 317-39.

Edward Dowden, *Essays, modern and Elizabethan* (London, 1910), pp. 26-60.

Archibald Henderson, *Interpreters of life and the modern spirit* (London, 1911), pp. 157-283.

Otto Heller, *Henrik Ibsen: plays and problems* (New York, 1912).

R. Ellis Roberts, *Henrik Ibsen: a critical study* (London, 1912).

Henry Rose, *Henrik Ibsen; poet, mystic and moralist* (London, 1913).

William Archer, 'The true greatness of Ibsen', a lecture delivered at University College, London. *Edda*, xii, 1919, pp. 175-91.

Carl Burchardt, *Norwegian life and literature* (London, 1920).

Storm Jameson, *Modern Drama in Europe* (London, 1920).

Janko Lavrin, *Ibsen and his creation. A psycho-critical study* (London, 1921).

T. M. Campbell, *Hebbel, Ibsen and the analytical exposition* (Heidelberg, 1922).

Basil King, 'Ibsen and Emilie Bardach', *Century Magazine* (New York), 1923: Oct. pp. 803-15, Nov. pp. 83-92.

Benedetto Croce, *European Literature in the Nineteenth Century* (London, 1924), pp. 326-43.

Hermann J. Weigand, *The modern Ibsen: a reconsideration* (New York, 1925).

Paul Henry Grumman, *Henrik Ibsen: an introduction to his life and works* (New York, 1928).

Elizabeth Robins, *Ibsen and the actress* (London, 1928).

Bonamy Dobrée, *The Lamp and the lute* (Oxford, 1929), pp. 1-20.

Harley Granville-Barker, 'The coming of Ibsen', in *The Eighteen Eighties*, Essays by Fellows of the Royal Society of Literature, ed. Walter de la Mare (Cambridge, 1930), pp. 159-96.

J. G. Robertson, *Essays and addresses on literature* (London, 1935), pp. 147-226.

A. Anstensen, *The Proverb in Ibsen* (Columbia U.P. and London, 1935).

E. M. Forster, *Abinger Harvest* (London, 1936), including chapter on 'Ibsen the Romantic'.

Theodore Jorgenson, *Henrik Ibsen: a study in art and personality* (Northfield, Minn., 1945).

Ronald Peacock, *The Poet in the Theatre* (London, 1946), pp. 65-71.

Brian W. Downs, *Ibsen: the intellectual background* (Cambridge, 1946).

M. C. Bradbrook, *Ibsen the Norwegian* (London, 1948).

P. F. D. Tennant, *Ibsen's Dramatic Technique* (Cambridge, 1948).

Alan Reynolds Thompson, *The Dry Mock* (Berkeley, Cal., 1948), pp. 197-244: 'Ibsen'.

Francis Fergusson, *The Idea of a Theater* (Princeton U.P. and London, 1949)—with special reference to *Ghosts*.

Brian W. Downs, *A study of six plays by Ibsen* (Cambridge, 1950).

Janko Lavrin, *Ibsen: an approach* (London, 1950).

Raymond Williams, *Drama from Ibsen to Eliot* (London, 1952).

John Northam, *Ibsen's Dramatic Method: a study of the prose dramas* (London, 1953).

G. K. Chesterton, *A Handful of Authors* (London, 1953), pp. 134–58: 'Henrik Ibsen', articles written in 1906 and 1928.

J. T. Farrell, *Reflections at Fifty, and other essays* (New York, 1954), pp. 66–96: 'Joyce and Ibsen'.

Francis Bull, *Ibsen: the man and the dramatist.* Taylorian Lecture (Oxford, 1954).

Eric Bentley, *In search of theatre* (London, 1954), pp. 365–80.

Eva Le Gallienne, *Hedda Gabler*, A preface . . . with a new translation (London, 1955); and *The Master Builder*, a translation . . . with a prefatory study (London, 1955).

Einar Haugen, 'Ibsen in America', *Edda*, lvi, 1956, pp. 270–88.

Una Ellis-Fermor, 'Ibsen and Shakespeare as dramatic artists', *Edda*, lvi, 1956, pp. 364–79.

T. R. Henn, *The Harvest of Tragedy* (London, 1956), pp. 172–88: 'A Note on Ibsen'.

F. W. Kaufmann, 'Ibsen's Conception of Truth', *Germanic Review*, xxxii (1957), pp. 83–92.

R. M. Adams, 'Henrik Ibsen: The Fifty-first Anniversary', *Hudson Review*, x (1957), pp. 415–23.

J. B. Priestley, *Literature and Western Man* (London, 1960), pp. 284–9.

J. W. McFarlane, *Ibsen and the Temper of Norwegian Literature* (London, 1960).

Una Ellis-Fermor, *Shakespeare the Dramatist* (London, 1961): chapter on 'Ibsen and Shakespeare as dramatic artists'.

J. Setterquist, *Ibsen and the Beginnings of Anglo-Irish Drama* (Harvard U.P., 1961).

Kenneth Muir, *Last Periods of Shakespeare, Racine and Ibsen* (Liverpool U.P., 1962).

F. L. Lucas, *The Drama of Ibsen and Strindberg* (London, 1962).

G. Wilson Knight, *Ibsen* (Edinburgh, 1962).

J. W. McFarlane (ed.), *Discussions of Ibsen* (Boston, Mass., 1962)—essays by various hands.

M. J. Valency, *The Flower and the Castle* (New York, 1964).

R. Brustein, *The Theatre of Revolt* (New York, 1964, and London, 1965), pp. 35–84: 'Henrik Ibsen'.

Rolf Fjelde (ed.), *Twentieth-Century Views on Ibsen* (New York, 1965)—essays by various hands.

Contemporary Approaches to Ibsen, ed. Daniel Haakonsen (Oslo, 1966)—essays by Francis Fergusson, James McFarlane, John Northam *et al.*

B. W. Downs, *Modern Norwegian Literature 1860–1918* (Cambridge U.P., 1966), pp. 43–64 and 116–32.

M. Meyer, *Henrik Ibsen: the Making of a Dramatist 1828–1864* (London, 1967).

Hans Heiberg, *Ibsen: a portrait of the artist* (London, 1969).

J. W. McFarlane (ed.), *Henrik Ibsen* (Penguin Critical Anthologies, London, 1970).

(ii) other studies of the three plays in this volume include:

Ivor Brown, Introduction to *An Enemy of the People*, trans. Eleanor Marx-Aveling (Heinemann, London, 1951).

P. D. F. Tennant, 'A critical study of Ibsen's *Vildanden*', *Edda*, xxxiv, 1934, pp. 327-54.

Otto Reinert, 'Sight Imagery in *The Wild Duck*', *Journal of English and Germanic Philology*, lv (1956), pp. 457-62.

T. C. Worsley, Introduction to *The Wild Duck*, trans. Max Faber (Heinemann, London, 1958).

Mary McCarthy, *Sights and Spectacles* (London, 1958), pp. 166-76: 'The Will and Testament of Ibsen' [on *The Wild Duck*].

Louis Crompton, 'The demonic in Ibsen's *The Wild Duck*', *Tulane Drama Review*, iv, 1959, pp. 96-103.

James McFarlane, 'A note on Ibsen's draft manuscripts to *Vildanden* and *Rosmersholm*', *Modern Language Review*, liv, 2, April 1959, pp. 244-5.

Robert Raphael, 'Illusion and the self in *The Wild Duck*, *Rosmersholm* and *The Lady from the Sea*', *Scandinavian Studies*, xxxv, 1963, pp. 37-50.

Karl S. Guthke, *Modern tragi-comedy* (New York, 1966), pp. 144-65: 'Analysis of *The Wild Duck*'.

Sydney Mendel, 'The revolt against the father: the adolescent hero in *Hamlet* and *The Wild Duck*', *Essays in Criticism*, xiv, 1964, pp. 171-8.

T. Støverud, *Milestones of Norwegian Literature* (Oslo, 1967), pp. 103-18: '*The Wild Duck*: a study in ambiguity'.

Brian Johnston, 'The metaphoric structure of *The Wild Duck*', in *Contemporary Approaches to Ibsen*, ed. D. Haakonsen (Oslo, 1966), pp. 72-95.

Dorothy Seyler, '*The Seagull* and *The Wild Duck*: Birds of a feather', *Modern Drama*, viii, 1965, pp. 167-73.

Gordon Craig, 'A Note on *Rosmersholm*'. In *Teatro della Pergola*. Rappresentazioni di Eleonora Duse. Dicembre 1906, etc. (Florence, [1906]).

Cleanth Brooks and Robert B. Heilman, *Understanding Drama* (New York, 1945), pp. 256-317: 'Rosmersholm'.

Harley Granville-Barker, *The use of the drama*. The substance of three lectures delivered at Princeton University, U.S.A., upon the Spencer Trask Foundation in 1944 (London, 1946), pp. 47-51: 'Ibsen and his "Rosmersholm" '.

Desmond MacCarthy, *Humanities* (London, 1953), pp. 65-70: 'Rosmersholm'.

K. Reichert, 'Tragedy of Idealism: Henrik Ibsen', in *Tragic Themes in Western Literature*, ed. Cleanth Brooks (Yale U.P. and London, 1955), pp. 128-49, mainly on *Rosmersholm*.

Robert R. Reed, Jr., 'Rebecca of Manningtree and Ibsen's Rebecca West', *Notes and Queries*, Nov. 1957, pp. 481-4.

John D. Hurrell, '*Rosmersholm*, the existentialist drama and the dilemma of modern tragedy', *Educational Theatre Journal* (Columbia, Mo.), xv, 1963, pp. 118–24.

Thomas F. van Laan, 'Art and structure in *Rosmersholm*', *Modern Drama*, vi, 1963, pp. 150–63.

Brian Johnston, 'The Dialectic of *Rosmersholm*', *Drama Survey*, vi, 1967, pp. 181–220.

John Northam, *Dividing Worlds* [*The Tempest* and *Rosmersholm*] (Oslo, 1965). Kristiansand Museum Pamphlets, no. 2.

Alrik Gustafson, 'Aspects of theme and form in *Rosmersholm*', in *Scandinavian Studies. Essays presented to Henry Goddard Leach* (Seattle, 1965), pp. 213–26.